Michael Marten and Katja Neumann (eds.)

Saints and Cultural Trans-/Mission

COLLECTANEA INSTITUTI ANTHROPOS

Editor: Anthropos Institut e. V.
Arnold-Janssen-Str. 20
D-53757 Sankt Augustin
Germany

Vol. 45

Michael Marten and Katja Neumann (eds.)

Saints
and
Cultural Trans-/Mission

2013

Academia Verlag ▲ Sankt Augustin

Bibliographische Information der Deutschen Bibliothek
Die Deutsche Bibliothek verzeichnet diese Publikation
in der Deutschen Nationalbibliografie; detaillierte bibliografische Daten
sind im Internet über http://dnb.d-nb.de abrufbar.

ISBN 978-3-89665-621-6

               Academia Verlag
               Bahnstraße 7
               D-53757 Sankt Augustin
               Germany

Herstellung: HD Ecker: TeXtservices, Bonn, Germany

Contents, Overview

Contents, Details

Introduction

Welcome to this edition of Collectanea on "Saints and Cultural Trans-/Mission". This collection of papers seeks to identify and problematise the conception and representation of saints in various cultural, social, historical and economic contexts. Anthropology, and in part historical anthropology, can serve to illuminate the place of saints in society, their adaptability and mutability across geographical and imaginative borders, and also in part to examine what it is that makes saints "religious" figures in different settings, thereby contributing to the discourse on religious/secular distinctions.

The various essays offered in this collection, each with their own unique and critical focus, enable a comparative glimpse into key problems that anthropological study is confronted with when engaging with the "cultural-religious matrix" spun around the discourse on saints. This happens by reflecting on the significance of the material form of the medium "saint" in the person, narrative, depiction or ritual that provides the basis for interpretation, thereby inviting academic, artistic and personal reflections on Western cultural perceptions and interactions with the saint's mediary situation. Although this "material form" is interpreted partly in literary, artistic and at times even entirely fictional form, its materiality effects and affects links beyond its representation to those connected in some way to the saint, whether as devotees, promulgators, artists or deconstructionists.

Key questions arise when addressing such issues, for example: who or what finds transmission in media and rituals surrounding instances of saint-depictions, worship and invocation? Can discourses on saints offer something more, something broader than theological debates? Is it possible and useful to seek to identify commonalities and differences in interpreting the place of saints in societies across historical, cultural and geographical boundaries? What motivates the construction or deconstruction of sainthood? Reflecting critically on questions such as these uncovers cultural and academic preconceptions in the construction and maintenance of qualities of sainthood, whilst the mode of investigation and choice of focus on boundaries, whether these be discursive, economic, historic, social or medial, develops this further. This collection continues the dialogue that originated around a workshop held at the University of Stirling by the *Translating Christianities* research group in May 2010; in bringing together this special edition, further papers have been solicited beyond those offered at the workshop.[1] In Stirling participants were left with a sense of curiosity about the intricacy of constructions of various saints as they had played themselves out across the disciplines represented: mate-

---

[1] See also <www.translatingchristianities.stir.ac.uk>.

rially distinct, diverse and present, and subverting and transcending normative or homogenous interpretations.

Stereotypically, saints are linked to notions of moral superiority and are the objects of personal devotion, pious reflection, and devotees' emulation. Such hagiographic accounts are frequently attached to historical persons who have received favour with ecclesiastical authority and are subsequently honoured by canonisation. The endorsement of saints inevitably results in a certain level of political and cultural currency, and yet the extent to which one can assume that saints are characterised by virtue of cultural conventions and local interests remains debatable, as Brian Murdoch's paper on St Gregorius makes clear. This particular saint sustains a narrative that remains playfully alluding to cultural and social conventions and popular myths, notably King Oedipus, to which his story continues to provide a contrapuntal narrative. As a marginal, "apocryphal" saint, without a cult or identifiable devotional practice attached to his person, his elusive presence as a fictional character is received with incessant narrative reworkings. Although these remain identifiably related to his person, all the while they evade "authoritative" canons or historical prototypes. In their dispersed and culturally diverse guises, the St Gregorius narratives convey the full authority of his sainthood, attached to his obedient behaviour in penance, thereby gaining favour with God. Thus, despite his fictional character and position outside the traditional canon, he serves as a concrete example of supposedly traditional values. From the appeal to Scriptural authority and popular biblical themes interwoven in his story, his ardent conviction in the reality of salvation by the power of (ecclesiastically legitimated) absolution is kept intact across cultural boundaries and plot adaptations. St Gregorius exemplifies the penitent, possibly encouraging the faithful to disclose themselves in confession, and to trust in the power of saintly intercession. By contrast to St Gregorius' perpetrations (however unwittingly), most crimes must seem redeemable. As a datum of cultural ingenuity, the fictional story of St Gregorius legitimises ecclesial authority over administering penance whilst relativising the ultimate importance of sin in the vision for salvation.

By comparison the legendary St Barbara offers a very different perspective and interpretation of both the role of ecclesial authority and divine mercy in relation to the cultural context of North Lebanon, as Christine Lindner demonstrates. Tracing variant interpretations of the St Barbara myth, Lindner describes the instability of such imagery, relating it to the specific circumstances of the community she is describing. Picking up on ideas of bricolage as an interpretative tool, she points to the ways in which interpretations accrue to St Barbara. The myths surrounding her are elaborated upon, and particular facets emphasised, contingent on the national, communal and local contexts, as can be seen in the representations of her in particular church traditions, or in the contrasts between the children's songs and actions relating to her in Lebanon and Syria. Lindner enables us to observe the fundamental instability of conceptions of sainthood in a contemporary setting, even to the point of celebrations of a saint being subsumed into other festivals due to migratory processes, as the incorporation of "Lebanese Halloween" illustrates.

As Emilia Ferraro's paper forcefully shows with the figure of San Juan in Northern Ecuador, the saint becomes the cultural locus of ethnic identity formation. No longer the herald of Christian doctrine in the guise of St John the Baptist, San Juan continues to change shape: a hybridised saint, placed at the crossroads of social, cultural and political boundaries which appear and disappear according to historical developments. Within the celebration to his honour, San Juan travels from the liturgical space of the church to the civic space of the square and the cultic space of private shrines. Thus, the ritualisation of economic dependencies, as they are reinforced in the traditional exchange of the *rama* that mark the social boundaries between peasantry and landowners, are patronised by the same saint who crosses over into the micro-economic unit of the family where the celebrations to San Juan finds altered expression. The mingling of native religious sensibilities with the characteristics of the imported saint make San Juan, as opposed to Saint John the Baptist, a distinctly kichwa patron. The associations of likening kichwa devotional behaviour to the Christian adoration of Christ marks another conceptual boundary that identifies the indebtedness to anthropologically discrete cultural archetypes for cross-reference, in turn borrowing and invoking Christian vestiges resonant with the history of transmission that this saint underwent, reinforcing this cultural transformation.

The play on the word "transmission", reflecting on yet another religio-cultural expression of interpretive power in association with its Christian "purpose" of mission, points to its ideological and political involvement. Missionary activities were profoundly entangled in colonial activity. While many of the papers in the present collection identify and discuss saints which were brought into new contexts via mission, the role of saints in the context of mission from a European perspective seems less obvious. With an official refusal to acknowledge saints as part of the devotional life of Protestant believers, Michael Marten's take on missionary biographies reinterprets what may be deemed the ideological side to hagiographic accounts. As Marten's essay shows in the case of Protestant missionary biographies, these texts harness a popular understanding of their quasi-saintly subject, which is to be found not in the work and mission abroad, but in the edification and education of the believers at home. Thus, their narratives epitomise the missionaries' lives by enforcing and exercising the virtues of Victorian society, justifying the colonial enterprise hand in hand with the assertion of the sanctity of the endeavours of mission.

Jason Hartford's detailed examination of interpretations of St Sebastian in 19th–century French art is connected to wider artistic innovations. The use of St Sebastian symbolising a broad discourse of sexual minority was long established, but the author demonstrates through the use of numerous artistic representations that this discourse has not always been stable. In the period in question here, it underwent substantial changes and adaptations; there were, at times, several simultaneous discourses that imagery of this particular saint carried, contingent upon the contexts in which such imagery was created. The fluidity of doctrinal and homoerotic discourses attached to particular representations across varying temporal and cultural boundaries did not necessarily entail the queering of Christianity or interpretations of it, but these mutative processes did call into question hermeneutical stabilities that had hitherto been accepted as normative. Hartford also shows that any level of automaticity in linking artistic licence and liberal interpretative patterns is misplaced in this particular field.

Beside the reception and use of saintly imagery treated so far, the act of creating these images merits further attention. Two papers that specifically treat of the material condition of the saint as a work of art are Lindy Richardson's work on re-interpreting ancient historical saint-myths in contemporary artistic creativity, and Jean Andrews' essay on 17th–century iconography. While it is not a given that non-Western cultures "handle" images and the images of the saints in the same way, or infer the same interpretive (theoretical?) significance to their being as what might broadly be characterised as Western traditions, creating these images has always relied on the artistic vision of the individual creator, even if that is interpreted in varying ways. Furthermore, such creations have usually been sanctioned and commissioned by religious authorities or entertained by private patronage. What we today understand as "the freedom of the artist" changes perceptions of images, including those that intentionally seek to re-interpret subjects that at one time would have been considered sacred. Such production processes have become a turning point to anthropological evaluation of saints in our Western context. Richardson, in creating an art work (that is represented here in photographs of selected pieces) and analysing some of her own intellectual and emotional processes in this creative endeavour, is exploring the place of the artist in the production, maintenance and demise of saints. Her fragile bones, made of paper, convey something of the fragility of the narratives around Saint Ursula, but also seek to restore something of the humanity of the saint, returning her from divine abstraction to human form. Her reflections on this process serve to illuminate something of the divine-human relationship in this kind of artistic creation.

Meanwhile, Andrews' essay on St Joseph in the paintings of Josefa de Óbidos (1630–1684) and Diego Quispe Tito (1611–1681) offers a critical historical perspective on diverging cultural perceptions away from colonial metropolitan centres, showcasing the popular aesthetics of the iconography of St Joseph. Josefa's life was notably reclusive and access to training and material limited, but her work displays a playful approach to the figure of St Joseph, even when she has to express herself in relatively small formats. Working for private commissions allowed her a free interpretive range beyond the strictures of authoritative ecclesiastical teachings and convention. Thus her interpretation – consonant on many aspects with tradition – allows itself to blend conventions by modelling the Holy Family in the soft and effeminate features commonly reserved in iconography for angels and cherubim, blurring the boundaries between the Holy Child and his mortal parent Joseph along lines of gender, age and sanctity. Without revoking the mortal status of St Joseph, his saintliness but also his visual dependence on and adoration to the graven image of the child, mature beyond his years and nurturing towards his tender carer, reflect a unique and personal vision of the artist to her subject matter. The contrast in depiction and continuity in character marked out by the discussion on St Joseph in relation to the work of Diego Quispe Tito (Cuzco, Peru) certainly serves to pose questions beyond artistic interpretation. Whereas Josefa de Óbidos was marginal to society in Lisbon, Diego Quispe Tito entertained a well-situated workshop in Cuzco, though this was removed from the artisan society of Western colonial import. His depictions likewise follow the trend of showing a youthful Joseph, with clearly indigenous coloration and posture usually reserved for the Virgin; Joseph is given sainthood by association. The inspiration drawn from artistic expression brought out by Andrews in her discussion of St Joseph, the otherwise marginal character in the Holy Family, exemplifies a crucial perspective on devotional practice for anthropological research.

The relationship to the Virgin that depictions of Saint Joseph draw upon find a markedly different engagement from that of the Virgin in an Andean setting – a strong contrast in both medium and function. The work of Sabine Dedenbach on Pachamama and the Virgin Mary offers a critical reflection of the level of inculturation from an Andean perspective. Different from the direction of research undertaken on San Juan, where a Christian saint became an indigenous patron, Dedenbach illustrates the elusive Pachamama in indigenous' attempts to express their relationship to her, disguised from colonial interference. Identifying the cultural impact of Catholicism in the Andes proves more than a linguistic challenge. The play in the devotional literatures with the colonial Spanish, Quechua and Latin offer remarkable insights into the role of the two figures, Pachamama and the Virgin Mary, who are shown to have a curious relationship involving processes of assimilation and to some extent at least, an interchange of identities, contingent upon the audiences' position and viewpoint. The strong emphasis of the feminine divinity likewise restructures the internal workings of saintly and ecclesial hierarchies unacceptable to colonial rule.

The cultural milieu that these papers identify, trace and comment on by way of considering the role of the saints in devotional practices, hagiography and iconography, offer a compelling vantage-point from which to consider and evaluate anthropological research in its doubly implicated socio-cultural embeddedness. The saints' semi-alien characters, as far as addressing a mystified conception of (formally) Christian origin, and their ambiguous relationship vis-à-vis the divine, places them in a vicissitudinous relationship to their cultural locus and the project of the researcher. This relationship implicates the terms of engagement. The authors have made no claims regarding the theological significance of anthropological research on saints, though the theological understanding that the saints' diverse and multifarious identities represent in various discourses and cultural contexts do, of course, invite further consideration. The characteristically interdisciplinary engagement facilitated by these studies on saints – in various media and cultures, and across cultural boundaries in legends, folklore and imagery as well as ritual practices – informs the divergent forms of cultural imagination that shape acts of artistic and social devotion surrounding saints. To be brought to light as saints, these figures need to be observed and discussed in their social functionality. The stereotypical position of saints within Christian culture, as humans of special sanctity transmuted by divine glory, rests between the realms ethereal and material and assures the autonomy of interpretative positions over against the direct control of ecclesial authorities. Being brought or finding their way into other cultures and societies, not least by virtue of colonial expansion, saints occupy a dual role in mission: in different settings both connected to and detached from westernising ideologies. We might even go so far as to say that saints, more than ideological and economic structures, have proven a tendency to resist their missionary masters and can be found to have taken on a life of their own within their respective communities, without being relegated to the status of cultural artefact, or (necessarily) becoming the blank canvas for newly articulated projections of verisimilitude. The fascination that emanates from the figure of the saint – approached in devotion, adored in artistic portrayals, or used in multiple other ways – has determined various forms of human interaction in the past, and continues to do so in certain circumstances in the present, as the papers here illustrate. Examining saints from a critical, often interdisciplinary or methodologically pluralist perspective that traverses and reflects the modi of productions indicates the ongoing importance of the study of saints in their cultural and historical contexts.

We would like to record our warm thanks to Joachim Piepke and his colleagues at *Anthropos* who have enabled the publication of this volume to proceed so smoothly.

Michael Marten / Katja Neumann, June 2013

The Dwindling Saint:
from Hagiography to Folktale

Brian Murdoch

Abstract. – The incestuously born and married saint (and pope) Gregorius is fictional, although his tale, which starts as a twelfth-century hagiographical romance in French, does appear in prose form in actual legendaries. It appears also in the *Gesta Romanorum*, survives to Thomas Mann and beyond, crossing many borders. There are later literary re-tellings and many (oral) folktales, in which it is changed, reduced and degenerated. Some cultures lose major portions (Spanish), preserve different identifiable elements of the story in separate versions (Serbian, Irish), or lose nearly all original elements (Hungarian). However, significant theological elements remain. Gregorius is not Oedipus. *[Gregorius, hagiography, incest, folk-tale, degeneration, secularisation]*

Brian Murdoch is Emeritus Professor of German at Stirling University, and has held visiting fellowships and lectureships at Cambridge and Oxford. He has published widely on medieval literature in German, English, the Celtic languages, and on a comparative basis (handbooks on Old High German and on Cornish literature). In the modern field he has written extensively on the literature of the world wars, notably on Erich Maria Remarque, and has published translations from Latin and from medieval and modern German. Recent relevant books include *Adam's Grace*, 2000, *The Medieval Popular Bible*, 2003, *The Apocryphal Adam and Eve*, 2009. His monograph *Gregorius*, for which this was a preliminary study, appeard in 2012 (OUP).

The saint (and pope) in question here – Gregorius – is a fictional one, although he has sometimes been linked somewhat over-enthusiastically with the genuine Gregory the Great (whose deeds, to be fair, are also occasionally fictionalised, praying Trajan out of hell or making otherwise unrecorded visits to Ireland). Even though the story of Gregorius, which starts as a literary work, a metrical hagiographical romance, does sometimes gain apparent authority by its inclusion in rather shorter prose form in actual legendaries, he never acquires the respectability of a cult, nor really a definite feast-day. In this he is unlike other equally apocryphal saints who did – ranging from those only recently removed from the canon, like St. Barbara or St. Christopher, to others who were never more than locally accepted anyway: St. Josaphat, whose name is probably a corrupted Bodhisattva, St. Uncumber, who is an abstract concept, and St. Guinefort, who is a greyhound. The story of Gregorius lasts for a very long time, however, and it crosses a great many borders. It becomes the substance of explicitly literary re-tellings, of legends, of exempla, and of (oral and written) folktales, in the course of which it is varied, reduced and changed. A recent study of different versions by Yoav Elstein (1986) refers to around thirty versions and points out that there are (possibly a good many) others, although Elstein's views on the antiquity of the legend are questionable.

Gregorius (the Latin name has to be retained to distinguish him from Gregory the Great and other historically attested figures) is the son of an incestuous relationship between a noble brother and sister, after which the brother departs in penance on a pilgrimage or crusade and dies, while the sister becomes the ruler of the land. The child is set out in a boat with money, rich cloth, tablets or documents containing (anonymous) details of his origin and a request for baptism, and is found by an abbot, who provides him with foster-parents, his own name of Gregorius, and a monastic education. The boy Gregorius accidentally hurts a foster-brother, whose mother accuses him of being a foundling vagabond. Gregorius leaves as a knight to seek the truth about his origins, rescues his mother's land from attack and (unknowingly) marries her, even though he is wearing clothes made from the cloth she had placed with him. When the sin is discovered by way of the tablets, he undertakes a 17-year penance chained up on a rocky islet, which he survives miraculously. A dream sends emissaries to find him after the death of the pope or bishop, the key to his shackles is equally miraculously discovered inside the traditional fish, and he is himself made pope (or as in some versions a bishop; in folktales from areas beyond the area covered by the Roman church he can become Patriarch, Catholicos or even a rabbi). He is then able to give absolution to his mother (and occasionally also to his late father/uncle/brother-in-law), and after death becomes a saint in heaven.

That the story has elements in common with that of Oedipus, is clear, but in fact Gregorius is really very unlike Oedipus in most respects, and the only fully shared motif is the marriage to the mother. There is no mutilation, prophecy or parricide, and Oedipus, on the other hand, is not the product of incest. The Greek hero's ending is tragic in his defiance of the gods, whereas Gregorius submits to the will of God and is rewarded on earth and after his death. The story of Gregorius as we have it begins with a twelfth-century French or Anglo-Norman poem, and in most early versions it is presented essentially to exemplify the concept that any sin can be forgiven through contrition, penance and grace, except the despair of forgiveness. An earlier – sometime very much earlier – prose legend, supposed to have passed from Greek to Latin and then to Western Europe, has been posited, but absolutely no evidence for this survives, and it is unlikely that it would have disappeared so completely. There is, on the other hand, a clear line of transmission for the tale from the west to the east.

The French poem was adapted in around 1200 by the German Hartmann von Aue in a striking poem, and his work was turned into Latin verse and also into High and Low German prose texts which appear in collections of saints' lives, the only point at which the tale enters even quasi-official hagiography. The tale was also adapted from these sources into prose versions used as short exempla, usually illustrating humility, in Gospel plenaria. A western geographical limit to the story is provided by the curious Icelandic *Book of Reykjahólar*, a manuscript hagiographical collection produced not only after the Reformation but also well after the invention of printing, in which the compiler has tried not very successfully to reconcile Gregorius's ultimate role as pope or, as happens in some texts, as bishop. This is not done, incidentally, by simply making him the Bishop of Rome, though a nineteenth-century German text did use that ploy.

Far more important overall than the eccentric and remote Icelandic text is the Latin prose version from the thirteenth or fourteenth century based probably on the French poems and incorporated into the extremely popular moralising story-book, the *Gesta Romanorum*, where it appears in two versions, one full (Oesterley 1872: 399–409) and the other very clearly truncated, since it lacks the entire penance section and the elevation, although Gregorius and his mother are pardoned directly by God (Dick 1890: 148–159). The *Gesta Romanorum* was translated in and after the Middle Ages into many other western and also eastern European languages (including Czech, Polish, Ukrainian, Hungarian and Russian) and this version, either in Latin or one of the vernaculars, probably served as the source not only for various literary works, but for a great number of folktales. A modern English translation of the *Gesta* appeared, in fact, as early as the 1820s, although even in the revised and much-reprinted version by Wynnard Hooper the moralisations attached to the individual stories were retained only in an abridged and sometimes amended form, and they are often different from the Latin (Swan 1877). In the nineteenth century and after, folktale analogues to the story of Gregorius, often based on the *Gesta*, began to be adduced from all over Europe and beyond, with material ranging from Ireland to Armenia, what is now Iraq, and Egypt. There is also, interestingly, a Jewish version in which the hero becomes a famous rabbi; it was printed in Poland in 1909 in Hebrew with some Yiddish, and crosses therefore yet another boundary. That Hassidic version is, moreover, of some importance in terms of folktale morphology and also of literary structuring (Elstein 1986). A nineteenth century song-cycle, an Austrian play in the 1950s, and especially the efforts of Thomas Mann, who used the tale in his *Doktor Faustus* before devoting a whole novel to the theme in 1951 as *Der Erwählte* (*The Holy Sinner*), which has in its turn been adapted for the theatre in the present century in places as far apart as Poland and New Zealand, all hand the story down to the present.

The folktale versions are of special interest, although there are several basic problems in assessing them. Precise dating is extremely difficult, and judgement is always required as to how close they are as analogues, or what relationship to the basic story they actually have, even though they have been presented in secondary studies either as parallels or sometimes even as evidence for (lost) original versions. Some, however remote, do still retain most of the original story. One in modern Syriac (Neo-Aramaic) was collected in Alqôsh, in what is now Iraq, by

Karl Eduard Sachau in the 1880s, and printed in German translation (Lizdbarski 1896: 56–64). Apparently originally from a written (Nestorian) source, it does, to be sure, have a number of oddities (including an afterthought ending in which the Pope makes the central figure a Patriarch), but it retains most of the elements found in the western versions, even though the central figure is called Alexander (a name which appears regularly in the *Gesta Romanorum*). In other cases, the change or loss of specific motifs can cause a shift in the balance of the narrative from theology to entertainment, although the theological aspects never entirely disappear; and even the role and relative position of the central figure may change. Further, within a given culture several versions may survive, each of which contains some of the elements of the original story. Two preliminary points may be noted, however. First the loss of the name Gregorius is not especially significant, particularly when we have moved away from the influence of the Roman Church, for which it is a significant papal name. Secondly, the chivalric aspects of Gregorius's career after he leaves the monastery, which are played up in the early western versions (which were often directed at an audience of lay nobility, often addressed as *seigneurs*, for example, in the French poems) are regularly lost in the folktales.

Terms such as reduction, degeneration and (most notably in the case of the folktale) morphology may all be applied to the Gregorius story. Indeed, the reduction of the earliest and extensive metrical versions to prose begins early, and in more straightforward terms continues with the loss or syncopation of episodes or motifs. There have been studies of textual degeneration with respect to medieval romances, for example (see Jacobs 1995). Vladímir Propp's *Morphology of the Folktale* is of course a structural study of fairy-tales (with implications for later literature), and in the case of Gregorius, the folktale versions sometimes reconfigure the motifs to conform to set models; but the assimilation of a hagiographic romance to the folktale presents interesting problems in terms of Propp's insights and the type-analysis of Antti Aarne and Stith Thompson. In the categorising work of the latter scholars, Gregorius is linked with the Oedipus saga however (Propp 1968; Aarne and Thompson 1961; Thompson 1955–1958; and see Ó Súilleabháin and Christiansen 1963; 184; Jolles 1930).

In view of the wealth of material available, demonstration of the process and results of reduction and change in the later stages of the tradition must necessarily be selective. Attention will be paid here to a literary text in which the reduction may be (in part) accidental; to some early folk-ballads (long known and noted as analogues); to some far later oral folktales (largely ignored in studies of the tradition), which are distant from the folk-ballads in chronological and geographical terms, although in both cases different elements of the original story have been preserved in separate versions; and finally to a folktale which, although still recognisable in terms of the preservation of a number of motifs, has shifted the hagiographical narrative to a point where only the superficiality of the shared motifs makes it part of the tradition, and which therefore tests the definition of analogue.

The Valencian writer Juan de Timoneda (ca. 1518–1583) published in 1567 a popular collection of prose novellas, *Patrañuelo*, which contains as his *patraño quinta* a version of the story of Gregorius based probably – at least up to a point – on that in the *Gesta Romanorum* (Referres 1979). The story was well-known in Spain, and a century later, in 1658, it was also used in thoroughly operatic fashion by the dramatist Juan de Matos Fragoso as *El marido de su madre san Gregorio*, a play which makes the first incest illusory (the pair prove not to be brother and sister) and avoids the second altogether (the marriage is not consummated) although Gregorius does penance anyway. Juan de Timoneda's version, however, though found in a well-known work, follows the original only until about the halfway point, when it replaces the second incest, penance, elevation and absolution with an unconvincing and abrupt alternative ending, which has a distinct effect on the tale as a saint's life, or indeed as a religious work at all. Why the change was made is far from clear, but the rhymed quatrain which heads the fifth novella in the collection already speaks simply of "a child put out to sea, the teachings of an abbot, the naming of Gregorius, who afterwards became king". There is no indication that this might be hagiographic or even moralising. For all that, what we *do* have of the original story is very close to the epitome: a sister becomes pregnant by her brother, she weeps for the sin and the brother leaves disguised as a poor pilgrim (which sounds rather like Gregorius himself later on) to seek pardon from the pope, but drowns on the way to Rome. The baby boy is set out to sea with silver and gold for his education, and a golden tablet, is found by a fisherman and baptized Gregorius by the abbot of a rich monastery. He is educated, learns of his background after the usual incident with his foster-brother, and is then trained as a knight and departs. Gregorius rescues his mother, whose lands are under attack, and as a reward the queen agrees to marry him. This sequence, the setting forth of the hero as a knight, the conquest and the marriage are all established parts of the folktale as such; the initial training of the central figure as a cleric in the monastery is not.

In the early versions of the tale there now follows the central sin of the principal character, the unwitting but nevertheless sinful act of incest with his mother, and Gregorius's awareness thereafter (since he has been clerically trained), that penance can cancel out even this dreadful sin, and help him to regain grace. In the *Patrañuelo*, Gregorius gives the queen the tablet indicating his background before the marriage is consummated, so that she realises at once that Gregorius is her son, nephew and now husband, something which usually happens after the sin has been committed. In this case it seems as if the writer simply found the second incest too much too take, but at all events a completely new and largely secular ending is provided, in which Gregorius marries the widow of the queen's steward instead, who had been killed in the battle to save the lands. The queen vows to remain chaste, and the whole matter is kept secret; all live happily and honourably for many years thereafter. The ending differs considerably from the truncated version of the *Gesta Romanorum*, so that it cannot be considered as a source; that version retains the second incest and Gregorius is pardoned by a voice from heaven, even if he does not become pope.

The real point of the work has been lost. The monastic education and the central figure's papal name (referred to more than once) point on to the papacy after the strikingly great penance for his incest, but none of that happens; Gregorius does no penance, becomes neither pope nor saint, and does not even go to heaven. All that remains of the theological background is the implicit punishment on the father of Gregorius, and the continued chastity of the mother. The overall effect of abrupt and unsatisfactory secularisation in a literary production, going further than the variant narrative in the *Gesta Romanorum* tradition anticipates, however, several later versions. The Jewish version recorded and discussed by Elstein avoids the second incest (in that case by divine intervention), and as noted, the later Spanish play manages to avoid, in effect, both instances of incest.

A degenerate but still comparable version of the story of Gregorius is provided in three separate Serbian ballads (in trochaic ten-syllable lines with formulaic repetitions), which seem to be early analogues, and two at least of which were adduced as such at an early stage in the scholarly study of the Gregorius tradition. The Serbian folk-ballad itself, which was the object of much attention in the context of oral-formulaic composition, structure and indeed variation by Milman Parry and Albert B. Lord, is a significant genre (Lord 1960), and it is of interest that the whole tale of Gregorius – albeit with some changes, and with the predictable loss of the name and the papal outcome – is nevertheless covered in the three surviving examples. All three have the mother-son incest, but the two versions first noted seem not to have the brother-sister incest, although in fact it may well be present in a distorted form in one of them, and may originally have been there in the other; it *is* present in the third version. As a separate matter, nationalism seems to have reshaped one of these Serbian songs to a certain extent. The central figure in all of them is *Nakhod Simeon*, Simeon the Foundling, and the songs were collected in the early nineteenth century by Vuk Stefanovič Karadźič (1787–1864) (1841–1865, II: nos. 14 and 15; VI: no. 5). They aroused interest in Germany from Goethe and later Jacob Grimm, and the two first identified were translated at an early stage into German (Talwj 1825–1826: I, 71–77; Gerhard 1828: 226–232). Their source is not clear, but reference has probably correctly been made in the context to the *Gesta Romanorum*, with considerable degeneration apart from the name-change. The date of the three songs is equally unclear, though they may go back to the fifteenth or sixteenth century. The apparent absence of the brother/sister incest in the two songs first translated and discussed seemed to move them away from the Gregorius-tradition, but in 1946 an English translation was published of a third Serbian ballad (also in Karadźič's collection) which does have that initial incest, and this completes the picture (Walshe 1946).

In the first song the birth of the central figure is not described at all, and the tale begins with the finding by an abbot or senior monk of a child in a basket, with a Gospel-book, by the Danube. Since we are told nothing of the background, it may be that the original incest was either left out deliberately, or has simply been lost in the process of transmission. The child is baptized Simeon, and a repeated formula indicates that the child is advanced by a specific number of years. Mocked at the monastery school as a foundling, he returns to the monastery, takes his Gospel-book and is given a horse and money to go and find out his identity. After a formulaic nine years he wishes to return to the monastery, but encounters instead the queen of Buda, who is taken with his beauty, plies him with wine and he kisses her, presumably a euphemistic avoidance for the incest. He flees in shame on the following morning, leaving his Gospel-book. He is not rescuing (or marrying) the lady, who is of course his mother. When he returns to find the book – which now serves as the recognition-token – he finds the queen weeping over it, and she tells him that he is her son. There has still been an unwitting sin, therefore. Simeon returns to the monastery, and as a penance is imprisoned in a cell with water up to his knees, the water filled with snakes and scorpions. The key is thrown into the Danube and he will be forgiven when it is found; after another formulaic nine years a fish is caught with the key in it, and Simeon is found in a dry cell, bathed in golden light, the Gospels in his hand. The mother receives no absolution, and indeed has a very limited role here except as a seductress. Nor is Simeon elevated to any ecclesiastical dignity.

The second song does provide a fore-tale, in which an emperor brings up a young girl so that he can marry her, which he does against her will, although there were other suitors. This slightly obscure opening is perhaps clarified by the third ballad, where a brother brings up a younger sister, and it is possible that this is intended in the second song, so that the initial incest may indeed be present after all. Certainly the girl sets her child out to sea, specifically for fear that he will turn out like his progenitor, so that she sees the child as wicked, rather than the act of begetting. The child is found by the patriarch Sava with writings and clothing, and is again named Simeon. Simeon takes the writings and clothing when he is sent out into the world to establish his parentage, reaches the court of his mother, who – as in the epitome – is being pursued by suitors, and they marry. The mother later recognises the writings and clothing and tells Simeon that he has married his own mother. Simeon confesses to the patriarch Sava, is placed in a stone tower and the key is thrown into the sea, again with the comment that he will be forgiven when it is found (this motif always indicates that forgiveness is possible after a potentially finite period, since the key always is found). After thirty years it is found in a golden-finned fish. Simeon is dead, but prayers and vigils are offered at the "church of Vilendar", so that here the central figure seems at least to have become a cultic saint. Some of these adaptations of the original tale are explained to an extent by Serbian history, which at least provides an explanation for the names: the early thirteenth-century St. Sava is the patron saint of Serbia and founder of the Orthodox monastery (Khiliandarion, Hilandar, Vilendar) on Mount Athos. His father, the Serbian king Stephen I Nemanja adopted the name Simeon as a monk and is known as St. Simeon.

In the shorter third song a brother keeps his younger sister as a mistress, rather than finding her a husband. Their child, set out with a christening robe, is found this time by Patriarch St. Dmitri, rather than the Serbian St. Sava. This presumably refers to the Russian Orthodox saint, Dmitri of Rostov (1684–1705), who was indeed popular in the South Slav world, and gives us a date from the eighteenth century or later. Simeon the Foundling is brought up as a knight, and Dmitri sends the boy to marry a widowed queen in Hungary, so that the theological education and later quest motifs are both lost. How the queen, Simeon's mother, came to be widowed and what happened to his father is unclear. Later she discovers and recognises the christening robe, and reveals the truth. She wonders then how they can be delivered from their sin, expressing thus an awareness of guilt. Simeon returns to Dmitri, who locks him in a dungeon and throws the keys into the sea, again with the prophecy that the sin will be forgiven when they are returned, so that motif of possible forgiveness is maintained as usual. Seven weeks later the keys are discovered on the shore, the dungeon is opened and Simeon is found there, Gospel in hand, but dies at once. Dmitri has a rose planted on his grave which provides solace for travellers. All three folk-ballads are still hagiographic, with some veneration of the central figure at the end, who is, even if not elevated to the papacy, able to confer grace or (in the weakest of the versions) at least offer some benefit for the traveller. Simeon's incest is unwitting (though the sexual guilt in the first song is not quite the same as in the body of the tradition), and penance is still presented as necessary. The theological implications of the tradition are still there, and indeed the addition of local-national elements simply adapts the hagiography without losing it.

A similar situation – of the preservation in several tales of discrete elements of the original story – obtains in a series of Irish folktales, collected from oral sources in the middle of the twentieth century. There is, in fact, an earlier written Irish prose version which clearly derives from the *Gesta Romanorum*, and which has the title *Geineamhain Ghrigóir* ("The birth of Gregorius"). The manuscript is dated 1678, but the Irish in which it is written is notoriously conservative in nature, so that a date for the original is very hard to determine. It has been placed in the late fifteenth century, but that may well be rather early. As with later folktales, it does show the loss of some major motifs, notably the absence of the cloth placed with the infant Gregorius which serves later on as a potential recognition-object. This motif, however, does occur in one of several oral folktales collected in the west of Ireland relatively recently and preserved in the collections of the Irish Folklore Commission, indicating that the full story was originally more widely-known in Ireland, something which gives us, with Iceland, the most westerly extent for the tale (Falconer 1958). The written version is fairly close to the *Gesta Romanorum*, with some local changes – Gregorius hurts his foster-brother during a game of hurling, for example, and the fish in which the key is found is a salmon – and some unusual deviations such as the naming of the central figure by his mother rather than by an abbot. The revelation of the incestuous marriage is also condensed. The letters placed with the child ask that he be educated and brought up as a prince, though he does become learned. Having read of his origins in the letters he sets out as a knight and eventually reaches his mother's lands, where she is under siege by the son of the King of Hungary (possibly a scribal confusion at some stage between Hungary and the usual Burgundy). Gregorius defeats him, but the queen's nobles and counsellors, afraid that the king of Hungary will come and avenge his son, want her to marry Gregorius, and when she refuses, having vowed permanent chastity, they threaten to withdraw their allegiance if she refuses, so that she is blackmailed into compliance. The revelation of the incest comes quickly, and the mother sends her son off on a pilgrimage, and this time he is locked into a church on a rock in the sea. This is unusual, although the fact that he stays there for eighteen years, instead of the seventeen common in early versions, may just be a slip from a misread Roman numeral. That he is in a church is a variation found in later folktales, however. He becomes pope and, having refused for some time to see his mother when she comes as a penitent, eventually grants absolution and reveals his identity. Gregorius is not, however, expressly described as a saint.

The editor of this written text has provided details of three oral versions, one from County Cork and two from County Galway, collected in the early 1940s. The first is in English, but has the Irish title *Pápa an Bhéil Órdha* ("The Pope with the Golden Mouth") and the second, in Irish, has a similar title. The epithet is applied elsewhere in Irish to Gregory the Great, but St. John Chrysostom (literally "golden-mouth") is linked with the story in the related legend of Paul of Caesarea, recorded in a Bulgarian manuscript, and published in Russian and then in German (Köhler 1870: 288–291). That legend is readily recognisable as an analogue in spite of the different names, and John Chrysostom actually appears in it, but the reference in the Irish titles may simply be a coincidence. In the body of these two oral Irish versions, the unnamed hero does not, in spite of the title, even become pope. The first has the hero, who is the child of a brother (who is a priest) and sister, but is never named, exposed like Oedipus rather than being set out to sea; there is throughout the tradition the possibility of interference from the familiar Greek tale, and the editor of the Irish material notes parallels with this and with other incest-legends (Falconer 1958). Eventually he becomes a priest and returns to his parents. He discovers his origins and does penance – for his birth sin, rather than for actual sin on this occasion, presumably – on a remote island, locked in a cave. The key is found in a fish, and he is released and returns to the world. There is no second incest here, but at the end the son does anoint his parents, after which all are changed into white doves, something which again happens in other folktales. The second oral tale begins with a father-daughter incest, which is rather more common than sibling incest in medieval incest-tales and folktales (Archibald 2001), but is of course very different from the Gregorius tradition. The second incest is as in the tradition, although the son and the mother have children. The central figure undertakes a penance under water, from which he is rescued by a papal emissary and pardoned by the pope, and he returns then to his wife/mother. His two sons become priests. The third oral tale is brief and corrupt (the mother's name in the title – *Gréige Ni Ghuaire do mháthair* ("[Greg-] Guaire is your mother") – seems to be a garbled version of Gregorius), and the child is again born from a father-daughter incest. What remains here is the marriage to the mother and the recognition by way of an embroidered cloth, which is a regular feature in the tradition, but not present in the other written or oral Irish versions. Of the oral tales, then, only one has a brother-sister incest, and that does not have the second incest. Two, however, have the penance, and their recent provenance demonstrates the longevity of the tale, but also its fragmentation, preserving different parts of the story in different versions.

Although there are many further variations on the narrative in those folktales which have been recorded, it is appropriate to end with one where a supposed analogue ceases to be, in effect, a story of Gregorius at all, quite apart from the loss of the name. The Hungarian folktale of "Janos the Crane" (available once more in German translation) has, in spite of having been claimed as a version of the Gregorius narrative, lost most (though not quite all) of the ecclesiastical elements. Moreover, not only is the supposed central figure no longer called Gregorius, but he is no longer really at the centre (Róna-Sklarek 1909: 269–271). Janos is born after an illicit but not incestuous liaison between a princess and a soldier, and put out in a golden casket, where he is found by a fisherman. Driven away after mockery, he encounters his mother and she seduces him. As soon as Janos reveals his background, the mother realises who he is, and in remorse they seek absolution from the pope. Janos is given a seven-year penance, while this time it is the mother who is locked inside a church and the key thrown away. After his own penance, Janos retrieves the key from the inevitable fish, but when the church is opened the mother is gone and a white dove flies out (a motif seen already in Irish and found elsewhere). Janos marries and lives happily.

Some elements are recognisable: a princess's illicit child, its removal by being put out to sea, the fisherman, the unwitting (and here brief) relationship with the mother, and the penances, which come from the pope. There was, indeed, a Hun-

garian version of the *Gesta Romanorum* made in the late seventeenth century by
János Haller (1626–1697), so that it is unsurprising that the story as such was
known (Katona 1900). But the folktale has no brother-sister incest, no abbot and
no ecclesiastical destiny, papal or otherwise, for Janos. In fact, his mother is at the
centre of the tale and is the subject of the real miracle. The child's conception is
different: the soldier hides inside a golden crane that had been made as a present
for the princess, and which forms the memorable tag for the story. The motif of
the key in the fish, which is part of the original tradition, is of course a familiar
staple of the folktale in any case. The mother alone turns into a white dove, which
does mean, presumably, that she has been given absolution directly from God for
her sin. The titular central character, no longer even Gregorius, is neither pope,
bishop, nor saint, and he lives happily ever after in this world. Unlike most of the
earlier versions, this one gives us no idea what happens to him in the next. A ficti-
tious saint, then, has been completely desanctified.

The tale of the apocryphal saint Gregorius has an extensive tradition, and in
spite of some inevitable overlaps he is not simply an Oedipus, indeed is not really an Oedipus figure at all, although he has sometimes been seen as a medieval
Oedipus. Oedipus, it must be recalled, is not the product of incest, and Gregorius
does not commit parricide, and certainly he does not blind himself in despair, but
argues precisely against *desperatio*. Indeed, his largely undeserved and certainly
unwitting fate may be linked equally well with that of Job (and the words of Job
regretting the day he was born are regularly voiced by all the main characters in the
story). Thomas Mann, too, was well aware that there were links between the central character and Faust: *es irrt der Mensch, so lang er strebt*, man will err, while
he strives. In spite of the extravagant nature of the double incest in the tradition,
Gregorius in terms of example is also an everyman figure. Initially the story provides less a hagiographic legend as such than an example for the forgiveness of all
sins, however extreme, provided one does not despair – something the monasti-
cally trained Gregorius usually points out to his mother after the discovery of their
incest in early versions. The initial brother-and-sister incest can be linked, too, with
Adam and Eve, themselves patently of one flesh, and the tale can be related both
to the response to original sin and to actual sin (Murdoch 2000: 50–75). The *Gesta
Romanorum* version of the tale links it firmly with divine providence, in which
apparent evil acts can lead to good endings. As the extensive tradition continues,
however, the crucial narrative elements which support the theology are trimmed
or lost, and eventually pretty well all the links to theological problems, most notably the response to unwitting sin – the accidental mother and son incest – in a
Christian context are suppressed. But in spite of the dwindling and fragmentation
of the story, the narrative remains a theological one, and even with the reduction
and indeed displacement of the central figure himself in the Hungarian folktale,
the mother, at least, embodies the concept of grace after penance.

The paper given at the Stirling symposium in May, 2010, of which this is a revised version, was part of the preliminary work for my book, *Gregorius*, which appeared with Oxford University Press in 2012, the fifth chapter of which contains a full survey of late reworkings and folktale versions.

References Cited

Aarne, Antti, and Stith Thompson
1961   The Types of the Folktale. Helsinki: Acad. Scien. Fennica.

Archibald, Elizabeth
2001   Incest and the Medieval Imagination. Oxford: OUP.

Dick, Wilhelm
1890   Die Gesta Romanorum, nach der Innsbrucker Hs. vom Jahre 1342 und vier Münchener Hss. Erlangen and Leipzig: Deichert. (repr. Amsterdam: Rodopi, 1970)

Elstein, Yoav
1986   The Gregorius Legend: Its Christian Versions and its Metamorphosis. In: The Hassidic Tale. *Fabula* 27: 195–215.

Falconer, Sheila
1958   An Irish Translation of the Gregory Legend. *Celtica* 4: 52–95.

Gerhard, Wilhelm
1828   Wila: Serbische Volkslieder und Heldenmährchen I. Leipzig: Barth.

Jacobs, Nicolas
1995   The Later Versions of Sir Degarre: A Study in Textual Degeneration. Oxford: SSMLL.

Jolles, André
1930   Einfache Formen. Tübingen: Niemeyer. (repr. Darmstadt: Wissenschaftliche Buchgesellschaft, 1958)

Karadžič, Vuk Stefanovič
1841–1865   Srpske narodne pyesme. Vienna: Yermenski manastir. (later editions in Belgrade in 1891, 1932–1936, 1976 and see the Projekat Rastko on the web: www.rastko.rs/knjizevnost/vuk/index.html)

Katona, Lajos
1900   Gesta Romanorum. Budapest: Franklin-Társulat.

Köhler, Reinhold
1870   Zur Legende von Gregorius auf dem Steine. *Germania* 15: 284–291.

Lidzbarski, Mark
1896   Geschichten und Lieder aus den neuaramäischen Handschriften der königlichen Bibliothek zu Berlin. Weimar: Felber.

Lord, Albert B.
1960   The Singer of Tales. Cambridge: Harvard University Press. (repr. New York: Athenaeum, 1968)

Murdoch, Brian
2000   Adam's Grace: Fall and Redemption in Medieval Literature. Cambridge: Brewer.

Oesterley, Hermann
1872   Gesta Romanorum. Berlin: Weidmann. (repr. Hildesheim: Olms, 1963)

Ó Súilleabháin, S., and R. Th. Christiansen
1963   The Types of the Irish Folktale. Helsinki: Acad. Scien. Fennica.

Propp, Vladímir
1968   The Morphology of the Folktale. 2nd ed. trans. Laurence Scott, Austin and London: University of Texas Press.

Referres, Rafael
1079   Juan de Timoneda, El Patrañuelo. Madrid: Castilia. (also in the Biblioteca virtual Miguel de Cervantes on the web)

Róna-Sklarek, Elisabet
1909   Ungarische Volksmärchen: Neue Folge. Leipzig: Diederich.

Swan, Charles
1877   Gesta Romanorum [1824]. rev., corr. Wynnard Hooper. London: Bell. (repr. London: Bell, 1905)

Talwj [i.e. **Therese Albertine Luise von Jacob**]
1825–1826   Volkslieder der Serben. Halle: Renger. (new ed. Leipzig: Brockhaus, 1853)

Thompson, Stith
1955–1958   A Motif Index of Folk Literature. Bloomington: Indiana University Press.

Walshe, M. O'C.
1946   Two Serbian Ballads. I. Simeon the Foundling. *Slavonic and East European Review* 24: 14–15.

"Hechli Berbara!":
Identity and the Celebration of Saint Barbara in North Lebanon

Christine B. Lindner

Abstract. – This article explores the popular hagiography and celebrations for Saint Barbara as practiced by Christians in North Lebanon. The unique nature of these commemorations illuminates the specific cultural, historical and political influences on this community, which is emphasized through a comparison to the commemorations for Saint Barbara at different geographic locations and historical periods. It is argued that these differences emerge through culturally specific readings of Saint Barbara's hagiography, through which certain themes are emphasized within the celebratory practices. As these are living traditions, changes to the population and culture of North Lebanon have influenced recent celebrations of Saint Barbara Feast. *[Saint Barbara, Popular Hagiography, Oral History, North Lebanon]*

Christine B. Lindner, Ph.D. is a historian of gender and transnational identities, focusing specifically on Christian communities that connect American and Middle Eastern societies. She is a co-organizer of the Christians in the Middle East research network. Publications include "'Making a way into the heart of the people': Women of the Early Protestant Church in Beirut" (2011); "The Flexibility of Home: Investigating the Spaces and Definitions for the Home and Family Employed by the ABCFM Missionaries in Ottoman Syria from 1823 to 1860" (Salt Lake City, 2011); "'In this religion I will live, and in this religion I will die': Performativity and the Protestant Identity in Late Ottoman Syria" (2010); "'Long, long will she be affectionately remembered': Gender and the Memorialization of an American Female Missionary" (2009).

While walking to my office at the University of Balamand in Lebanon, on a bright December day in 2010, I came across two female undergraduate students. Both were fitted in fancy dress costumes, while one carried a large serving bowl. I noticed decorations that resembled those displayed by my own mother in her New York suburban home and remembered the date. This was the day of the university's celebration of *Eid il-Berbara*: the Feast for the Great Martyr Barbara.

Commemorations for saints, like Barbara, are important facets through which religion is personally experienced and collectively performed. Although often based upon "official" hagiographies, religious celebrations and popular iconographies are part of a community's "lived religion" (Hermkens, Jansen and Notermans 2009: 3). As such, these practices are not static, but evolve to reflect the changes unfolding within and outside of the community (Jansen 2009: 36). They can be considered "bricolage" events through which divergent elements are selectively appropriated and adapted to create new religious experiences that illuminate the hybrid identity of its participants.[1] Comparing the commemorations for a particular saint from culture to culture, and across time periods, can uncover the ways that historical, social and political changes are personally embodied and performed. Religious traditions are thus individual performances of a collective identity.

This article will explore the traditions for the annual commemoration of Saint Barbara practiced by Christians in North Lebanon. In addition to the University of Balamand, this area encompasses the districts of Koura, Zhgarta-Ehden, Tripoli, Dinnieh and Akkar, with a population that is predominately Sunni Muslim, Greek Orthodox and Maronite Christian, with smaller pockets of other sectarian communities. The data for this research stems from an Oral History project conducted with university students who interviewed older relatives or neighbors about religious and cultural traditions.[2] Three of the students selected Saint Barbara's Feast for their Oral History project, and represent the Greek Orthodox and Maronite communities from the villages of Zgharta, Kulhat, and Kafarhazir (Barakat 2010, Dib 2010, Fadel 2010). Additional interviews and research supplement these texts to fully explore the Christian identity of North Lebanon (Abboud 2011, Jabbra 2011, Najjar 2011, Teeny 2011a, 2011b).

In order to identify the celebratory elements that are as specific to North Lebanon, comparisons will be made to other commemorations of Saint Barbara. These include celebratory events, such as songs and parades, as well as iconographic images. Comparing these remembrances demonstrates that Saint Barbara is a highly adaptable saint, for the nature of these commemorations varies greatly over time and across geographic locations. This diversity stems from the malleability of Barbara's hagiography to local interpretations. It will be argued that this diversity reflects the way that the political, social and historical contexts influence a community's celebration, through the selective emphasis of specific themes within Barbara's hagiography.

From this it is possible to re-examine the celebrations for Saint Barbara in North Lebanon, identifying how established traditions and current changes draw upon certain themes within her story. However, these recent transformations illuminate the multiple and sometimes conflicting influences on contemporary Christians in North Lebanon. As the celebrations for Saint Barbara are constructed through "bricolage", recent changes in political structuring, immigration and social capital have affected the popular performances of these celebrations. The Feast for Saint Barbara thus continues to be a living and evolving tradition.

---

[1] For an important discussion on the use of the term "bricolage", as defined according to Roger Bastide (rather than the use by Claude Lévi-Strauss), over the term "syncretism", see Schmidt 2006: 236–243.

[2] This project was organized in collaboration with Souad Slim and Robert Wise.

Hechli Berbara

On the eve of Saint Barbara's Feast day, which is celebrated on the fourth of December (according to the Gregorian calendar),[3] the shouts of children can be heard throughout the Christian villages of North Lebanon. As children pass from neighbor to neighbor, they sing a traditional song:

Hachli Berbara maa' banat el hara.
E'refta men 'iinayha, wa men laftit Idayha, wa men haik el iswara!

Barbara is fleeing with the neighborhood girls.
I recognize her from her eyes and from the gesture of her hands and from that bracelet!
(Najjar 2011)[4]

Singing this song and dressed in different costumes, the children ask for money and sweets, particularly "hameh el berbara", the staple dish of barley wheat soaked in rose water (Barakat 2010; Hussein 2010).

The respondents of the Oral History project explained that these traditions celebrate the life of the Great Martyr Barbara and have been repeated for at least three generations, which is the definition of a "tradition" employed in this study. The respondents recalled the story of Saint Barbara as such: "Barbara was the daughter of a pagan, a person who doesn't believe in the same God she believed in, our one and only God. He used to worship statues and isolate her in a tower to preserve her beauty and virginity and to keep her from the outside world" (Dib 2010). Another explained that "the curiosity of Barbara pushed her to ask and to learn more about Jesus, and believed in him as the son of God and the saver of humanity" (Barakat 2010). The story continues that:

Once, her father ordered to build an extension to the tower so she messed with [sic] the design and put three windows instead of two as a symbol of the Trinity. After her father was sure [that] she was a Christian, he denounced her to the Roman province [sic] where they treated her badly and tortured her (Dib 2010).

In some accounts, Barbara's wounds from the torture were miraculously healed (Dib 2010). In one version, Barbara was "made [to] walk nude in front of all the people of the kingdom, according to Barbara's father['s] request. For this reason, she decided to cover her face with a mask so that no one can recognize her" (Barakat 2010). Another respondent stated that "Saint Barbara used to disguise herself in multiple characters to mislead the Romans who used to follow her and

---

[3] The Julian Calendar sets Saint Barbara's Feast on the 17 December, when the Alawites of Turkey (a heterodox Shia Muslim community who integrate various Christian saints into their worship) celebrate her festival (Procházka-Eisl and Procházka, 2010: 102 note 292).

[4] I have chosen to transliterate the Arabic songs in a manner that keeps the colloquial intonations of words instead of homogenizing the Arabic.

to be able to meet with other Christians without her father knowing" (Dib 2010). One concluded the story stating that: "[t]hey say that her father was struck by lightning after they beheaded her since he preferred her death over [her] remaining a Christian" (Dib 2010).

Analyzing these responses, we can identify three major characteristics that guide the traditions and popular hagiography of Saint Barbara in North Lebanon. Firstly, children are the central component of the traditions. It is the children who dress up, sing the songs, visit neighbors and collect treats. The celebrations center upon the children's activities and encourage them to participate in reenacting elements of Barbara's story.

Second, there is a strong emphasis on community. Familial and communal ties are important in Lebanon, where *wasta* (connection) is commonly employed for social maneuvering (Stamn 2006: 23, 28–31). All three respondents illuminate the communal nature of these traditions. The celebrations could not be properly performed alone: they require interaction amongst people and the movement within the public sphere. Celebrating Saint Barbara's Feast is an important time to bring together young and old within a village, reconnecting communities and providing an opportunity to give to the local poor (Fadel 2010).

Nevertheless, the traditions performed in North Lebanon require individual identification with both Barbara and the saints who helped her, which is the third characteristic. By putting on masks and "running" from house to house, the children individually recreate the acts of Barbara in her flight from her father. As one respondent explained: "Her energy and light [are represented] by the makeup people wear. Her stubborn[ness] in defending her religion with candles. Her persistence in her religion even though she was in so much pain with wheat [that we eat]" (Fadel 2010). Drawing upon the theories of Judith Butler (1990), the enactment of these events can be read as a performative icon, through which the children connect to God through individually reenacting the life of this Martyr-Saint.[5]

Moreover, by giving gifts and joining in the singing of songs, the villagers themselves become part of the Barbara story: as her protectors and assistants. Although not identified by the respondents, some hagiographies identify another woman, Juliana, as having helped Barbara and who also died a martyr (Saint John of Damascus Institute of Theology n. d.). Nevertheless, there is a clear emphasis on helping Barbara within the described celebrations. The chanted song encourages: "Hechli Berbara!", which one respondent translated as "Run away Barbara!" (Dib 2010). The song also recognizes that it was only the believers who were able to correctly identify Barbara from behind her disguises; by recognizing her eyes, hands and bracelet. Likewise, it is only one from within the community who can

---

[5] This differs from Pentceva's use of the phrase "performative icon" to describe the belief that icons are "living paintings" through their evocation of the senses (Pentcheva 2006).

correctly identify the children from behind their masks and properly respond with suitable sweets and treats. But as the children now represent Barbara, aiding them thus aids the saint, and affirms the villagers' communion within the church.

Although not referenced to by the respondents of the Oral History project, four churches or chapels dedicated to Saint Barbara are located in North Lebanon. The first is the ruined Church of Saint Barbara, located in Barghoun along the coast. These ruins are dated to the fourteenth or fifteenth century, suggesting that the commemoration of Saint Barbara in North Lebanon dates to the Mamluk period of the late Middle Ages (Davie et al. 2010d). The three other churches dedicated to Saint Barbara are located in Amioun, Ras Masqa and Kousba and were erected in the early twentieth century upon the foundations of ruins dating to the Middle Ages (Davie et al. 2010a, 2010b, 2010c, 2010e). While it is unclear from the sources if these ancient churches were also dedicated to Saint Barbara, the (re)construction of the three churches in her honor reveals an increased interest in the saint amongst Christians of North Lebanon during the early twentieth century.

In accordance with Orthodox tradition, the three churches place an icon for Saint Barbara on their iconostases. Noticeably though, the icons of the three churches vary. The icon from Amioun, which was painted in the late 1960s by Greek Orthodox nuns from the nearby Mar Yaccoub (Saint James) Monastery in Dideh, has Greek writing and follows traditional Orthodox imagery of linear features and a golden background (Davie et al. 2010a). The icons from Ras Masqa and Kousba however, include European symbolism; the details of which will be discussed below (Davie et al. 2010b, 2010e). Noticeably, these three icons differ from the paper icon reproductions that are popularly sold and privately held by Christians.[6] These appear to be based upon recent Russian or Greek icons, for they fuse traditional Orthodox and European symbolism, but in a manner that differs from the icons of the three churches. While the practices for celebrating Saint Barbara are relatively uniform in North Lebanon, her iconographic representation is varied.

Comparing Traditions

The traditions for celebrating the Feast of Saint Barbara in North Lebanon have been repeated from generation to generation, but differ from the commemorations for Saint Barbara performed by Christian communities around the world and over time.

The earliest commemorations for Saint Barbara emerged in Turkey, where many, although not those in Lebanon, identify as the setting for her story. As described by Pfannkuch (1987: 41), her remains were deposited in Constantinople during the sixth century and churches were named in her honor during the ninth

---

[6] Two private icons were shared with the author by Bianca Teeny and Michelli Lakkis.

and tenth centuries. A Coptic church for Saint Barbara was established in Egypt during the seventh century, while a holiday for her in Syria is dated to the tenth century. Pfannkuch argues (1987: 41) that while these commemorations for Saint Barbara were exported from the eastern Mediterranean to Europe in the Middle Ages, he does not provide details about them, limiting our understanding of the ancient traditions. As such, it is possible, but difficult to determine if the North Lebanese traditions stem from the ancient traditions, or if they are imported and adapted from later European traditions.

After arriving in Europe, Saint Barbara became a popular saint throughout the late Middle Ages. She was included as one of the fourteen saintly intercessors as well as one of the four Virgin Saints, who often accompanied the Virgin Mary in paintings (Pfannkuch 1987: 41). Images depicting Saint Barbara are profound, dating from the fourteenth to seventeenth centuries. Many of these show her wearing a crown, holding a book (presumably the Bible), a long feather or palm branch, and standing near a tower (Anon 1450, Anon 1490a, Anon 1490b, Memling 1480). The crown reflects her elevated status, as a daughter of a Roman governor (Pfannkuch 1987: 40). The book may reference the hagiographical detail that Barbara became a Christian through study and by aid of a tutor (Assaf n. d.: 323–329).[7] The feather is associated with immortality, arguing that she gained immortality through Christ. It also represents purity, symbolizing her virginal death (O'Grady 2002: 55). The tower is an indentifying aspect of Barbara's story, for she rebelled against her father's paganism by having a third window cut into the tower representing the Trinity.[8] The popular hagiographies of North Lebanon also mention Barbara's elevated status, her learning of Christianity, rejuvenation from wounds and contestation over the tower windows. These elements are most clearly displayed in the icons of the Ras Masqa and Kousba churches that were produced during the past one hundred years. Thus the presence of these European symbols may be foreign imports, adapted by Christians in North Lebanon, similar to the way that European Marian imagery has been appropriated by Arab Christians (Jansen 2009: 33–48; Jabbra 2009: 291–295).

In some parts of Europe, Saint Barbara is regarded as the patron saint of artillerymen and miners. Pfannkuch (1987) argues that these associations are rooted in the historical transformation of the central European mining industry when Barbara replaced local saints through the selective emphasis or adaptation of her hagiography to support mining culture. The link with artillery is based upon the belief that her father was killed by lightening as punishment for his act of beheading Barbara. While both the Lebanese and European accounts describe the death of

---

[7] This detail is not currently part of the present day Roman Catholic hagiography, but is present in the Greek Catholic version.

[8] For a feminist interpretation of this symbolism see Caprio (1982).

Barbara's father by lightening, it is within the European context that this is used to link Barbara with artillery. The mining association stems from the detail that Barbara hid in a rock while escaping her father (Pfannkuch 1987: 42; Kirsch 1907). It is interesting to note that although hiding is an important characteristic of the Lebanese tradition, the element of hiding in a rock differs from the hagiography in Lebanon, where she hid in the wheat fields. The link between artillery, mining and Saint Barbara is thus a characteristic of European hagiography. The greatest example of this connection is the Gothic Cathedral of Saint Barbara in Kutná Hora, Czech Republic, which was financed by the wealth of nearby silver mines (Pfannkuch 1987: 42; Jaritz 2009: 131; Kulich 2002). This may also explain the association of Saint Barbara with the Holy Eucharist that is also found in Europe. It was believed that Saint Barbara protected individuals from instantaneous death, such as in explosions, so that they could receive their last rites (Kirsch 1907). As a result, some fourteenth and fifteenth century images of Saint Barbara depict her as a young woman holding a chalice (Anon 1490a), which is also found in some of the icons of North Lebanon.

An interesting example of how localized celebrations of Saint Barbara were selectively adapted from different cultural backgrounds, including European traditions, lies with Caribbean traditions. In the religion referred to as *Santería* or *la Religión de los Orichas* (the Religion of the African Saints), African Yoruba saints and beliefs were selectively fused with elements from European (specifically Spanish and Portuguese) Catholicism (Schmidt 2006; Murphy 2011). This "bricolage" created a new religion by adapting elements from both cultures in response to a specific historical context: the transportation of slaves from Africa and the organization of resistance movements. As the worship of African religions was forbidden, slaves would hide or fuse their worship of *orichas* under the cloak of an affiliated Catholic saint; the worship of the latter being acceptable by slave owners (Schmidt 2006: 240–242). This also reflected the Yoruba belief that that *orichas* most often manifested themselves through a human or another anthropomorphic medium (Murphy 2011: 155). Drawing upon the association with lightening mentioned above, Saint Barbara was believed to be the mask of the *oricha* Shango, the (male) god of thunder (Schmidt 2006: 239; Murphy 2011: 150–161). As a result, traditional Caribbean processions for Saint Barbara's Feast show her statues dressed in distinctive red, the color of Shango, and wearing a crown (Pérez y Mena 1998: 21; Murphy 2011: 150–161). These traditions reflect the unique adaptation of her story within Afro-Caribbean society and vary greatly from the historical trajectory and traditions found in North Lebanon. However the symbiosis of two religious traditions within one saint may help us to understand the apparent "contradictions" found in recent changes to the North Lebanese celebrations discussed below.

The traditional celebrations for Saint Barbara in North Lebanon are unique even in relation to the celebrations by nearby communities. Christians in neighboring

Syria share some of the traditions, particularly the wearing of masks and the collection of sweets. However, the song that children sing differs, for it emphasizes the benefits of giving sweets to the children and the curses for those who do not.

W yalle bte'te wehdeh, ma betshouf shahdeh; W yalle bte'te tnen, allah biyoufe 'anna ed-den ...
W yalle ma bte'te she, byek-hata jawza men lfarsheh; Byek-hata 'alsireh, w bitebbo 'layya lhasireh, w bet'awwe 'layya lje'laneh.

The woman who gives to one [person], she never has to beg; the woman who gives to two, God will wipe out her debts ...
and the woman who does not give anything, her husband will kick her out of bed and he will kick her out to the farm and wrap her up in a carpet and dogs will howl on top of her (Abboud 2011).

Within the Syrian context, emphasis is placed more upon the benefits of giving communal support for Barbara (embodied by the children) than on the children's performance of Barbara's flight, as in the North Lebanese tradition. This may reflect the differing political environment of the two nations, which will be discussed below.

The traditions performed by Christians in the Biqa' Valley of Lebanon also differ from those of North Lebanon.[9] While most hagiographies situate Barbara in Nicomedia or Heliopolis of northern Anatolia (Pfannkuch 1987: 41), Greek Catholics in the Biqa' believe that Saint Barbara lived in a nearby village, claiming that her father was the Roman governor of Heliopolis (present day Ba'albak). They support their assertion with reference to an ancient church dedicated to Barbara in Ba'albak (Jabbra 2009: 289). While the Biqa' traditions also focuses on children visiting neighbors, during the 1970s they collected wheat instead of sweets, possibly reflecting the importance of wheat and grain to this region. The wheat would later be exchanged for sweats (Jabbra 2009: 289–290). A similar song was sung, but with subtle differences.

Harij, Harij Berbara! 'amoundayn w menchera; Khel l kys w 'tina, law la l sheikh ma jina.

Flee, Flee, Barbara [or the mask, the mask of Barbara]; Two columns and a saw; Fill the sack and give us; If it weren't for the Shaykh [Barbara's father] we wouldn't have come (Teeny 2011a; Jabbra 2009: 289).

In addition to referencing the particular practice of distributing wheat, the Biqa' song places more emphasis on the communal support against a collective enemy: Barbara's pagan father. Similarly, the costumes worn during the 1970s did not significantly alter the children's appearance, but consisted of the addition of a silly hat or mask to everyday attire (Jabbra 2011). The element of fear (through hiding)

---

[9] The Biqa' is the narrow strip of land between the Lebanon and Anti-Lebanon mount ranges. The climate and culture varies greatly from that found along the coast and on the west side of the Lebanon mountains, where the North region is located.

is thus not as dominant in the Biqa' traditions as they are in the traditions of North Lebanon, which reveals the divergent experiences of Christian communities, even within the same country.

Official Hagiography and Thematic Interpretation of Saint Barbara

One explanation for the variances in the celebrations for Saint Barbara lies with the possibility of divergent hagiographies promoted by the different churches affiliated with the above examples. The practices discussed above span from Medieval Europe to the present day Caribbean, Syria and Lebanon. They are affiliated with the Greek Orthodox, Greek Catholic, Maronite and Roman Catholic churches.[10] The first record of Saint Barbara's hagiography is with the Menologion collection of saints' lives by the Byzantine Simeon Metaphrastes.[11] This was reproduced in J. P. Migne's *Patrologia Graeca* during the mid-nineteenth century. I have been unable to access this hagiography for analysis, although Pfannkuch argues that it was not Metaphrastes' version, but the thirteenth century hagiography by Jacobius a Vorgina, Archbishop of Genoa, that is the source for the European version (Pfannkuch 1987: 40). It is possible that two (or more) hagiographies of Saint Barbara existed, but that one has been officially erased. This alternative, Byzantine version might have included the disguising of Saint Barbara and the exchange of gifts, which are present in the North Lebanese and Syrian traditions, but not in the official hagiography currently circulated by the different churches.

Despite this exception, both the popular hagiography of North Lebanon and the official hagiography of the different churches uphold many of the same narrative elements. These include her virginal and youthful death, the rejection of her father's paganism, persecution at the hands of the Romans, death by her father, and the subsequent punishment of her father with death by a lightning strike (Saint John of Damascus Institute of Theology n. d.; Assaf n. d.; Kirsh 1907). While these elements are consistent features, the story's meaning is left open for individual interpretations and cultural adaptation. The hagiography is thus read and performed through culturally specific lenses (Pfannkuch 1987: 41).[12]

I would like to propose that these divergences emerge through a community's strategic emphasis on certain themes found within the saint's story, which are

---

[10] Greek Catholic and Maronite churches are officially united with the Roman Catholic church, but uphold certain Eastern Christian practices and traditions.

[11] An interesting photograph for the Saint Barbara service at Saint Marina Church in Amoiun shows the priest holding an icon for Saint Barbara in one hand and that for Saint Simeon Metaphrastes in the other (Anon 2010).

[12] Pfannkuch (1987) promotes a similar argument to explain why Barbara became the patron saint of different European artisan communities, ranging from Librarians to firefighters and miners.

based upon, but adapted from the narrative elements outlined above. I have identified five themes within Barbara's hagiography that can be employed. The first is the purity and virginity of Barbara's youth. Barbara remained a virgin by rejecting an earthly husband and by dying at a young age. The second is the subservient nature of Barbara's womanhood, particularly her stoic acceptance of death and commitment to Christ. For Barabara, Christ became her eternal protector, supplanting the role of her father and any potential earthly husband. The third is the persistent strength of Barbara's inquiry and commitment to Christian theology, which demanded sacrifice and martyrdom. The fourth is the rejection by Barbara of her father's non-Christian faith and lifestyle, revealed in her ordering of the third tower window. The fifth is the ever present threat from non-Christian authority, represented in both her father and the Roman government, who collectively caused her torture and death. Through focusing on one or a combination of these themes, unique interpretations of Saint Barbara's hagiography developed, which were supported by culturally specific celebrations.

Re-examining the Celebrations for Saint Barbara in North Lebanon

Despite being central elements of the Lebanese and Syrian traditions, masking and gift exchange are neither narrative elements in the other communities' commemorations, nor a common theme within the official hagiography. This provokes questions about their source. As suggested above, these practices may be based upon an ancient hagiography for Barbara that was lost or mitigated in the saint's migration to Europe. The practices may be a remnant of a celebration for another saint that was appropriated into Barbara's story (similar to the Caribbean traditions) (Jabbra 2011). Another hypothesis is that they are unique interpretations of the abovementioned themes that draw upon culturally significant references: wheat cultivation and collective fear. This would be similar to how central Europeans emphasized lightening to justify Barbara's role as patron saint of artillerymen and hiding in a rock to support her affiliation with mining. Regardless of its origin, the current justification for the masking and gift giving in North Lebanon folds into the official hagiography to emphasize the themes outlined above.

Masking and gift exchange are central characteristics in the ritualistic reenactment of fleeing and protecting "Barbara" within the North Lebanese traditions. The children, by putting on masks, symbolically become Barbara, and in so doing highlight their persistence and commitment to the Christian faith despite the dangers that it may cause (theme three). The neighbors recognize the children as pure and innocent from behind the masks (theme one) and dispense sweets to the children-Barbara. Through this act, they contrast those who are outside of the community, who do not recognize the children and will not give out sweets. This creates a division, of "us", who are within the community of believers, are safe and can be trusted, against "them", who are outside of the community, non-believers, who are not safe and cannot be trusted. Since non-Christians did not historically participate in the traditions, they are to be rejected from the community, just as Barbara rejected the culture of her pagan father and society (theme four). These non-Christian, non-participating "outsiders" are not only different, but are potential threats to the community's security, and represent the threatening Roman authority (theme five).

This emphasis on fleeing from danger and the community's role in protecting other members parallels the ever-present fear expressed by Christian communities in Lebanon, but in a manner that overcomes ecclesiastical differences. The celebrations for Saint Barbara are one of the few traditions that are shared amongst Greek Orthodox, Maronite and Greek Catholic Christians in the region (Jabbra 2009: 298).[13] Despite their theological and social divisions, Christians in Lebanon are united in their shared position as minorities under a Muslim majority and the ever-present fear of unpredictable persecution from the non-Christian authority, be it the traditionally dominant Sunni community or the rising power of the Shia community. Their fear is reflected in the traditional song that encourages "Run Away Barbara". While fear and hiding pervades the North Lebanese chant, the Biqa' song emphasizes communal support in the face of fear, revealing the long standing solidarity and strength of the Christian communities of this region (Fawaz 1988; Harris 1985). This sense of fear contrasts the mood of the song sung in Syria, which emphasizes gift giving to encourage prosperity as well as curses to those who do not give gifts. Many Christians in Syria express a relative sense of security under the secular Baathist regime, which is employed to buttress their support of Bashar al-Assad during the recent uprisings (Anon 2011a). However, recent political events, such as the rise of Hezbollah within the Lebanese politics[14] and the uprisings in Syria, augment the sense of fear of the "unknown outsider" by Christians in Lebanon and Syria (Aline 2011; Anon 2011a). Noticeably, these events also provide opportunities for Christian religious leaders to meet and express Christian solidarity in the face of the unknown future if the present Syrian government should fall (Amreih 2011).[15]

---

[13] Due to different historical pasts, traditions within these churches tend to diverge in a manner that reflects their specific historical backgrounds.

[14] Lebanese Christians are not unified in their relationship with Hezbollah. Many of the Maronite political parties are aligned with the March 14 movement, while the "secular" Michel Aoun and Christian members of the SSNP have been active members of the March 8 coalition with Hezbollah. While the former Greek Orthodox Patriarch met with both Hezbollah representatives and Michel Aoun at the Patriarchal residency at Balamand Monastery, suggesting his support of their coalition, the views of the new Greek Orthodox Patriarch are yet to be determined (Anon 2011b).

[15] Two conferences have also been held *Reviving the Christian Role in the Arab Levant* (American University of Beirut: 25–27 September 2011) and *The Future of Christians in the Middle East: A step forward to religious freedom* (Holy Spirit University, Kaslik: 18 November 2011).

Another recent transformation of the Saint Barbara celebrations illuminates a trend that contradicts this move towards Christian ecumenicalism (in the face of fear), but nevertheless, also reflects the social-historic context of Lebanese Christians. Saint Barbara's Day is commonly referred to as "Lebanese Halloween" (Barakat 2010; Hussein 2010; Jabbra 2009: 290–291, 299). The costumes worn by children and the sweets that are distributed are increasingly merged with the American version of Halloween in its references to trick-or-treating (or the collection of mass produced candies by children in fancy dress), but maintains its emphasis on the innocence of youth (theme one). This transformation highlights both a strong link many Lebanese have with the United States and American culture, as well as a trend towards secularization via Lebanese nationalism and consumerism. For various reasons, many of the Lebanese who emigrated during the Civil War, for education or employment, are returning,[16] bringing with them American culture and activities.[17] This, coupled with the increased access to American culture through television and the internet, has turned Saint Barbara's Feast into "Lebanese Halloween", granting individuals in North Lebanon an opportunity to express their hybrid and globalized identities (Stamm 2006: 20–40; Jabbra 2009: 299).

Return-emigration is not isolated to Christians however, for it is a cross-sectarian experience (Stamm 2006: 18). In some instances, life in the diaspora emphasized Lebanese national identity regardless of religious affiliation (Abdelhady 2008: 61; Hourani 2007). Just as Halloween celebrations in the United States have been secularized from their Christian/pagan origins to encourage national uniformity, recent Lebanese celebrations of Saint Barbara's Feast allows non-Christians to participate in this "national" holiday (Llewellyn-Davies 2008). This is evident in the semantic shift from "Saint Barbara's Feast" to "Lebanese Halloween", during which all children, Christian and Muslim, can enjoy the collection of mass produced "American" candies as well as "traditional Lebanese" sweets. As a result, the Saint Barbara's Feast traditions can be performed by my Orthodox and Maronite students from Koura with their Sunni friends from Tripoli during the university's "Lebanese Halloween" activities, as I observed in December 2010.

Nevertheless, this change has evoked criticism, not against its inclusion of individuals from other religions directly, but of its secularized association with wealth and greed. Consumerism and the display of wealth have emerged as important forms of social capital within post-war Lebanese society. Following the example of Rafic Hariri and the objectives of his construction company Solidere (Bădescu

---

[16] Due to the lack of record keeping, the number of returned Lebanese is unknown. However, Lebanon has a long history of emigration and return immigration (Khater 2001; Hourani 2007; Stamm 2006).

[17] It is interesting to note that at the Faculty Housing at the University of Balamand, the (American) Halloween tradition of trick-or-treating on the 31 October was initiated by a Lebanese-British family who recently "returned" to Lebanon in 2010.

2011; Gebhardt et al. 2005), individualized displays of wealth are presented as unifying forces that mitigate sectarian divisions in favor of a nationalized consumer identity. The tradition of giving children sweets and money during the Saint Barbara celebrations reinforces this consumerist trend, while the relabeling of the holiday as "Lebanese Halloween" encourages the dissolution of sectarian divisions through the emergence of a shared capitalistic, national identity.

It is this change that has been criticized by local religious leaders in North Lebanon. The secularization of the holiday is challenged through the reinstatement of Barbara's religious identity. In his 2010 sermon, Metropolitan Ephram Kyriakos, Archbishop of Tripoli, argued that the Roman idols of Barbara's father, have been replaced by the worship of "money", "authority and worldly glory." Instead of statues, people today "worship lust. They worship entertainment and all the other vices" (Kyriakos 2010). He explained that what is demanded of Christians is not a sacrifice of blood, like Barbara's, but for the celebrants to become "white martyrs", by being "aware and watchful over our spiritual life and not let material life overpower us and conquer our minds" (Kyriakos 2010). While this may be a coated criticism against cross-sectarian mingling, the overt message is to curtail the transformation of the celebrations into a purely secular holiday. This is done however by weakening (or possibly erasing) the popular hagiography for Saint Barbara, which is indigenous to North Lebanon, through emphasizing a "universal" Christian message. For example, the paper reproductions of icons for Saint Barbara that are locally sold and purchased by Christians in North Lebanon show her wearing a crown, or a veil, holding a cross and a book. These evoke a general Christian message, not the particularities of the local, popular interpretation. This is also evident in the religious hymn sung at churches, which varies greatly from the popular song and does not reference traditional practices. It has been translated as such:

Once upon a time, in the old time, a girl named Barbara was full of faith;
Barbara did not desire any money and she did not care about beauty, only the love of Truth was worrying her;
She loved the wounded Jesus, whose words feed the soul, and in front of the people and her father, she was not scared to reveal her secret;
Jesus told her "my daughter, since you believed in me, in your heart I have a home and in my heart you are living";
and she kept her love and her faith that cannot be hidden, so she won the crown of glory and her Lord took her to Him (Teeny 2011b).

Thus, the push to re-sanctify Saint Barbara and her feast in North Lebanon is done in a manner that mitigates the unique nature of the local, popular traditions.

Conclusion

The aim of this paper was to explore the celebrations for Saint Barbara as practiced by Christians in North Lebanon. The unique aspects of these traditions, including children songs, the wearing of masks, and the exchange of gifts, prompted inquiry into their sources. After making comparisons with commemorations from other cultures and time periods, it was argued that culturally specific traditions reflect the historical, political and social environment through which particular celebratory practices emerged. The differences lay with the selective emphasis a community places upon the different themes found within Barbara's hagiography. Emphasizing or deemphasizing elements of Barbara's narrative justifies cultural traditions that are performed during the celebrations, which represents how Barbara's story is popularly remembered.

This reinforces the theory upheld by many of the authors within this special issue, that saints are adaptable to local contexts. The veneration and commemoration of saints varies greatly, illuminating the global and heterogeneous nature of Christianity. It also reveals that, despite a push towards standardization, saints can be adapted to fit local trajectories and possibly fused with other deities and religious systems, as seen with the Caribbean *la Religión de los Orichas*.

However, the nature of these localized traditions may challenge orthodox interpretations. The tradition of gift exchange and masking may be indigenous to North Lebanon, but the current stress on these elements within recent celebrations is being identified by local clergy as a (negative) secularization of the holiday that needs to be reformed. This is done by reinforcing the shared "official" hagiography for Barbara, which is based upon European texts from the Middle Ages. Doing so curtails the unique practices and the popular hagiographical that are indigenous to the region. In order to curtail the globalization and secularization of Saint Barbara's Feast into Lebanese Halloween, religious leaders may erase the culturally specific elements that make the traditions unique to the region. One form of globalization will be replaced by another.

Lastly, tracing the history of Saint Barbara's hagiography reveals the interesting movement of her story: from the eastern Mediterranean to Europe. From there it moved onto the Caribbean and back to eastern Mediterranean. While the diversity of sources makes it easy to isolate the European features, the lack of sources about the ancient traditions frustrates our understanding of the original story and traditions. More research of this facet is needed to properly explain the origin the Lebanese customs. This may reveal that the masking and exchange of gifts was an element found within the original hagiography, which was lost in the story's migration to Europe, or, that it was an indigenous practice grafted onto Barbara's hagiography. This might be achieved through investigating current practices for celebrating Saint Barbara in Turkey, which is the most probable setting of her story, as well as in the Balkans, which was an important passageway between east and west.

Since originally submitting this article, the 2011 celebration of *Eid al-Berbara* took place at the University of Balamand. Advertisements for the event described it as "Saint Barbara Day: The Traditional Lebanese Way". In the university's central courtyard, local artisans displayed their crafts, while two stands were erected to distribute "hameh el berbara": the traditional barley sweet. One stand was located next to a space to carve pumpkins into jack-o-lanterns. Students here were dressed in costumes and distributed their hameh el berbara that was cooked in a large cauldron like a "witches brew". On the opposite side of the square, was another group of students who wore everyday attire to distribute their hameh el berbara. Behind this group was a poster, recounting the story of Saint Barbara and the reasons for the wheat and costumes. Thus the divergent elements of the traditional celebrations in North Lebanon were presented to university students to selectively employ for their annual celebration for Saint Barbara, thus creating and recreating their own traditions.

This article was originally presented at the "Relations between Christian churches in the Near and Middle East – theological, historical and political-cultural aspects" Conference, 15 to 17 September 2011, which was jointly hosted by the Christians in the Middle East research network and the Katholische Universität, Eichstätt-Ingolstadt, Germany. I must thank the participants for their feedback and comments. Tarek Abboud, Nizar Najjar, Bianca Teeny, Julie Saba and Michelli Lakkis provided essential help in translating and transliterating the Arabic texts, as well as providing additional texts for analysis. I am also grateful to Nancy Jabbra for sharing her research on Christian communities in the Biqa' as well as Kifah Hanna and Zayde Antrim for letting me share my findings at a special lecture at Trinity College (Hartford, CT, USA) in February 2012.

References Cited

Abboud, Tarek
2011   Saint Barbara Song (Safita, Syria). [email] (Personal Correspondence, 19 July).

Abdelhady, Dalia
2008   Representing the Homeland: Lebanese Disaporic Notions of Home and Return in a Global Context. *Cultural Dynamics* 20: 53–72.

Aline, Sara
2011   The Church's vow of silence. *Now Lebanon* [online] Available at   <http://www.nowlebanon.com/Print.aspx?ID=304715> [Accessed 25 August 2011].

Amreih, Antoine
2011   Christian church leaders urge unity at Balamand meeting. *The Daily Star Lebanon*, 21 September. p. 2.

Anon

1450   Saint Barbara [glass-stained] (Metropolitan Museum of Art). Available at: <http://www.metmuseum.org/Collections/search-the-collections/70012449> [Accessed on 31 October 2011].

Anon

1490a   Private Devotional Shrine. [sculpture-wood] (Metropolitan Museum of Art). Available at: <http://www.metmuseum.org/Collections/search-the-collections/70009934> [Accessed on 31 October 2011].

Anon

1490b   Saint Barbara. [Statue] (Metropolitan Museum of Art). Available at: <http://www.metmuseum.org/Collections/search-the-collections/70011072> [Accessed 31 October 2011].

Anon

2010   [Priest holding icons of Saint Simeon Metaphrastes and Saint Barbara at Saint Barbara-Amioun Marina]. [image online] Available at: <https://picasaweb.google.com/arch.antonios/StBarbaraAmiounMarina#5412443853287687698> [Accessed on 20 November 2011].

Anon

2011a   Fearing Change, Many Christians in Syria Back Assad. *New York Times*, 28 September, p. A1.

Anon

2011b   Patriarch Ignatius IV Meets with Representatives from Hezbollah. *Notes on Arab Orthodoxy* [blog] 6 October. Available at: <http://araborthodoxy.blogspot.com/2011/10/patriarch-ignatius-iv-meets-with.html> [Accessed on: 9 November 2011].

Assaf, Mikhayil

n. d.   Kitab As-sinaksar Al-mouthanmal 'ala Siyar. Beirut: Markaz ad-dirassat al-orthozoksi al-antaki.

Bădescu, Gruia

2011   Beyond the Green Line: Sustainability and Beirut's post-war reconstruction. *Development* 54: 358–367.

Barakat, Rody

2010   "The Lebanese Halloween" (Zgharta, North Lebanon): Interview of Janette Rached (Tripoli, Lebanon, 2010). [unpublished essay].

Butler, Judith

1990   Gender Trouble: Feminism and the Subversion of Identity. New York and London: Routledge.

Caprio, Betsy

1982   The Woman Sealed in the Tower: A Psychological Approach to Feminine Spirituality. New York: Paulist Press.

Davie, May, et al.

2010a   Chapelle Sainte Barbe (Qiddisé Berbara) d'Amioun. *ARPOA: Architecture Religieuse du Patriarcat Orthodoxe d'Antioche.* [online] Available at: <http://www.balamand.edu.lb/english/ARPOA.asp?id=11282&fid=270> [Accessed on 19 November 2011].

2010b Chapelle Sainte Barbe (Qiddisé Berbara) de Kousba. *ARPOA: Architecture Religieuse du Patriarcat Orthodoxe d'Antioche.* [online] Available at: <http://www.balamand.edu.lb/english/ARPOA.asp?id=11165&fid=270> [Accessed on 19 November 2011].

2010c Église Sainte Barbe (Qiddisé Berbara al-Qadimé) de Ras Masqa.*ARPOA: Architecture Religieuse du Patriarcat Orthodoxe d'Antioche.* [online] Available at: <http://www.balamand.edu.lb/english/ARPOA.asp?id=10288&fid=270> [Accessed on 19 November 2011].

2010d Église Sainte Barbe (Qiddisé Berbara) de Barghoun. *ARPOA: Architecture Religieuse du Patriarcat Orthodoxe d'Antioche.* [online] Available at: <http://www.balamand.edu.lb/english/ARPOA.asp?id=7922&fid=270> [Accessed on 19 November 2011].

2010e Église Sainte Barbe (Qiddisé Berbara) de Ras Masqa. *ARPOA: Architecture Religieuse du Patriarcat Orthodoxe d'Antioche.* [online] Available at: <http://www.balamand.edu.lb/english/ARPOA.asp?id=10284&fid=270> [Accessed on 19 November 2011].

Dib, Nicole
2010 "Saint Barbara Remembered ...: Interview of Afifeh el Khoury" (Kulhat, Lebanon, 2010). [unpublished essay].

Fadel, Christina
2010 "Saint Barbara Holiday: Interview of Joulia" (Kafarhazir, Lebanon, 2010). [unpublished essay].

Fawaz, Leila
1988 Zahle and Dayr al-Qamar: Two Market Towns of Mount Lebanon during the Civil War of 1860. In: N. Shehadi and D. Haffar Mills (eds.), Lebanon: A History of Conflict and Consensus; pp. 29–63. London: I. B. Taurus.

Gebhardt, Hans, et al.
2005 History, Space and Social Conflict in Beirut: The Quarter of Zokak el-Blat Beirut: Orient-Institut.

Harris, William
1985 The View from Zahle: Security and Economic Conditions in the Central Bekaa 1980–1985. *Middle East Journal* 39: 270–286.

Hermkens, Anna-Karina, **Willy Jansen** and **Catrien Notermans**
2009 Introduction: The Power of Marian Pilgrimage. In: In: A. Hermkens, W. Jansen and C. Notermans (eds.) Moved by Mary: The Power of Pilgrimage in the Modern World; pp. 1–16. Farnham: Ashgate.

Hourani, Guita
2007 Lebanese Diaspora and Homeland Relations, paper presented at the *Migration and Refugee Movements in the Middle East and North Africa Conference* (Cairo: 23–25 October 2007) [online] Available at: <http://www.ndu.edu.lb/Lerc/publications/Lebanese%20Diaspora%20and%20Homeland%20Relations.pdf> [Accessed 14 November 2011].

Hussein (al), Marwa
2010 Balamand Students Celebrate Halloween, *Balamandiyoun* [online] 8 December. Available at: <http://balamandiyoun.blogspot.com/2010/12/balamand-students-celebrated-halloween.html> [Accessed on 20 August 2011].

Jabbra, Nancy W.
2009   Globalization and Christian Practice in Lebanon's Biqa' Valley. *Middle East Critique*. 18: 285–299.
2011   Correspondence about Saint Barbara Celebrations in Biqa Valley. [email] (Personal Correspondence, 13 October 2011).

Jansen, Willy
2009   Marian Images and Religious Identities in the Middle East. In: A. Hermkens, W. Jansen and C. Notermans (eds.) Moved by Mary: The Power of Pilgrimage in the Modern World; pp. 33–48. Farnham: Ashgate.

Jaritz, Gerhard
2009   The Visual Representation of Late Medieval Work: Patterns of Context, People and Action. In: J. Ehmer and C. Lis (eds.), The Idea of Work in Europe from Antiquity to Modern Times; pp. 125–148. Farnham, UK: Ashgate.

Khater, Akram Fouad
2001   Inventing Home: Emigration, Gender, and the Middle Class in Lebanon, 1870–1920. Berkeley, Los Angeles and London: University of California Press.

Kirsch, Johann Peter
1907   St. Barbara. *The Catholic Encyclopedia. Vol. 2*. New York: Robert Appleton Company [online] Available at <http://www.newadvent.org/cathen/02284d.htm> [Accessed 20 August 2011].

Kulich, Ján
2002   Kutná Hora: St. Barbara Cathedral and the town. Prague: Gloriet.

Kyriakos, Ephrem
2010   Met. Ephrem on the Feast of St. Barbara. *Notes on Arab Orthodoxy* [blog] 9 Dec. Available at: <http://araborthodoxy.blogspot.com/2010/12/met-ephrem-on-feast-of-st-barbara.html> [Accessed on 30 July 2011].

Llewellyn-Davies, Sabina
2008   The Lebanese Halloween. *NOW Lebanon* [online] 3 December. Available at: <http://www.nowlebanon.com/NewsArchiveDetails.aspx?ID=69508#> [Accessed on 14 November 2010].

Memling, Hans
1480   Virgin and Child with Saints Catherine of Alexandria and Barbara. [painting] (Metropolitan Museum of Art) Available at: <http://www.metmuseum.org/Collections/search-the-collections/110001501> [Accessed 31 October 2011].

Murphy, Joseph M.
2011   Santa Barbara Africana: Beyond Syncretism in Cuba. In: D. Lindenfeld and M. Richardson (eds.), Beyond Conversion and Syncretism: Indigenous Encounters with Missionary Christianity, 1800–2000, pp. 137–165. New York and Oxford: Berghahn Books.

Najjar, Nizar
2011   Interview with author. Tripoli, Lebanon (Personal Correspondence, 19 August).

O'Grady, Kathleen
2002   The Tower and the Chalice: Julia Kristeva and the Story of Santa Barbara. *Feminist Theology* 10: 40–60.

Pentcheva, Bissera V.
2006   The Performative Icon. *The Art Bulletin* 88: 631–655.

Pérez y Mena, Andrés I.
1998   Cuban Santería, Haitian Vodun, Puerto Rican Spiritualism: A Multiculturalist Inquiry into Syncretism. *Journal for the Scientific Study of Religion* 37: 15–27.

Pfannkuch, H. O.
1987   Medieval Saint Barbara Worship and Professional Traditions in Early Mining and Applied Earth Sciences. In: C. S. Gillmor (ed.), History of Geophysics. Volume 3: History of Hydrology; pp. 39–48. Washington, D.C.: American Geological Union.

Procházka-Eisl, Gisela and **Stephan Procházka**
2010   The Plain of Saints and Prophets: The Nusayri-Alawi Community of Cilicia (Southern Turkey) and its Sacred Places. Wiesbaden: Harrassowitz-Verlag.

Saint John of Damascus Institute of Theology
n. d.   December 4: The Holy Great Martyr Barbara together with Julianna (c. 306) St. John of Damascus, Father and Hymnographer (776). [online] Available at: < http:// www.balamand.edu.lb/theology/JohnDLiturService.htm > [Accessed on: 20 August 2011].

Schmidt, Bettina E.
2006   The Creation of Afro-Caribbean Religions and their Incorporation of Christian Elements: A Critique against Syncretism. *Transformation: An International Dialogue on Mission and Ethics* 23: 236–243.

Stamm, Sibylle
2006   Social Networks Among Return Migrants to Post-War Lebanon. *CIS Working Paper* 9. Available at: <http://www.cis.ethz.ch/publications/WP9_stamm.pdf> [Accessed 7 February 2012].

Teeny, Biany
2011a Interview with Author. Balamand, Lebanon (personal communication 15 November).
2011b Translation of Saint Barbara Hymn by Nicolas Malek. (personal communication 16 November).

Saint John the Baptist in Northern Ecuador, or the Ritual Making and Fostering of Ethnic Identity

Emilia Ferraro

Abstract. – This paper describes and analyses the celebration of Saint John the Baptist (San Juan) among the indigenous villagers of Northern Ecuador. Through time, the changing ethnic, social and economic boundaries have been incorporated into, and reflected by the celebration of San Juan. San Juan stands at the apex of an ordered indigenous universe, and every year in June Kichwa peasants organize a celebration in his honour. The paper argues that this celebration is a way to manifest people's devotion to the saint, and also an important opportunity to reinforce and ritually map ethnic differences. *[Ecuador; Hacienda; Hacienda Rituals; Agrarian Reform; Andean Christianity; Saint John the Baptist]*

Emilia Ferraro, Lecturer in Sustainable Development and Anthropology. Director. Undergraduate Programme of Sustainable Development. Department of Geography and SD. University of St. Andrews, UK. Selected Publications:
2011a. *Trueque.* An Ethnographic Account of Barter, Trade and Money in Andean Ecuador. *Journal of Latin American and Caribbean Anthropology* vol. 16 (1): 168–184.
2009. Money, Credit and Faith. Narratives and Images of Money, Fertility, and Salvation in the Northern Andes. In: R. Wright and A. Villaça (eds.), Native Christians: Modes and Effects of Christianity among Indigenous Peoples of the Americas. Oxford: Ashgate.
2008. Kneading Life. Women and the Celebration of the Dead in the Andes. *Journal of the Royal Anthropological Institute* vol. 14 (2): 262–277.
2006. Culture and Economy. The Milk Market in the Northern Andes of Ecuador. *Ethnology* Vol. XLV (1): 25–40.
2004a. Reciprocidad, Don y Deuda. Formas y relaciones de intercambios en los Andes del Norte del Ecuador. Quito: FLACSO & Abya Yala. ISBN Flacso: 9978-67-083-1. ISBN Abya Yala: 9978-22-393-2.
2004b. Owing and Being in Debt. A Contribution from the Northern Andes of Ecuador. *Social Anthropology* Vol. 12 (1): 77–94.
2004c. (with H.Jácome and J. Sanchez) Microfinanzas en la economía ecuatoriana: una alternativa para el desarrollo. Quito: FLACSO-Ecuador. ISBN: 9978-67-081-5.
2000. (with M. Cuvi and A. Martínez) Género y ruralidad en el Ecuador de la década de 1990. Quito: CONAMU. ISBN: 9978-41-4274.

This paper is an ethnographic account of the celebration of Saint John the Baptist, as it takes place among the indigenous villagers of Northern Ecuador. The kichwa peasants of the Pichincha province consider the saint, locally and affectionately called *San Juan*, as the most important character of their religious universe, and every year in June organize a celebration in his honour that involves huge expenditures and resources. The celebration is not only a way to manifest people's devotion to the saint, essential to put in motion his good will, but is also an important opportunity to reaffirm a specifically "indigenous" identity and sense of belonging through both the ritual renewal of the relationship with the saint, and the mapping of ethnic territorial and symbolic boundaries. Through time, these changing ethnic, social and economic boundaries have been incorporated into, and reflected by the celebration of San Juan.

Socio-economic Characteristics of the Area

The focus of this paper is the kichwa village of Pesillo, in the parish of Olmedo, Cayambe Canton. The area lies in the Northern Highlands of Ecuador, in the ecological zone known as *Andes de Páramo*, between 2800 and 3400 m. a. s. l. It is characterised by a "typically" Andean weather, with temperatures varying between 5 ° and 22 °C throughout the year, dropping dramatically at higher altitudes and at night. Heavy showers in the rainy season and prolonged droughts, chill dry winds, and frosts in the dry season, represent a great challenge to agriculture, which until very recently was the main source of livelihood. Currently, people survive on a mixed economy, combining agriculture with a number of "non-traditional" activities such as cattle breeding; the sale of cow's milk to local cheese factories; wage labour in urban centre across the country, and employment in the local flower plantations for export (cf. Korovkin 2003).

The village of Pesillo is grouped around the former *hacienda* buildings which include the church, some small shops and offices. The only recognised local authority is the Central Committee, i.e. the village directorate. Its members are elected once a year in a general assembly and its principal responsibility is the management of common resources (e.g., Páramo land) and administration of internal affairs, such as the organisation of communal festivals and events that involve the whole community. Administratively, Pesillo includes also six scattered hamlets (*sectores*); however, residents of these hamlets consider themselves as independent villages (*comunidades*) thus showing that legal, territorial, and administrative divisions do not always fit local perceptions.

Besides Pesillo, the parish of Olmedo includes several kichwa villages and the parish seat, the *mestizo* town of Olmedo. The main differences between "indigenous" and "mestizo" people (i.e. of mixed origins) are linked to general economic criteria, such as for example, the level of control over basic resources (e.g., land, pasture), but they are also defined by the level of engagement and dependence upon the national society, external markers such as the use of specific clothes/garments, and residential patterns: characteristically *mestizos* live in the parish seat only, while indigenous people live in the villages around it. However, local ethnic categories are very fluid, and to a great extent people self-appoint themselves to one or another category. *Mestizo* people define themselves by their refusal of indigenous markers: they despise indigenous people whom they consider, among other things, ignorant and not intelligent. On their part, indigenous people, Pesillanos especially, have always felt superior to *mestizos* because in the past the latter were economically and administratively dependent upon the *hacienda*, situated in Pesillo (see below). Nowadays, the relationship between the two groups is very close, and their respective members maintain a variety of social, labour and economic arrangements. Yet, it is also a problematic relationship, characterised by mutual resentment and racism (Ferraro 2006; 2011). As we shall see later on, the celebration of San Juan is significant in ritually reinforcing these ethnic distinctions.

Socio-economic History of Pesillo

The socio-economic history of Pesillo is intimately connected to its peculiar history as a Church/State property that has granted it a unique position within the Ecuadorian panorama (Crespi 1968).

The Time of the Fathers

Pesillanos divide their history according to the succession of owners and managers of the land (Yanez del Pozo, 1988). Such history unfolds chronologically from an original "Time of the Fathers", when the area was a vast *hacienda* owned over time by different Catholic orders. The *hacienda* system of land tenancy was based upon a system of debt peonage for which indigenous peons were granted the residency and usufruct of a small plot of land (*huasipungo*), together with a small sum in cash (*suplido*) that they had to return in the form of days of labour (Crespi 1968; Costales 1987). Through the centuries, the original Catholic estate grew thanks to gifts of surrounding land and purchases by the Orders, especially the Mercedario Catholic Fathers who were the last private landowners of Pesillo. By the close of the colonial period, the *hacienda* included the area currently comprising the entire Olmedo parish.

At the time, Pesillo was a large complex housing a numerous population of *huasipungueros* (resident indigenous peons), non-resident *hacienda* employees with their families, and *mestizo* "apegados". *Apegados* – literally the "stuck on" – were *mestizo* landless families who lived along the roadside near Pesillo. Having no labor contract with the *hacienda*, they had no plot to work for their subsistence and to reside on, so they were accommodated by indigenous households under a variety of labor arrangements. This original condition of landless people still informs current ethnic relationships between the two groups, since indigenous people appeal to this past history to justify their sense of superiority over *mestizos*

(Cf. Crespi 1968; Ferraro 2004a). Several subdivisions and an administrative, re-ligious and ceremonial centre completed the complex. The monastery, chapel and cemetery served the surrounding *hacienda* hamlets as well, as did its storehouses and mills. The only recognised authority in Pesillo was represented by the Church personnel, especially the resident fathers, who were directly responsible for the management of the estate.

The Time of the Tenants

In 1908, during the administration of liberal president Eloy Alfaro Moreno, Church properties were expropriated. Hence, Pesillo became a State property under the control and responsibility of the Ecuadorian Ministry of Social Welfare (*Asistencia Social*). The estate was divided into five smaller *haciendas*, and rented out to indi-vidual tenants (*arrendatarios*). Pesillanos refer to this as the "Time of the Tenants". However, the change from a private to a State property did not fundamentally alter either the economic organization of the *hacienda* or the social organization of la-bour within it, and the relationship between the indigenous peons and the manag-ers/tenants continued to be hierarchical and highly exploitative.

The *hacienda* system went far beyond the economic order. It was indigenous peons' "native land" (Guerrero 1991: 134), and its culture remained in place even when its socio-economic structure was dismantled. The *hacienda* provided a sym-bolic as much as a physical space of production and reproduction of ethnic identity and differences which, to a great extent are still in place nowadays. Both the socio-economic organization of labour, and ethnic boundaries were reinforced by rituals, among which the celebration of San Juan was the most important one, as we shall see.

The Time of the Cooperative

In 1964, under the military government, the Agrarian Reform redistributed the land more equally across the country, and legally ended the *hacienda* land tenancy sys-tem. As Pesillo was already a State property, the land was distributed to the *hua-sipungueros* who now became owners of their *huasipungos*, while the rest of the land was sold to peasant cooperatives specifically established for this purpose (See Guerrero 1991; Crespi 1968; Landázuri 1980; Yanez del Pozo 1988; Prieto 1978; Martínez 1995; Becker 1999). This is the time that Pesillanos define as "Time of the Cooperatives".[1] By the end of the 1980s, peasant cooperatives had fully repaid

---

[1] Peasants Cooperatives were associations of producers who had collective use of the common means of production; they also had collective access, storage and sale of all assets. The law regulating coop-eratives dates back to the 1930s, but it is only since the Agrarian Reform, with the 1966 "Law of Co-operatives" that cooperatives came to the fore in the Sierra region of Ecuador.

their land and from the early 1990s they started to divide their common assets, including land, among their members, a process currently culminated.[2]

San Juan: Catholic Saint, Mountain Spirit, and Andean Christ

Saint John the Baptist (from now on San Juan) is the most important, respected, and feared character of the entire local pantheon of superior beings, and the protagonist of the most important celebration of the year, so much so that a number of authors have suggested the existence of a "San Juan culture" in the Cayambe-Imbabura region.[3]

Pesillanos and the villagers in the area worship a variety of saints. To a certain extent, each household has its own "tutelary" saint for protection and help. However, San Juan stands at the apex of this ordered indigenous universe, fulfilling *de facto* the role of "Patron Saint" of the area.[4] Sallnow (1991: 142) claimed that, unlike Andean pilgrimage shrines, Andean local patron saints generally are not very important, since they are not miraculous, "their cosmological role is unstressed and their cults are observed as a matter of routine (…) they are largely devoid of symbolic content, whether orthodox or syncretic". San Juan belies this claim, representing the structural equivalent of the Mountain Spirits that inhabit Andean shrines. His constant presence in households and his constant participation in people's everyday activities make him very "domestic" and a member of the family, thus very close to people who approach him with affection calling him "*el Santito*" or "*San Juanito*", i.e. dear little San Juan. Throughout the year, people "feed" him with masses, and take care of him by adorning his image with candles, flowers, rosaries. His image is kept in the main room of the house, and the night before his celebration, all around Pesillo, people light fires, called "San Juan's fires", in order to warm him up:

On the eve of the celebration for San Juan (23rd June), we say "let's keep the dear little saint warm". We gather wood and we light fires in each household. This is our custom, we

---

[2] This involved a legal process of change from the juridical status of "community" to "association" (*asociación*) which is a more flexible model that places fewer demands on its members (Bretón 1997: 91). Since the late 1980s peasant cooperatives have virtually disappeared in favour of newly formed communities and especially *asociaciones* (Cf. Zamosc 1995: 55–60).

[3] Nevertheless, the modalities and styles of the celebration vary among the different communities in the region (cf. Crespi 1981: 489).

[4] The Mercedario Catholic Order is named after Our Lady of Mercy who, consequently, was Pesillo's patron Saint, and officially still is. However, after the Mercedario Fathers left, gradually she has lost prominence in the area, and although still remembered and occasionally celebrated by individual households, such celebration goes unnoticed by the general community, and is not comparable to the splendour of the celebrations in honour of San Juan.

believe San Juan comes back from the year behind with cold, and all houses are lit up to
warm him up (F. Q., village of Muyurco Dec. 1996).[5]

San Juan, then, appears to be a highly personalised and "humanised" saint who
needs to be dressed, kept warm, and fed.

Pesillanos believe San Juan to be very powerful, in other words, very miraculous. People ask him for protection and help with all types of problems, needs and
general matters concerning humans, animals, crops and even "business" affairs.
But they also fear his anger and punishment. Like many other Andean Superior
Beings, San Juan manifests the contradictions and tensions that characterise local
religious perceptions and practices. As Taussig (1980: 113) has demonstrated, in
those areas where – as part of a process of political conquest – Catholicism replaced autochthonous religious practices by force, local people appropriated the
Catholic reification of Good and Evil as essences symbolised by God and Satan in
a *quasi*-Manichean vision of the world. In this vision Good and Evil are not opposed but, rather, they complement each other. Following such patterns, San Juan
is very miraculous and very angry at the same time. Like the Bolivian *Tío*, owner
of the silver mines, San Juan's power is two-edged, positive and negative, and his
attitude depends on people's actions towards him. People's devotion (*devoción*) is
an essential notion in structuring this relationship with the saint who will respond
positively to requests if and when the faithful prove their devotion. As an indigenous friend told me, "San Juan is for everything and his response depends on one's
will to have a feast" (J., village of Pesillo, December 1996).[6]

The belief that life and human prosperity is an effect of Superior Beings' good
will is widespread in the Andes. These Beings are the owners of all forms of life:
they can send rain and make the land fertile, or withhold it and make it sterile; they
can send diseases to animals, crops and humans, or send abundance and prosperity (cf. Bastien 1978; Nash 1979; Sallnow 1989; Harris 1989, 1995; Gose 1986,
1994; Rösing 1994, 1995). Humans are in debt to them and therefore must show
devotion in tangible ways, in order to avoid their anger and punishment which is
severe and affects the whole group (Gose 1994; Rösing 1994; Ferraro 2004; Dillon and Abercrombie 1988). San Juan is no exception. Local accidents and mis-
fortunes are explained as the Saint's anger sparked by the lack of the material
manifestation of people's devotion to him, such as for example, paid masses in his
honour:

---

[5] "En las vísperas de San Juan decimos 'hacémosle calentar al santito'. Nos hacemos un montón de
chamisas en cada casa y le quemamos. Esta es nuestra costumbre, que San Juan viene del año con frío
y todas las casas están encendidas para calentarle al santito". Unless otherwise stated, all translations
from Spanish are mine.

[6] "San Juan es para todo y depende de la voluntad de uno tener la fiesta".

People say that last June the transport cooperative had not offered a mass to San Juan and one of its buses turned upside down because, people say, they had not paid for the mass to San Juan, and the same happened to another, which also crashed. Two buses almost fell into the river and this because, people say, they do not believe in San Juan. After this, surely they must have paid for a mass to him (…) When one promises him something, for example a mass on a certain date, and then the day comes and the person has not fulfilled his/her promise, then anything can happen to him/her. San Juan will punish him/her (E. C., village of Pesillo, July 1997).[7]

It is my contention, therefore, that San Juan represents the fusion of the categories of Andean Mountain Spirits and Catholic characters such as saints and even Jesus himself. In fact, San Juan has the appearance of a Catholic saint, the power and functions of a Mountain Spirit, and following a common practice in the Andes, on some occasions he is also equated to Christ. Indeed, the equation between the Inca Sun (*Inti*) and Christ is not uncommon in the Andes, revealing that from the earliest time of the Spanish conquest, Andeans began to translate foreign imposed religious concepts and forms into local structures (cf. Dillon and Abercrombie 1988; Silverblatt 1988; MacCormack 1991a). Superior and human beings are therefore in constant negotiation and mutual exchange. This is the reason why their relationship has been traditionally subsumed under the category of "reciprocity", that is to say, a contract to all effects that obliges the parties to fulfil their mutual obligations. The yearly sponsorship and organization of a celebration in his honour is possibly the main obligation Pesillanos have towards San Juan, which they must fulfil to keep him happy, avoid his terrible anger, and thus renew their good relationship with him.

The Celebration of San Juan

In Pesillo there is no other event comparable to the feast of San Juan, in the week of 24th June, which represents the major celebration of the local and catholic calendar. There is evidence that the Catholic celebration of San Juan replaced the pre-Hispanic *Inti Raymi* harvest festival of the sun, as happened with many other Inca religious festivals according to the chroniclers (cf. also Dillon and Abercrombie 1988; MacCormack 1991a, 1991b; Guerrero 1991; Cervone 1996).[8]

---

[7] "Dicen que ahora en Junio la cooperativa de transporte [named after the Saint] no le ha pasado la misa y [San Juan] ha virado un bus de la cooperativa, porque dicen que no le ha pasado la misa a San Juanito. Dos buses casi se fueron al rio y esto dicen por no creer en San Juanito. Ahí seguramente ya le han pasado una misa (…) Por ejemplo, cuando se le ofrece algo [to the Saint], por ejemplo 'en tal fecha voy a pagar misa' y si es que en esta fecha no lo hizo, le pasa cualquier cosa. Le castiga, dicen".

[8] As early as 1551–1552, Garcilaso de la Vega reported the replacement of the Inca celebration for the sun, *Inti Raymi*, with the catholic celebration of *Corpus Christi* which he witnessed in Cuzco (in Mac Cormack 1991a: 59).

The celebration of San Juan is a year-long affair. People await it with impatience and excitement, becoming more animated as the date approaches, their eyes sparkling when they talk about it. This feast, in fact, represents the highlight of the year, and migrants from across the country come back for the occasion:

As we say here, as potatoes grow [as time goes by] we count the months [to the feast]. Almost … almost there, [the feast of] San Juan is arriving, only 12 months less … 11 months … In the new year we say "only six months to the dancing …" (J. M., village of Pesillo, July 1997)[9].

The Central Committee is in charge of organizing the calendar of activities for the feast, as well as of raising funds throughout the year in order to provide food and drink for all participants who arrive in Pesillo from the surrounding villages.

Rather than a single event, the celebration comprises a series of rituals and ceremonies that take place during the whole summer, starting the week before the 24th June (the day the Catholic calendar remembers the saint) until August. Such events take place separately and in different spaces, but their common denominator is the saint. In the week leading to the 24th June, every night vigils (*visperas*) in honour of the Saint are held in private houses which become real chapels dedicated to the saint. An altar is prepared for him, with his image adorned with flowers, candles, money, and other offerings that participants bring. In fact, these vigils are open to all devotees who, besides offerings, also bring with them pleadings and requests of help; a catechist leads the prayer of the rosary before the feast starts. The host of the vigil offers some food and drink, and people sing and dance around the altar of the saint:

We have a wake every night … People come and bring candles, money and the likes [and] we pray the rosary (E. C., village of Pesillo, July 1997).[10]

At the same time, bonfires are lit everywhere, both to welcome the saint and keep him warm, and to "call the rain" essential to prepare the soil for sowing after the harvest. The official celebrations for the Saint start on the late afternoon of the 23rd June with mass at church, attended by a crowd of devotees who take along their own images of the saint which in the days approaching the celebration have been further decorated with candles, flowers and money. An additional sign of the identification of San Juan with Jesus in indigenous contexts is the fact that similar vigils are held around Christmas in the *mestizo* town of Olmedo, but in honour of Baby Jesus for whom also bonfires are lit to keep him warm.

---

[9] "Como decimos por aquí, papas andan y estamos ya contando los meses. Ya…Ya mismo llega San Juan, que faltan solo 12 meses … 11 meses … En el año nuevo decimos ya son 6 meses que faltan para seguir bailando …"

[10] "Se va velando cada noche, [la gente acude] a dejar la espermita, el dinero, así. Rezan el rosario".

The 24th June is the *Dia Grande*, the day of the main celebrations. It starts again with the mass at church, where the image of San Juan is kept:

> The image of Saint John the Baptist belonged to our fathers. We keep it in the church, in order to praise it year after year. The whole community and the Central Committee offer the mass to San Juan. No, it would be impossible not to offer him the mass. This is our tradition, it must be respected. In the programme of the feast, year after year, the mass comes first, then the dances and the drinks ... There is no feast without the mass; we must always start with the mass and go to the mass first, at least for a moment (J. M., village of Pesillo, June 1992).[11]

This shows the extent to which the mass as ritual is clearly perceived as providing a sanctified space as well as a physical proximity that is shared with the saint by virtue of "passing" presence(s).[12]

After the mass, the image of the saint is carried outside the church, in a procession received by a respectful and solemn silence. The procession "seizes" the *patio* that the church building shares with the old *hacienda* house, and which still is Pesillo's main square. This small scale procession is not insignificant; instead – as we shall see farther- reinforces the ethnic character that marks the festivities surrounding San Juan. The procession around the village square is, in fact, a symbolic appropriation of a social and ethnic space, namely the space where the temporal and religious powers that have historically run Pesillo become visible, a constant reminder of the unique character of Pesillo as a "theocratic" *hacienda*. Here, the Church and the State still meet and intervene in local indigenous affairs, and the activities that legitimize authority and define the "polity", i.e. the identity of the village as differentiated from others, still take place. Marking the perimeter of the square, therefore, is also a symbolic act of "conquering" a space where indigenous people would once enter only from a subordinate and inferior position. Once the procession has "seized" the whole perimeter of the square, the saint's image is brought back into the church which will remain open until the following day, to allow people to pay visits to the saint during the whole day and night. The end of the procession marks the beginning of the ludic part of the feast, characterized by drinking and dancing, and which includes a programme of activities that varies every year but always includes the two main rituals of *la toma del patio* (the taking over of the square) or "entering of the communities" to the village square, and the offering of a pole of twelve live roosters (*rama de gallos*) to the central Committee and other local authorities, in acknowledgment of their authority and good dealings for the community.

---

[11] "La imágen de San Juan Bautista era de nuestros antepasados, la tenemos ahí (en la iglesia) de año tras año para recordarle. Toda la comunidad y el Comité Central le pasan la misa a San Juan. No ... no ... no puede ser que no le pasan misa, es una costumbre que tiene que pasar. En los programas que realizamos año tras año primero está la misa, después de la misa el baile, el trago ... Sin la misa no hay la fiesta tampoco, porque siempre hay que acercarse a la misa, siquiera a ver".

[12] I want to thank Katja Neumann for this thoughtful insight.

La entrada de las comunidades, or the Mapping of Ethnic Boundaries

While processions are a common element of Catholic celebrations, and are frequent throughout Ecuador, including the *mestizo* town of Olmedo, they are unusual
in the indigenous villages of the area, where the only processions I have ever encountered are in honour of San Juan. This is an additional sign of the significance
San Juan holds for Pesillanos.

During the year, each village belonging to the Olmedo parish organizes a team
that will represent it to the competition organized for the celebration of San Juan.
On the 24th June, after the mass, all village teams gather outside Pesillo. Each team
wears a visible mark of identity, such as a ribbon, or a coloured collar; each team
is preceded by two members carrying a banner with the name of the village. Each
party singing on its own, and accompanied by the guitars of one or more musi-
cians dressed as *aruchicos*,[13] the parade starts its slow march towards the village
square, where each party will perform in front of the audience. A jury will declare
the winning party and will grant it a prize and an honorific title that bears a huge
prestige for the winners.

More than the procession outside the church, this parade has a clear ethnic
character. Notably, *mestizo* people from Olmedo are completely excluded: neither
do they participate in the procession, nor do they attend the feast as spectators.
Instead, they organize their own celebrations for San Juan, which are more modest than the ones in Pesillo, and include the mass and some festive activities from
which indigenous villagers are excluded. The distance between the indigenous
village of Pesillo and the *mestizo* town of Olmedo is no longer than two km, and
to an outsider the two settlements may appear to be one the prolongation of the
other. This short distance is covered daily in both directions by both indigenous
and *mestizo* peoples (even by foot) who have close economic and social relationships. That the two groups are so evidently apart during the celebrations for San
Juan is, therefore, telling. Never does this short distance between the two locations
appear so wide as during this celebration, when the villagers' parade takes over one
hour to reach the village of Pesillo from the outskirt of Olmedo, through a long
detour that physically maps the boundaries of the "indigenous" area of the parish
and avoids all inhabited space, especially the town of Olmedo.

Unlike most Andean villages, where the traditional spatial divisions (of Inca
origins) between higher and lower sectors are still in place, in Pesillo and other
Ecuadorian highland villages space is organized concentrically around a centre
(cf. also Bourque, 1994: 229). The town of Olmedo being the parish seat, it hosts

---

[13] The *aruchico*, *chinucas*, and *diablouma* are traditional characters of the celebration of San Juan.
Some people disguise as such for the duration of the celebration, lending it a carnival-like quality. Such
characters are represented in different ways and have each a specific meaning. For a more detailed account see Ferraro (2004a).

the offices of the national authorities' representatives, and is inhabited by non-indigenous people. The parade for San Juan starts, therefore, from the "periphery" and progressively maps and delimits the physical boundaries of an indigenous space whose centre is the village of Pesillo, and whose square has always represented the heart of indigenous socio-economic and ritual life. The parade, therefore, is a statement about ethnic identity that establishes a frontier of exclusion and inclusion.

Both processions for San Juan, therefore, map not only religious but also social and ethnic boundaries. By emphasising the physical distance from Olmedo, the procession seems to mark also a "wider" and historical distance based on spatial and ethnic belonging. But more than this, both processions are a symbolic re-appropriation of an ethnic space. On-going music and singing accompany the parade, so that from a distance the impression is of a long dancing tail, and – borrowing Sallnow's words – "the entire journey has a surreal, dance-like quality" which is a fundamental characteristic of pilgrimages to Andean shrines (1991: 148). As Sallnow wrote regarding other Andean settings, so also the processions for San Juan perform a "kinaesthetic mapping of the space, a charting by bodily movement of the contours of the religious landscape … from the peripheral homelands to a sacred centre, a specially hallowed site where Christian divinities have begun to fuse with the tellurian Andean powers" (ibid). The slow march toward the village square is also a ritual passage across the land, from the "peripheral homelands" outside the inhabited area to the village sacred/civic centre, namely the patio outside both the *hacienda* house and the church which, in Pesillo history, have always represented a unified material and symbolic space. It is in this space at the junction of the sacred and civic space that San Juan physically resides. Like pilgrimages to a sacred shrine, the processions in honour of the saint are symbolic re-appropriations of the all-powerful, animated landscape.

Dancing and drinking characterise every event, and have a ceremonial character that may be seen as a synecdoche for the entire celebration. Their importance is illustrated by the following episode: An indigenous friend told me that she and her husband used to work for an Evangelical family in Quito, and were happy with them until asked to convert to the Evangelical faith. Then, they refused and returned to their village. My friend explained to me that "they wanted us to become Evangelical and I didn't like it. They [Evangelicals] do not like drinking and do not want us to dance and get drunk. They don't like *trago* (alcohol) and the feast" (R. M., Pesillo, June 2002). Evangelical withdrawal from drinking and dancing is seen as a lack of faith and devotion. This is further confirmed by the comments of another friend who on one occasion attributed the long-term draught affecting the crops to the action of some newly converted villagers who had thrown the images of San Juan into the river, thus causing the saint's anger who withdrew the rain for one year, causing people to lose their crops: "They repented. They begged the saint for forgiveness and abandoned the evangelical faith" (R. I., village of Pesillo, 2002).[14]

Rama de gallos: the Ritual Offering of the Pole of Roosters

The ritual offering of the roosters represents the climax of the *Dia Grande*. As a matter of fact, such ritual starts one year before, always during the celebration of San Juan, when an individual or a group asks the Central Committee or other recipients for a single rooster. This will be given back on the following celebration of San Juan in the form of a pole (*rama*) of twelve roosters. In order to gather the resources to return the full *rama*, the individual or group in question will resort to their social network of neighbours, kin and *compadres* to help them with cash mainly, thus starting a relationship of debt. In accepting to "help" the initiator and provider of the roosters, people share both the costs and the prestige associated with the *rama*, together with the moral entitlement to request the same help at some later stage, when necessary. These material and moral debts have a ritual counterpart in the practice of *el Castillo*. This consists in a series of ritual borrowing and lending of cash between individual households, which – given and taken in the name of the saint – must be returned doubled only and exclusively during the following year celebration of San Juan (cf. Ferraro 2004a; 2004; 2009). Hence, to a certain extent, the feast has retained some of the original meaning of the pre-Hispanic *inti raymi* celebration of the sun that included thanksgiving, propitiatory, and fertility rites.

The offering of the *rama* to the Central Committee or other authority takes place in the main square of the village and has a collective character. However, compared to past celebrations, current offerings appear very poor and void of any deep meaning. Instead, smaller versions of the same ritual take place in the more private and domestic space of individual households, between individuals who become ritual kin (*compadres*) through the offering of the *rama* that establishes a lifelong relationship. The household version of the *rama* finds only a marginal mention in the literature on the topic which, on the contrary, has always focussed on the principal "central" ritual of the offering of the roosters. At the time of my fieldwork however, the significance of such individual rituals had outgrown, both in number and in importance, the principal ritual. Nowadays, they take place all over Pesillo and nearby villages, and people invest significant amount of resources into such rituals that include the offering of huge quantities of food and drink to the respective helping parties.

---

[14] "Esta gente se arrepintió'. Rogo' perdón al Santo y dejaron de ser evangélicos".

The Celebration of San Juan through Time

It is impossible to understand fully such complex set of celebrations apart from the socio-economic and political context in which they take place. Past descriptions of the feast in Pesillo report that the ritual offering of the *rama de gallos* would take place in the *patio* of the *hacienda*, where all parties would gather around their respective leaders, and each would offer the *hacendado* (be he a priest under Church management or an *arrendatario*/tenant under state management) the pole of roosters. Under Church management (until 1908), such offering to the priests/landlord was compulsory, as were other offerings in the *hacienda*. With the management shift from Church to State (1908 to 1964) and the subdivision of the *latifundio* into five smaller *haciendas*, these offerings became voluntary and each family focused its attention on the manager of each *hacienda* (cf. Crespi 1968; 1981).

Scholars agree that as any *hacienda* festivals, also the celebration of San Juan in Pesillo and surrounding area played a key role in maintaining hierarchical relationships. It was a ritual of community integration; of reaffirmation of the existing social hierarchy, while also of subordination and acceptance of the *status quo* (Parsons 1945; Carvalho Neto 1964; Hassaurek 1967; Crespi 1968, 1981; Crain 1990; Guerrero 1991). The ritual "taking of the square" (*toma del patio*) – possibly a "revised" version or a reminiscence of the pre-Hispanic *tinqui*, the ritual fight among indigenous people of rival moieties – represented the symbolic appropriation of the space where the hegemonic power that sustained the *hacienda* system would become manifest. This was a space forbidden to indigenous people at ordinary times (cf. Crespi 1968, 1981; Crain 1990; Guerrero 1991; Cervone 1996; Bourque 1995). The ritual exchange of one rooster for twelve was a clear symbol of the unequal reciprocity that shaped relations within the hierarchical world of the *hacienda*. In offering twelve roosters to the landlord/priest, people recognised their superiority and authority, thus accepting it. For his part, by agreeing to initiate the celebration, the landlord accepted to sponsor the feast, thus giving clear signs of the "institutionalised generosity" that is expected to accompany power in the Andes (Guerrero 1991).

At the "Time of the Fathers", when Pesillo was a theocratic *hacienda*, the language, ideology and rituals of Catholicism articulated the hierarchical organisation and relationships of the traditional *hacienda* system. The celebration of San Juan ritually fostered the social context of patronage relationships between indigenous, *mestizo* and white people (Crespi 1981: 495). Both the "seizing of the square" and the offering of the roosters represented the symbolic and ritual imitation and inversion of the traditional hierarchical roles, which were thus affirmed and renewed each year. While providing a privileged mirror of the inequalities of the world at the time, San Juan was "instrumental" to all who played a role in it, by providing both sides (patron and peons) with material benefits. To the landlord, the celebration of San Juan would offer a covert strategy for exercising social control by trapping indigenous peasants and leaders of the *rama* into a monetary debt. To Indians, it offered the possibility of entering into a "waiting game that promised valuable and otherwise unobtainable rewards to the best public performers" (Crespi 1981: 498–499).

Around the 1950s, during the "Time of the Tenants", the corporate lessees of the Pesillo *hacienda* put an end to these ceremonies, refusing to play their traditional role as recipients and simultaneously initiators of the offerings. Consequently, people turned to their white/*mestizo compadres* from the nearby towns to fulfil these roles, moving the ritual focus from a single *rama* recipient to several ones. When, after the Agrarian Reform, the cooperative took full responsibility for the management of the land granted by the State (at "The Time of the Cooperative") it also took over full management of the costs of the celebration. Initially, cooperative funds were used to pay for the feast but after a while, the cooperative managers started searching elsewhere for contributions, in the form of prizes or cash donations from prosperous outsiders, and so the participation of white *compadres* declined. Crespi (1981) reports that the managers of the Ecuadorian Institute for Agrarian Reform and Colonisation (IERAC) imported new forms of entertainment, and attendance by outsiders increased. However, the whole celebration suffered a dramatic decline, according to this scholar, due to the disappearance of the traditional structures of power which provided justification and coherence for the celebration, and to the high costs of the *rama* rituals which were beyond the economic wherewithal of local peasants.

The Contemporary Celebration of San Juan

However poor it might comparatively appear, the contemporary celebration of San Juan is not bereft of profound meaning and still holds a tremendous significance for indigenous villagers. Residents suspend all routine activities to participate in the feast, migrants come back home for the occasion, and local NGOs plan their annual activities around the celebration, knowing that for local people it takes priority over any other activity. This becomes evident when attention is shifting away from the "public" space of the old *hacienda patio* to the more domestic and discreet space of individual households where individual *rama* offerings take place.

It is my contention that far from disappearing or becoming meaningless, such celebration still provides a mirror into contemporary social dynamics. The Agrarian Reform intensified the process of decentralisation put in motion by the partition of the former Church/*hacienda*, when the once centrally organized economic, social, and ritual life was then reconstituted around each of the five individual *haciendas*. With the total dismantling of the *hacienda* system, indigenous lives are no longer organised around a material and symbolic "centre". Former *huasipungueros* gained a degree of independence, and leaders (former non-resident *hacienda* workers) exhibited a higher degree of autonomy. The Agrarian Reform, thus, speeded up the process of social and economic fragmentation. The land freed by the Reform was accessible only to members of cooperatives, while former *huasipungueros* were excluded. The result was a further differentiation between indigenous people with and without land (cf. Martínez 1995; Bretón 1997). Members of families with little land, especially young men, left the local community in search of jobs.

Initially, the cooperative took over the role performed by the *hacienda* and became the organising centre of its members' lives. Families with access to co-operative land did not have to rely on one another, since they could turn to the co-operative for help. In the ledgers of Pesillo's "Atahualpa" cooperative, for instance, I found records of the cooperative granting *suplidos* and *socorros*, that is to say, concessions in the forms of cash and goods that the landlord would grant to his peons, and that would play a vital role in legitimating and reproducing the social organization of power within the *hacienda* cultural system. However, the stagnation of the land market blocked the new generation's access to independent parcels, causing greater pressure on the land of the cooperatives and accelerating the process of division. With the end of the cooperative and the division of its common properties among its former members, also the land was redistributed among villagers, and households took full and individual control over their parcels. With the redistribution of all land, former *huasipungueros* became more involved in market activities. This generated the strengthening of nuclear families, and granted a new and central role to kinship as the organizing knot of socio-economic life. The shifting role of the "community" (*comunidad*), as a result of the changing post-Reform socio economic context, has also meant a shift in the strategies and means by which the community relates to the Saint. While once the community was a legal and symbolic entity that represented the centre of indigenous economic and social life, this role is now performed by kinship, which has become the central axis of inter and intra community relationships. That is to say, because of the changing socio-economic context, individual families have more agency in so far as their economic strategies are concerned. Consequently, individuals have acquired increased importance in terms of ethnic claims (cf. Bretón 1997; Cervone 1996). In this process, the sector that once was considered as "peripheral" to the *hacienda* space, has strengthened its social and economic links through ritual and consanguineal ties. Consequentially, the ritual emphasis of the celebration of San Juan has shifted from the centrally performed *rama* offering to the central authority, to the "decentralised" *rama* rituals among individual households.

Conclusions

The redistribution of land to indigenous peasants through the Agrarian reform, has led to the physical and symbolic disarticulation of the *hacienda* cultural system with visible repercussions also at the level of the celebration of San Juan. Without a patron, there was no central authority that could be ritually acknowledged, legitimised and reproduced. The old centre of indigenous life – the *hacienda patio* – became a delegitimized and peripheral space, while on the contrary, what once was the periphery now enjoys a new vitality and strength. Currently, indigenous life takes place in more fragmented economic, social and therefore ritual spaces around individual households. The celebration of San Juan has readjusted accordingly. Since now more than in the past, relationships between villagers are essential for the socio-economic life of indigenous households, the celebrations around households have taken on a new and more important meaning. This is the "new feast" that celebrates, strengthens and seals a different and internally more fragmented sense of community. Such community is a more "individuated" entity; nevertheless, it forges a strong sense of collective belonging by emphasising ethnic spaces from which non-indigenous people are excluded. It ritually establishes ethnic boundaries that shape social relationships.

The celebration of San Juan has become, therefore, a privileged space to create, consolidate and make visible an indigenous identity that would otherwise remain understated, and could easily be diluted outside of its community boundaries. It represents a way to create a sense of social cohesion in front of the daily "des-indigenizing" pressures that indigenous people face by national globalized society. In so doing, it also shows once more that identities are ascribed to places. Pesillanos' identity has been challenged by the many and rapid socio-economic changes that the area has suffered in the last forty years. Local identities based upon the *hacienda* socio-cultural system of land tenancy have been dramatically altered by its dismantling. San Juan provides, therefore, the opportunity of fostering a new sense of belonging and differentiation at the same time.

Finally, the character of San Juan himself makes clear that the characters of the Catholic world have been "Andeanized" in more than one way. Not only has San Juan been invested with the qualities of both the Catholic and the Andean worlds, but his celebration is a privileged observatory of the changing socio-economic and ethnic relations in the area. Its persistence and changing over time are closely linked to the changing land tenancy systems, economic strategies, and social relations in the area.

References

Bastien, J. W.
1978 Mountain of the Condor: Metaphor and Ritual in an Andean Ayllu. St. Paul: West Publishing Co.

Becker, M.
1999 Comunas and Indigenous Protest in Cayambe, Ecuador. *The Americas* 55 (4): 531–559.

Bourque, N.
1994 Spatial Meaning in Andean festivals: Corpus Christi and Octavo. *Ethnology* 33 (3): 229–243.
1995 Savages and Angels: the Spiritual, Social and Physical Development of Individuals and Households in Andean Life-cycle Festivals. *Ethnos* 60 (1–2): 99–114.

Bretón, V.
1997 Capitalismo, Reforma Agraria y Organización Comunal en los Andes. Una Introducción al Caso Ecuatoriano. Lleida: Adreça Científica.

Carvalho-Neto, P.
1964 Diccionario del Folklore Ecuatoriano. Quito: Casa de la Cultura Ecuatoriana.

Cervone, E.
1996 El Retorno de Atahualpa. Ph.D. Thesis. University of San Andrew, UK.

Costales, P., and **Alfredo Costales**
1987 Pesillo. Documentos para su Historia. Quito: Abya Yala.

Crain, M.
1990 Ritual, Memoria Popular y Proceso Político en la Sierra Ecuatoriana. Quito: Abya-Yala – C. E. N.

Crespi, M.
1968 The Patrons and Peons of Pesillo. A Traditional Hacienda System in Highland Ecuador. Ph.D. Thesis. Ann Arbor: Michigan University.
1981 St. John the Baptist: The Ritual Looking Glass of Hacienda Indian Ethnic and Power Relations. In N. Whitten (ed.), Cultural Transformations and Ethnicity in Modern Ecuador; pp. 477–505. Champaign-Urbana: University of Illinois Press.

Dillon, Mary and **Thomas Abercrombie**
1988 The Destroying Christ: An Aymara Myth of Conquest. In J. D. Hill (ed.) Rethinking History and Myth. Indigenous South American Perspectives on the Past; pp. 50–77. Urbana: University of Illinois Press.

Ferraro, E.
2004a Reciprocidad Don y Deuda. Formas y Relaciones de Intercambios en los Andes Ecuatorianos. Quito: Flacso-Abya Yala.
2004b Owing and Being in Debt. A Contribution from the Northern Andes of Ecuador. *Social Anthropology* 12 (1):77–94.
2006 Culture and Economy: The Case of the Milk Market in the Northern Andes of Ecuador. *Ethnology* 45 (1):25–39.

2009 Money, Loans and Faith. Narratives and Images of Wealth, Fertility, and Salvation in the Northern Andes. In: R. Wright and A. Villaça (eds.), Modes and Effects of Christianity among Indigenous Peoples of the Americas; pp. 71–88. Farnham: Ashgate Publishing.
2011 Trueque: An Ethnographic Account of Barter, Trade and Money in Andean Ecuador. *JLACA* 16(1): 168–184.

Gose, P.
1986 Sacrifice and the Commodity Form in the Andes. *Man* 21: 296– 310.
1994 Deathly Waters and Hungry Mountains. Agrarian Ritual and Class Formation in an Andean Town. Toronto: University of Toronto Press.

Guerrero, A.
1991 La Semántica de la Dominación. El Concertaje de Indios. Quito: Libri Mundi.

Harris, O.
1989 The Earth and the State: The Sources and Meanings of Money in Northern Potosí, Bolivia. In: J. Parry and M. Bloch (eds.), Money and the Morality of Exchange; pp. 232–268. Cambridge: Cambridge University Press.
1995 The Sources and Meanings of Money: Beyond the Market Paradigm in an Ayllu of Northern Potosí. In B. Larson and O. Harris (eds.), Ethnicity, Markets and Migration in the Andes; pp. 297–328. Durham: Duke University Press.

Hassaurek, F.
1967 Four Years among the Ecuadorians. Carbondale: Southern Illinois University Press.

Korovkin, T.
2003 Flower Exports, Female Labor, and Community Participation in Highland Ecuador. *Latin American Perspectives* 30 (4): 18–42.

Landázuri, C.
1980 La Hacienda Estatal y Su Transformación en Cooperativa Agraria: El Caso de Pesillo 1913–1977. Tesis de Antropología. Quito: Universidad Católica (PUCE).

MacCormack, S.
1991a Religion in the Andes. Vision and Imagination in Early Colonial Peru. Princeton: Princeton University Press.
1991b Ritual, Conflicto y Comunidad en el Perú Colonial Temprano. In S. Moreno Y. and F. Salomon (eds.), Reproducción y Transformación de las Sociedades Andinas, Siglos XVI–XX; pp. 47–67, vol. 1. Quito: Abya Yala.

Martínez, L.
1995 Familia Campesina y Comportamiento Demográfico. El Caso de las Cooperativas Indígenas de Cayambe. *Colección Avances* n. 1. Número Monográfico. Quito: Asociación Ecuatoriana de Población (AEPO).

Nash, J.
1979 We Eat the Mines and the Mines Eat Us. New York: Columbia University Press.

Parsons, E. C.
1945 Peguche, Canton of Otavalo, Province of Imbabura, Ecuador: A Study of Andean Indians. Chicago: University of Chicago Press.

Prieto, M.
1978 Condicionamientos de la Movilización Campesina: El Caso de las Haciendas Ol-medo-Ecuador (1926–1948). Tesis de Antropología. Quito: Universidad Católica (PUCE).

Rösing, I.
1994 La Deuda de Ofrenda: Un Concepto Central de la Religión Andina. *Revista Andina* 12 (1): 191–216.
1995 Paraman Purina-Going for Rain. Mute Anthropology Versus Speaking Anthropology. Lessons from an Andean Collective Scarcity Ritual in the Quechua-Speaking Kallawaya and Aymara. *Anthropos* 90 (1–3): 69–88.

Sallnow, M.
1989 Precious metals in the Andean moral economy. In: J. Parry and M. Bloch (eds.), Money and the Morality of Exchange; pp. 209–231. Cambridge: Cambridge University Press.
1991 Pilgrimage and Cultural Fracture in the Andes. In J. Eade and M. Sallnow (eds.), Contesting the Sacred. The Anthropology of Christian Pilgrimages; pp. 137–153. London: Routledge.

Silverblatt, I.
1988 Political Memories and Colonizing Symbols: Santiago and the Mountain Gods of Colonial Peru. In J. D. Hill (ed.), Rethinking History and Myth: Indigenous South American Perspectives on the Past; pp. 174–194. Urbana: University of Illinois Press.

Taussig, M. T.
1980 The Devil and Commodity Fetishism in South America. Chapel Hill: The University of North Carolina Press.

Yanez del Pozo, J.
1988 Yo Declaro con Franqueza. Quito: Abya Yala.

Zamosc, L.
1995 Estadísticas de las Áreas de Predominio Étnico de la Sierra Ecuatoriana: Población Rural, Indicadores Cantonales y organizaciones de Base. Quito: Abya Yala.

"The Loneliest Woman in Africa"

Missionary Biography as a Form of Scottish Protestant Sainthood

Michael Marten

Abstract. – The article analyses a tradition of Scottish Protestant missionary biography from the early 20th century, with a view to contextualising these works within a broad paradigm of sainthood. Commonalities in themes, stylistic interpretations and motivations are elucidated upon and compared. It is argued that this genre of missionary biography acts as a form of canonisation for popular sainthood, with the missionaries acting as role models for the reader. *[missionary biography, sainthood, canonisation, Scotland, Celtic, Africa]*

Michael Marten is Lecturer in Postcolonial Studies in the Critical Religion Research Group at the University of Stirling. His research focuses primarily on missions and churches of the Middle East. He has published *Attempting to Bring the Gospel Home: Scottish Missions to Palestine, 1839–1917* (London: I. B. Tauris, 2006), and is currently working on a new book on missions and gender questions in Palestine.

Introduction

Scottish Protestants usually claim that they do not venerate saints, and many might barely acknowledge them in the way that, for example, adherents within Catholic traditions do. It may therefore seem rather odd to speak of saints in this context, but I want to show that processes of veneration – particularly in displaced contexts such as missionary centres – existed, and were developed with a very particular purpose that effectively made them a form of canonisation.

In defining my terms, I will begin by pointing to the broad interpretation of "saints" that the Call for Papers specified which first prompted this paper: "Within Christianity they are conceived of as mediators between humankind and the divine; they are teachers, models, missionaries, martyrs, patrons and after death their relics can still achieve miracles". This can be traced to early veneration – almost always of martyrs – as early as the second century, and tended to be local, often with a focus on the tomb. Dying for beliefs one holds would, it was presumed, result in closeness to God, and intercession to a saint who might intercede on behalf of the believer was therefore a way of approaching God (of course, it was usually not being suggested that saints themselves bestowed blessings). The growth of Egyptian monasticism and the spread of ideals about the ascetic life led to an increase in those venerated as saints. A trade in the relics of saints gradually developed, as it was believed these bestowed divine blessings on the owner. Cathedrals and churches vied for influence, with relic collections becoming significant markers of importance.[1]

Of course, over time more intricate processes developed which entailed greater clarity in discerning who should or should not be regarded as a saint. It was only in the aftermath of the Reformation and Counter-Reformation that complete control over these processes was achieved, at least in theory: papal approval was required for canonisation, with key criteria being evidence that the proposed saint had lived a pious life, and had performed some miracle. Nonetheless, in popular culture – especially away from the Church's metropolitan centres – there have been particularly pious individuals who have been treated as saints, whether the hierarchy has recognised them as such or not: they have been venerated, and could be asked to intercede before God on behalf of an individual or a community. Farmer notes that from the early Middle Ages, Scotland, Ireland, Wales and Cornwall (the "Celtic areas") had a great many saints, in part because the word had been broadened in usage to "mean hardly more than pious church-founder or learned ecclesiastic" (1978/2004: xvii).[2] This is a usage that waxed and waned over the centuries, but at the latest with Alexander Carmichael's great collection of Gaelic prayers and poetry from the Outer Hebridean islands published at the end of the 19th century, the *Carmina Gadelica*, an increasing sense of the place of Celtic saints as mentors and aids who could "combine miraculous powers with human foibles" (de Waal 1988: 9) entered into broader Christian discourse in Scotland. Amongst the most well-known Protestant ministers from the inter-war years who developed the idea of saints in such contexts is perhaps George MacLeod, the founder of the Iona Community, whose prayers and liturgical writings invoked saints and angels in a way that regularly seemed to transgress the accepted norms of his tradition. However, I want to argue here that this kind of thinking arose not only in the context of Carmichael's work, but also came about in the context of missionary biography.

In 2003, the late, great missionary scholar Andrew C. Ross drew my attention to the book from which the first part of the title of this article is taken. We were discussing the place and value of early 20th century missionary biography, and the extent to which such works might be used today to understand the place of missions in popular understandings of the time.[3] The book he mentioned is by William Pringle Livingstone: entitled *Christina Forsyth of Fingoland: The story of the loneliest woman in Africa*; it was published in 1918. The introductory note tells

---

[1] For an introduction to Coptic monasticism, see Ghabra 2002: 1. Farmer 1978/2004 discusses some of the issues mentioned here and in the subsequent paragraph in his introductory notes.

[2] Other essays in this special issue point to phenomena of this nature occurring in other contexts.

[3] At the time he pointedly said that I should write about this topic and that he looked forward to reading something on it before long. Sadly, he died in 2008 and so I am too late for that, but I would like to think that some of what I argue here might have interested or even amused him.

us much of what we need to know about this book: "It is a simple human story", Livingstone claims (Livingstone 1918: vii).

Of course, the supposed loneliness that Forsyth experienced was of a particular kind, as Livingstone makes clear: she "lived alone for thirty years ... amongst a wild and dissolute tribe of heathens ... She seldom saw a white face ..." (Livingstone 1918: vii). In other words, the company of the "wild and dissolute heathens" with whom she lived for three decades counted for nothing – she was lonely, he thought, because there were no "white faces" for her to relate to. Forsyth retired at the age of 72, so in these statements, Livingstone is negating entirely the company and agency of Africans, which she seems to have found perfectly acceptable for much of her adult life. Clearly, for Livingstone, Africans could not possibly provide adequate company for a European woman, and as there were no Europeans nearby, or ones that she saw regularly, she must have been the "loneliest woman in Africa".

There were a number of more or less prolific missionary biographers in this period, but Livingstone's output on this front is undoubtedly rather impressive. Not only did he write about Forsyth, but he also wrote:

– a biography of Robert Laws, a missionary in Southern Africa: *Laws of Livingstonia: A Narrative of Missionary Adventure and Achievement* (1912?)
– two biographies of Mary Slessor, one an adult version entitled *Mary Slessor of Calabar: Pioneer Missionary* (1915), and one a children's version, with the far more exciting title *Mary Slessor: the White Queen of Okoyong – a true story of Adventure, Heroism, and Faith*; (1916?)
– a biography of David Torrance *A Galilee Doctor. Being a Sketch of the Career of Dr D. W. Torrance of Tiberias* (1923)
– a life of Jesus that he entitled *The Master Life – the Story of Jesus for Today* (1925).[4]

Livingstone was, inter alia, the editor of the monthly *Record of the United Free Church of Scotland*, the general church publication of the denomination to which the missionaries belonged (or they eventually became a part of through church unions), becoming editor of *Life and Work* when the United Free Church of Scotland and the Church of Scotland reunited in 1929, a post he then held until 1934. This would have given him relatively easy access both to the individuals he wanted to write about, and relevant sources about them.

---

[4] Incidentally, he also wrote a book on *Shetland and Shetlanders* (1947), which I have not read.

The Context of Missionary Biography in the Early 20th Century

Whilst in the Scottish context particularly, Livingstone was prolific and successful (all his books went into multiple editions, and sold thousands upon thousands of copies), he was one of many similar authors. Sometimes, returning missionaries would write about their colleagues – as happened with William Ewing's biography of Alexander Paterson (1930?) or Constance Padwick's famous biography of William Temple Gairdner (1929/1930) – or they would simply trawl documents and speak to the missionary and/or their friends and write on that basis, as happened with James Wells' biography of James Stewart (1909).

These biographies appeared in a very particular context, of course. Missionary book publishing in Britain alone at times rivalled the output of what we might call "secular" publishers. It is probably safe to say that every literate church-going household in Britain would encounter missionary stories in some form – a veritable onslaught of missionary communication. Whatever pedagogic, spiritual or theological thinking behind the publication of these books, we can certainly point to attempts to replenish missionary resources as a coherent reason for their proliferation: we know that despite the popular image of numerous missionaries and widespread mission work, at the end of the 19th and beginning of the 20th century, there were too few missionaries and not enough money for the tasks the mission boards and existing missionaries wanted to carry out:

The period … [1874–1914] saw brilliant work done by Church of Scotland missionaries in many countries, but it was not a period in which there was any widespread concern in the Church for the work these men and women were sent to do. A small minority of congregations contained within them minority groups who supplied the support that allowed this work to go ahead.

… what has been seen as a time of supreme interest in the mission of the church overseas appeared very differently to the men concerned with carrying it out. Dull indifference was the mood of Scotland in their view (Ross 1972: 57).

Ross explains why missions in church life and in the national press achieved such prominence by pointing to news issues and social factors: today we might think of internet, cinema, radio and television as sources of news and entertainment, but in this period missionary news provided what was seen as a reliable source of information about the expansion of the British empire (even though support for such expansion was not universal, interest in it was, as Said argued in 1993: 76). Of course, the "church-going middle-class Scot would seem to have favoured neither the theatre nor the pub" (Ross 1972: 71), and so the social function of missionary meetings and writings should not be overlooked.

Although he is addressing primarily the Church of Scotland's Blantyre mission, the picture he presents is not "a peculiar one" but applies to the church as a whole (Ross 1972: 52–53; 67–71). This is not new: for example, an 1882 article in the

Church of Scotland *Life and Work* magazine warned "that missions were unpopular in the sense that every congregation had people who were not only indifferent, but hostile" – quite aside from an issue of patience with the apparent slow progress of missions: "What with our steam engines, our telegraphs, and our telephones, we are so accustomed to rapidity of movement and quick results that we lose patience with every undertaking that does not move to a speedy issue" (Kernohan 1979: 35).

Therefore, publishing motivational biographies was certainly something that the churches supported. Indeed, in some Evangelical[5] contexts, it was almost automatically assumed that one would serve the church overseas unless called to serve at home, so missionary biographies that encouraged such thinking were promoted by many. As a result, publishers in turn found them to be a profitable venture.[6] However, Jonathan Bonk points out that this emphasis on the western missionary was in fact misplaced in terms of actual results:

despite the very modest results accruing from the prodigious efforts of nineteenth-century missionaries like David Livingstone, Robert Moffat, Mary Slessor, and C. T. Studd, these names are household words today; in contrast, while Christian numerical growth in Africa has burgeoned from an estimated 8.8 million in 1900 to 382.8 million in 2004, scarcely anything is known about the persons chiefly responsible for this astonishing growth – African catechists and evangelists (Bonk 2004: 153–154).

So in addition to the "easy racism" I have already pointed to in the title and premise of Livingstone's book on Forsyth, we can also observe a more complex but deeper racism: the profiling of European missionaries over (in this instance) Africans who were far more than a footnote in the missionary endeavour. This is replicated throughout the books in question, which should come as no great surprise, given the European understandings of race at the time these books were being written.[7]

---

[5] It is worth noting that I am using the term Evangelical to denote the revivalist movement that dominated much of 19th century Protestant life; Bebbington's 1989 text is a comprehensive guide.

[6] It is notable that the market in such publications was dominated by a handful of publishers, with Hodder & Stoughton probably the most significant. I would like to see an examination of the proportion of various publishers' income based on biographical publications such as those mentioned here, as they were clearly profitable for a long time. I am not aware of any such work having been carried out, but if the appropriate source material were available, it could be a very interesting exercise for an appropriately qualified scholar to pursue.

It is also worth noting that many of these books, even about Scottish missionaries, were published by London-based publishers. We can point here to the over-riding Evangelical understandings in Britain that were more significant than the national or denominational divisions which existed (cf. e.g., Bebbington, London / New York, 1989, who points to the wide range of interactions between Evangelicals all across Britain in the 19th and 20th centuries, often regardless of the denominational background).

[7] I have discussed this in more detail as it relates to the missionary context at this time in Marten 2006: chapter 5.

Questions of Gender and Class – Patterns in Missionary Biography

Having briefly mentioned race, I want to examine more closely the portrayal of
gender and class in these biographies. By way of example, I will look at two texts,
one Livingstone's biography of Mary Slessor (1915), the other his biography of
David Torrance (1923). There is a general pattern to these biographies that we can
describe as a discourse: we can see normative forms of childhood, life-choices,
missionary beginnings and so on, which suggest a clear agenda on the part of the
missionary biographer; this will be discussed in more detail below.

Livingstone describes Mary Slessor's early life in some detail, which I can
only summarise here: she was born on 2.12.1848 to an alcoholic father who was
a shoemaker and drove the family to penury through his drinking, resulting in both
mother and daughter working as weavers in a factory in Dundee. Slessor was 11 at
this time, and great emphasis is placed on her initially working half-days with the
other half-day being given over to school attendance, and then, once she worked
full time, attending school at night. The trauma of her father's addiction is something her mother shared only with Mary, but:

All the endearments of his wife and daughter were powerless to save the man whose heart
was tender enough when he was sober, but whose moral sensibilities continued to be sapped
by his indulgence in drink … The fact that the family was never disgraced in public was attributed to prayer. The mother prayed, the daughter prayed, ceaselessly, with utter simplicity of belief, and they were never once left stranded or put to shame (Livingstone 1915: 6).

In Livingstone's portrayal, Victorian moral codes around drunkenness are upheld because of the prayers of the mother and daughter, pointing to a deep piety
on the part of the mother, something she in turn communicated to her daughter.

Slessor's father died whilst she was probably still in her teens. Her early life
is portrayed by Livingstone as one of "misery", with her Bible and attendance at
the United Presbyterian Church of Scotland and Sunday School as her only con-
solation. She went to Old Calabar (Nigeria) in August 1876 aged 28, famously the
only woman on the ship, having pursued, against all the odds, some limited further education in Edinburgh once she had applied and been accepted for overseas
work in May 1875.[8]

We can contrast Slessor's background with that of David Torrance, missionary to Palestine. Born on 6.11.1862, his father was a doctor in Airdrie, a Justice

---

[8] The extent of her education is only hinted at: according to Livingstone, she read voraciously, and
attended for a short period the Normal School in Edinburgh's Canongate, but was not formally regis-
tered as a student (1915: 11–12, 18).

Aside from Livingstone's book, brief summaries of her life story can also be found in more recent texts, such as Orr Macdonald (2000): 140–142 and Trollope (1983): 194–199, amongst others.
However, the extent to which they might rely on Livingstone for their information is not clear to me.

of the Peace and for a time a town councillor and burgh treasurer. An enthusiastic Freemason, he was also an elder in the Church of Scotland, though his wife and children went to the Free Church. Torrance attended "the Academy" and when his father died, his mother moved the family to Glasgow, where Torrance, aged 16, immediately started his medical training at the university, whilst working in the public dispensary with the purpose, according to his biographer, of relieving his family of the costs of his studies:

He toiled hard, and at times the struggle was severe, but he had other interests which relieved the strain and kept his mind fresh; he played football, worked with his hands, and attended the Church and University choirs ... he had been born into the life of the spirit through his mother's love and piety, and the course of his aspiration and action had been, from the beginning, definitely in the right direction ... When he joined the Church, she sat beside him at his first Communion and cried softly in her joy. He became a teacher in the Sunday school, took part in the various activities of the congregation, and exercised an inspiring influence on the young people (Livingstone 1923: 18–19; see also 12–13; 16–17).

Again, we see here the important role of the mother in relation to the piety of her child. It is no doubt reasonable to assume that the early death of the father played a role in the increased importance of the mother.[9]

Torrance received an invitation to work for the Free Church of Scotland Jewish Mission Committee whilst sight-seeing in New York and in February 1884 set off on his first exploratory trip to Palestine (Livingstone 1923: 21, 23). So we have here the classical hallmarks of the middle classes – the father a doctor, a JP, a town councillor and burgh treasurer, a Freemason and a member of the Church of Scotland. His widowed mother seems to have struggled to pay for her son to study medicine; but on the other hand, Livingstone describes him receiving the call to pursue missionary work whilst he was sight-seeing in New York – such financially demanding leisure activity, no matter how educational it might have been perceived to be, would have been inconceivable for Slessor.

In terms of gender and class, these two examples appear to represent a significant contrast to one another. However, beyond the coincidence of both fathers dying early, their commonalities are also striking: the fathers' deaths marked difficult personal circumstances – obviously, this is relative, as Slessor was undoubtedly markedly poorer than Torrance – but an emphasis is placed on classical virtues of the Victorian era in both narratives: hard work (weaving and in school work), and steadfastness in prayer and a godly life. The mothers play a significant role in the encouragement of this piety.

Furthermore, in both volumes, over several hundred pages, we are guided through a number of key markers:

---

[9] Interestingly, the mothers of Slessor and Torrance are barely mentioned by Livingstone once the missionaries have left for their mission stations.

– their calling to mission work, which is initially something they are modest and
  hesitant about, relying on the wisdom of others for guidance, even though they
  both appear to see this as something they really want to do;
– their careers in their chosen mission fields, which are punctuated by periods of
  doubt and despair, with corresponding experiences of piety and kindness that
  revived their spirits;
– their humble and reluctant acceptance of honours bestowed upon them for their
  work; these took various forms, e.g., Slessor received, amongst other signs of
  gratitude for her work, royal recognition as an Honorary Associate of the Order
  of the Hospital of St. John of Jerusalem (Livingstone 1915: 303–308), whilst
  Torrance, upon completing 25 years in Tiberias, was celebrated in a ceremony
  by local Jews, Muslims and Christians, to which "the Doctor could only make
  a brief reply" (Livingstone 1923: 219–222);
– their eventual deaths are presented as highly significant events, embodying all
  that the individual's life has represented. The loving spouse or wider family and
  friends are often present, and whether the missionary died in service or after
  retiring to Scotland, there is not only a physical, but also a meta-narrative of
  closure: whilst being someone to emulate (more will be said about this below)
  this individual was so special that their life's work cannot be replaced, even if
  the mission they founded or worked for continues under the direction of another
  individual. There is a uniformity to these death narratives that reminds one of
  the uniformity of converts' redemption narratives that Griffiths has described
  (2005).

These are some of the markers of their lives in terms of events. I have deliberately chosen two biographies by the same author, and will shortly turn to another
of his books. Choosing books by the same author not only makes the differences
that might exist more significant, but emphasises even more their similarities: difference and similarity are not simply a result of a preference of writing style, but
reflect a literary politics that correlates with social norms and boundaries regarding gender and other markers. In a wider sense, however, these books also represent a typos: other missionary biographers wrote in similar ways, though not many
were as prolific as Livingstone. Of course, the biographies under discussion here
are all from a very particular time period, and any reading of biographies by these
missionaries would inevitably have been older works, rather than these particular
books – in part because the subjects were contemporaries of one another. Whilst
the meta-narrative of their reading material might have been similar, they would
have been different in style, as evidenced by something like Marshall's more sum-
mative work (1863).

Having described briefly some aspects of the lives of Slessor and Torrance,
more general patterns of this form of biography can be highlighted. All of these

markers communicate a wider message that represents key values of perseverance, faith, dedication, and unwavering commitment to the cause. Of course, many of the missionaries will have thought of their lives in the terms outlined here and described their experiences in such ways, in part because of the prevalence of meta-narratives that dominated the purpose and drive of missionary life – there is a dialectical relationship between the (expected) narrative forms and the missionaries' accounts of their experiences.[10] The connection to the childhood and familial expressions of piety that I noted earlier dominate in this literary genre, and is carried forward throughout adulthood.

First of all, we can note that mission work is often marked by treacherous beginnings, perhaps characterised by duplicitous locals or untrustworthy officials – despite this, the missionary succeeds in setting up a rudimentary mission station (see for example, Torrance's turbulent dealings with customs officials when he sought to import medical items without paying bakshīsh,[11] as Livingstone describes in 1923: 59–65).

After a while, a small number of people become interested in the work, and perhaps even convert – this is taken as evidence of the viability of expanding the work, and perhaps further recruits join from the sending body as happened in Tiberias, when a Scottish woman, Helen Fenton, arrived to initiate a girls' school (Livingstone 1923: 78). However, just as substantial success appears to be imminent, serious opposition manifests itself in the form of a local religious or civic leader, who threatens to close the mission either through recourse to officialdom, withdrawal of school pupils or patients, or even raw violence. Some semi-miraculous event averts this catastrophe, however, and the threat is overcome, for example, in Tiberias, northern Palestine, a rabbi

whose hostility to the mission was peculiarly virulent had a daughter-in-law suffering from a deranged mind ... [another rabbi tried to cure her but failed, and] the husband became impatient and sought the advice of Dr. Torrance, whose rational treatment soon restored her to her right mind ... [when the rabbi also fell ill, the son/husband brought Torrance to him:] Immediate relief was given ... no man could have been more grateful, and he never afterwards opposed the Mission (Livingstone 1923: 78–79).

---

[10] Griffiths' essay (2005) on the typical forms that conversion narratives took suggests the sort of pattern that I am referring to here – there is no reason to assume that this did not occur in the contexts I am describing, though further work to link missionary narratives to other missionaries would be an interesting pursuit: it is known that Ion Keith-Falconer's life-story was inspirational for many missionaries, but whether the likes of Torrance or Slessor would have had access to, and interest in, other missionaries' life stories, is not completely clear. Certainly, although they rarely had the opportunity to meet missionaries in other parts of the world, when they did manage to do so (for example, missionaries in India sometimes travelled to and from Europe via the Middle East), such meetings are often portrayed as occasions of considerable personal enrichment and mutual support.

[11] Although this cannot be defined and discussed in detail here, this was often understood to be a "bribe" by westerners, but it is more of a gratuity or a tip that will speed a transaction along a little.

Whilst facing such problems in the field, the missionaries also struggle with the lack of support from home after the initial enthusiasm for the mission has worn away – "if only more support were forthcoming, think of what could be done!" is a frequent refrain – but despite this, they valiantly carry on. For example, Slessor hoped that further missionaries could be sent to a particular area, and although the responsible individual in Scotland was sympathetic,

[f]or a quarter of a century the supply of men had not sufficed for the existing needs of the Mission, and extension had been impossible. The givings … for foreign missions had been far below the urgent requirements. Either … staff and income must be largely increased, or they would have to step aside … No adequate response was made to this … [appeal], and the lonely pioneer was forced onwards upon her lonely path (Livingstone 1915: 200).

The outcomes of the missionary labours were unpredictable: depending on their environment, the work may or may not have resulted in many converts. For example, there were relatively few in the Middle East, whereas many missions in Africa recorded high numbers of converts. However, it is worth bearing in mind Jonathan Bonk's point referred to above about African mission work: it was mostly Africans who led other Africans to conversion. The biographies occasionally let this slip out too; there is, of course, an element of racism at play here on the part of the author. Of Forsyth, for example, Livingstone notes that her reports home never included "anything in them about *her* service … She very seldom used the personal pronoun, preferring the word 'we.'" (Livingstone 1918: 146) – in the same way that he was unable to accept that she might not have been lonely with Africans around her, it seemed incomprehensible to him that Africans might be active in the work she is pursuing, even being seen as partners, as Forsyth perhaps wanted to imply through her usage of "we". Of course, in keeping with the tradition of piety these biographies came from, ultimate responsibility for any achievements is attributed by the missionary to divine assistance, e.g., Livingstone on Forsyth: "For the results attained Mrs. Forsyth herself took not an atom of credit. She held that she was only an instrument; the power and the strength came from above" (Livingstone 1918: 226).

Affirmation of the missionaries' work is key: often, after many years there is a significant event that includes the approval of local dignitaries, even if they are not converts; in fact, there do not even need to have been many converts for the event to serve to further validate the work (see the example mentioned above for Torrance; I have discussed this event in more detail in Marten 2006: 93–94).

Eventually, the missionary either retires to Scotland (and often continues to engage with the issues and serve the church with devotion as best they are able to do), or they die in post. In either case, the death itself is a ritualised narrative drama: it is barely a caricature to say that all these missionaries die peacefully, remembering to the last minute their service in foreign fields, dying with the wish that, as

Forsyth is supposed to have said, "I should like to do better than I have done" (Livingstone 1918: 234). The presence of family at the moment of death is frequently highlighted: for example, in Padwick's account, Temple Gairdner,

> lay there, half in heaven, but supremely normal, commenting on his children's letters, greeting his eldest son from India with a quaint jesting tenderness; wholesome and humorous to the very last, when on the evening of May 21st he fell asleep and very early next morning slept his life away on his wife's shoulder. His son, as he looked on the sleeping face, could only say, "Your joy no man taketh from you" (Padwick 1929/1930: 325).

Whilst such a collation of literary traits invariably results in a certain level of over-simplification, my point here has been to point to general trends in the writing of missionary biography in the early part of the twentieth century; there are many more examples of such writing that could serve to substantiate the patterns being described here. It is not just that origins are portrayed in similar ways, even if the contexts are substantially different (as with Slessor and Torrance), but the patterns their lives take – according to these missionary biographies – are remarkably similar in outlook and the kinds of interpretation that can be derived from them, even when describing missionaries working in very different parts of the world. All these accounts are related.

The Role Model

If they are related, we might ask: to what, or to whom? I want to argue that they are related not just to one another: it is worthwhile looking beyond the missionaries to identify the role model for this standardised type of writing. It is no great surprise that a clue lies in another one of Livingstone's books: his biography of Jesus, published in 1925.

However, before turning to this question, it is necessary to examine the wider context of his book. In 1906 Albert Schweitzer published his *Geschichte der Leben-Jesu-Forschung*, translated into English by William Montgomery in 1910 under the title *The Quest of the Historical Jesus*. The German title gives a better summary of the intent of the book: it is a "history of the life-of-Jesus-research", in which Schweitzer seeks to show how all modern interpretations of the life of Jesus have reflected the norms and values of the society they were written in. Schweitzer argued that as a consequence, Jesus' life needed to be interpreted anew by placing him firmly in the context of the time in which he lived.[12] It is now perhaps diffi-

---

[12] Of course, subsequent hermeneutical developments called this very aim itself into question, challenging any attempt at identifying the historical Jesus. But in the context of the time, Schweitzer's work is key and is an essential reference point here.

cult to comprehend the significance of such an argument at that time, but the controversy surrounding Schweitzer's book and his dismissal of many hitherto highly regarded works ensured that it was read widely in German and then also translated into other languages. By the 1920s it is almost inevitable that Livingstone would have either read Schweitzer's book, or have heard of it and the key arguments it advanced. It is worth citing a longer passage from Livingstone's aptly-titled introduction ("The Reason for the Book") to see the connection being made to Schweitzer's work:

Exact knowledge of Jesus and His teaching is uncommon even amongst those who are His followers ...

The picture still too often presented of Him is that of a sad and emaciated figure, meek, gentle-spoken, lamb-like, treading a grey and stony way, accompanied by a group of middle-aged men and drooping women, talking mysteriously of a mystical kingdom, and suffering at last, willingly yet shrinkingly, a shameful death in atonement for the sins of the world. It is a conception fitted less to inspire and help than to draw out wonder and pity, and it does not appeal to the modern spirit ...

In these days, as often before, a tired and perplexed humanity is turning from organised forms of religion and examining with a fresh and independent interest the claim that Jesus is the spiritual hope of the world. No one ... can fail to be impressed by the need for a clear-cut presentation of His life and aims disassociated from the professional ideas and phraseology that have ruled in the past ...

The present book is a contribution towards meeting the need. Written from the standpoint of the time in which He lived – which is the only possible way to recover the actual atmosphere, and to appreciate what He was and the significance of His teaching – it seeks to make the real Jesus live anew before the eyes of old and young, and to portray in some sort of intelligible manner the unbroken sequence of His career, though one does not suppose that this, or any, harmony reproduces the original order of events ...

Nothing, it is believed, is stated that is inconsistent with His nature or the spirit and circumstances of the age (Livingstone 1925: ix–xi).

Clearly, Livingstone is placing his effort directly into the kind of approach Schweitzer advocated, or at least, he saw himself as doing so. Recovering "the actual atmosphere" does not necessarily involve reproducing "the original order of events", but simply means ensuring that what is written in the narrative is consistent "with His nature". But what was Jesus' nature, in Livingstone's view?

The picture is of one in whom there was no drab or effeminate feature; whose life rather was aflame with beauty and colour, and dynamic with energy and intellectual power; who bore Himself with incomparable distinction and authority and drew to Him the young and virile, and all that was buoyant and robust and noble in human nature; who established no religion and formulated no scheme of salvation, but waged with practical purpose and utter fearlessness a revolutionary campaign against age-long conservative evils in the cause of simplicity, purity, freedom, progress and brotherhood; who faced alone with unshakable courage that most formidable and implacable of all mobs, a priesthood alarmed for the integrity of its order and the security of its privileges; and who only gave up when His mission was accomplished and His fate unescapable (Livingstone 1925: x).

This muscular and masculinised form of belief fits perfectly into a certain post-World War One worldview: whilst the vision of continual human progress had been called into serious question by the unprecedented carnage of the war, Britain, on the victorious side, found itself apparently regaining its strength during the 1920s, and with societal upheavals such as the suffragette movement seeming to point a way forwards for society (whether church members approved of it or not is irrelevant here, it was taken as a clear sign of the onward march of modernity), a Jesus-image of the kind Livingstone describes would fit well into such a societal worldview.[13]

However, this model of Jesus is not simply a product of post-World War One thinking and engagement with Schweitzer's work. When we compare this book to the missionary biographies, we find a great many parallels. The outline of the missionary life – apart from the omission of the violent death of Jesus[14] – is not dissimilar in outline and reaction to the life of Jesus Livingstone describes in his *Master Life*.

Of course, it is important to differentiate between this work and his missionary biographies (and those of other authors). Although Livingstone creates a unified narrative from the four gospel stories for his life-of-Jesus, he is not primarily concerned about creating a historical narrative, but an inspirational one. The story is meant to speak to the readers and encourage them in their faith, and the explanation he gives for writing the book in the first place gives an indication of the kind of faith he is hoping to foster – a parallel to the "beauty and colour, ... dynamic with energy and intellectual power" of Jesus, and certainly not "drab or effeminate", as the quotation above puts it. The masculinised heteronormativity that Livingstone

---

[13] That such a vision of Britain's place in the world was largely an illusion took some time to become apparent. To present this in a very simplistic way: the early 1920s – after the Versailles peace treaty, the awarding of League of Nations' mandates, and the gradual return to a kind of economic and industrial prosperity – saw many in Britain perceive themselves as returning to a pre-war status of global dominance after an initial period of concern immediately after the war. There was a realisation that in the post-war era France and the USA might need to share more fully in the control of the world's economy and political arrangements, but whilst worries about the 1917 Communist revolution in Russia complicated this vision, it was not until the 1929 Wall Street financial crisis (that then spread around the western world) that significant doubts about modernity resurfaced.

Of course, such a vision of global dominance, even if slightly tempered by new realities, would have been impossible for someone like the German-French Schweitzer from the contested territory of Alsace-Lorraine to hold in the aftermath of the First World War. There was – unsurprisingly – considerably more introspection in German society as a whole about the war and the reasons for defeat than there was in Britain about the war and victory.

[14] This is not to say that no missionaries died unexpectedly, or even violently: some did, but they were the exception; see, for example, Ritchie (2006) for details of Ion Keith-Falconer's death from illness in Aden, and the dramatic consequences that had for the mission there, and missions from Scotland more broadly. One of the motivating factors behind the creation of medical missions was the desire to preserve the good health of clerical missionaries.

is propagating is not unusual for this period, and fits into a context of wider understandings about the body and ways in which it represents certain kinds of emotional aspirations.[15] Another missionary biographer, James Wells, writing about James Stewart who worked in South Africa, begins a chapter entitled "The Man: His Outer Life": "His manliness must be a prominent feature in every just and living portrait of Stewart. He was every inch a man". He goes on to cite a woman colleague to substantiate this, as if a woman's opinion would serve to emphasise the point still further:

"Dr. Jane Waterston, for many years his colleague, says, 'It was the main characteristic of the Doctor that, first and foremost, before being clergyman, doctor, or missionary, he was a most manly man, with great physical strength, and no fear of man or beast. It was this distinguishing trait that so commended him to the natives of this country'" (Wells 1909: 378).

At the end of his life-of-Jesus narrative, Livingstone includes a chapter on "What Came After". The penultimate lines from the previous chapter, narrativising the resurrection stories from the gospels and the Acts of the Apostles, point to the direction this will take: "He left them [the disciples] only a clarified idea of God and a vision of a Better Way of Life" (Livingstone 1925: 311). This is the theme that Livingstone picks up on in his concluding chapter. Tainted by viscerally expressed sentiments against Judaism, Islam, the established Church,[16] and even Paul, he notes that,

Man's [sic] relation to God had always existed; the perfect system of love and law had been in operation since the beginning. The object of Jesus was to reveal it more clearly to men and women that they might act upon it; to make them see that to act upon it would solve all their ills. It was the true path and direction of activity which He pointed out, and how each day's requirements in it could be met with courage and joy and peace. He called it The Way. This idea of the right Way ran through all His teaching. It was the way of salvation for which men [sic] had always been seeking. There was no need therefore to propose any new plan of salvation; the Way He taught led naturally to life, fuller life here, and higher life hereafter …
… the Way of Life has not failed. It has never failed wherever it has been tried (Livingstone 1925: 312–313; 318).

In Livingstone's virulently anti-establishment polemic, he is pointing to what he thinks is the overwhelming importance of the role model function Jesus should have for Christians. After all, his book is even entitled *The Master Life* – "master" here signifying not only a lord or ruler, but also, surely, someone with complete

---

[15] Kirk (1998) and others have shown the importance of the body in creating a certain moral and societal understanding in this period. The inter-war physicality of masculinity and femininity is, of course, not just restricted to the Anglo-Saxon world: it took on more far-reaching forms in Germany, as numerous scholars have shown, Mouton (2007) serving as a representative example of others here.

[16] He rails against both Catholic and Protestant traditions – rather an ironic position to take, given his many years at the heart of the (United Free) Church of Scotland establishment!

knowledge, the pure original from which copies are made. This is clearly a life to emulate and follow, in Livingstone's eyes.

It is a very particular, ideologically-driven role model that Livingstone is seeking to present in this context. The muscular Christianity he is invoking is embodied, we might say, in a muscular Christ, a common pattern in these biographies. The extent to which such masculinised norms were meant to speak to women might seem questionable at first, but as the comments from Jane Waterston about James Stewart cited above illustrate, Wells was (apparently) not simply expressing a man's view that a particular form of "manliness" was a desirable characteristic of a Christian. Strength, not only of character and personality, but also physical, was lauded in this discourse, and is to be found in many of the biographies of missionary men in this period. When writing about the missionary women, this was also raised, but it was usually expressed in terms of tenacity and courage, for example, pointing to what we might term "an inner strength".

We can observe this in the approach Livingstone takes to his biographies of Slessor and Forsyth. In this context we can also point out that whilst his life-of-Jesus seeks only to inspire, with his missionary biographies Livingstone claims he is seeking to do two things: create an historical account, and write something that is also inspirational to the reader. For example, in the "Prefatory Note" to his Mary Slessor biography, he mentions that she was asked to write an autobiography. She reluctantly agreed, but died before being able to work on it, leading him to develop this project: "from many sources, and chiefly from her own letters, it has been possible to piece together the main facts of her wonderful career" (Livingstone 1915: iv). He goes on to write of her complex and at times rather contradictory character, but then adds:

But when her life is viewed as a whole, and in the light of what she achieved, all these angles and oddities fall away, and she stands out, a woman of unique and inspiring personality, and one of the most heroic figures of the age.

Some have said that she was in a sense a miracle, and not, therefore, for ordinary people to emulate. Such an estimate she would have stoutly repudiated ... [She argued that] "God is ready to take every act and motive and work through them to the formation of character and the development of holy and useful lives that will convey grace to the world." It was so in her case, and hence the value of her example, and the warrant for telling the story of her life, so that others may be influenced to follow aims as noble, and to strive, if not always in the same manner, at least with a like courage, and in the same patient and indomitable spirit (Livingstone, 1915: v–vi).

Forsyth's (supposed) loneliness was a marker of her dedication, commitment and perseverance to the missionary cause that she gave her life to – this self-sacrificial act, as Livingstone portrayed it, was an intrinsic part of her deeply pious commitment to Jesus. Bearing in mind that he wrote Slessor's biography before Forsyth's, Livingstone directly compares and contrasts Forsyth, "the loneliest woman in Africa", with Slessor, arguing that Forsyth herself emulated, but re-interpreted, Slessor's work:

… in the whole range of missionary biography one will find few figures who are at once so lovable and so strong, so lonely and yet so happy, so humble and yet so great.

Mrs. Forsyth was very like Miss Slessor … in character, faith, humour, patience, and courage, and there are some curious parallelisms in their careers, but the two differed greatly in their methods. Miss Slessor was a worker on a large stage and touched thousands of lives … she thought in terms of towns and districts. Mrs. Forsyth was an intensive worker, thinking in terms of individuals … She was as brave and tenacious in seeking to conquer a man or woman as Miss Slessor was to win a tribe.

… the record of Mrs. Forsyth's career may complete a picture which Miss Slessor's life began … (Livingstone 1918: vii–viii).

Emulation of a way of life was a theme other biographers picked up too. Wells writes of James Stewart: "'The just shall live by faith,' that is, he shall make a *life* of it" (Wells 1909: 288). In response to his death, Wells records numerous complimentary reminiscences of Stewart, many of which pick up on this theme. For example, "The Rev. F. W. King of Alice writes: 'His departure is a loss not only to our own community, but to the whole Church of God …. We all drew inspiration from his consecrated life'" (Wells 1909: 402).

We can see from these few excerpts that the primary concern of these authors is the representation of a pious life that others may emulate, thereby enabling the readers to live more pious lives themselves. In other words: whilst the examples of Forsyth, Slessor and the others might appear to be beyond the reach of ordinary Christians – very few of the readers of these mission biographies would seek to follow their example and go off to serve as missionaries in Africa or anywhere else – their attributes were what the biographers sought to emphasise in their discourse: Forsyth's "character, faith, humour, patience and courage" (Livingstone 1918: vii) and Slessor's "courage, and … patient and indomitable spirit" (Livingstone, 1915: v–vi) and so on were something that all Christians could emulate no matter what their context might be. We can see the parallel to Jesus: his example appears to be beyond that of the ordinary Christian, but in fact his life – as Livingstone portrayed it – was about showing a better "Way" to live.

Conclusions – Questions of Sainthood and "Canonisation"

The *Carmina Gadelica*, Carmichael's multi-volume collection of Gaelic prayers, pointed to the omnipresent nature of saints long dead who might be looked to for help and guidance. There was a particular emphasis on certain saints who might offer guidance in particular contexts (de Waal 1988: 189–191). Whilst the missionary biographies clearly do not create sainthood in the same way, I want to argue that they nonetheless do so, albeit in a different context and with other purposes, centred on the idea of emulation.

Of course, the sainthood that I am describing here is not connected to the formal sainthood and canonisation processes in Catholic tradition. Whilst these missionaries may be venerated in certain ways, there is no sense that this is linked to particular artefacts or locations, such as tombs or relics. Tombs exist, of course, but have never been sites of veneration: the photograph here shows David Torrance's tomb, photographed in February 2010, in the church graveyard in Tiberias,

Fig. 1: David Watt Torrance's tomb, Church of Scotland graveyard, Tiberias (photograph: Michael Marten, February 2010).

now in Israel. It was reasonably well-kept, but the weeds and general vegetation around it – and the fact that the graveyard has long only been accessible through a locked entrance – clearly point to a dearth of visitors, a situation that has not changed over the years.

However, tombs aside, I would argue that these missionary biographies sought to create a kind of saint in order to serve at least *some* similar purposes to traditional Catholic saints. Given that Protestants have tended not to pursue the idea of saints as mediators with God, this assertion requires re-thinking questions about the usage of saints as helpers or guides in the popular or Celtic traditions mentioned at the beginning of this article, away from the control of metropolitan ecclesial centres. This then also enables a reassessment of the missionary biographies' purpose.

The comparison of the volumes I have been describing with *The Master Life* point to significant commonality: whilst the missionaries in question are not venerated and beseeched in prayer as intercessors, they are – not unlike the ultimate divine role model, Jesus – individuals to be emulated by the believer who wants to come closer to God. It is likely that none of these missionaries would have been very comfortable with such a comparison, but they had little choice in the matter: the comparison was made for them by their biographers, often after they had died and no longer had any say in how they might be represented.[17] Livingstone's biography of Torrance is even entitled in such a way as to remind Christians of the healing role of Jesus in the Gospel narratives: *A Galilee Doctor: The Life of Dr Torrance of Tiberias*.[18] If, as noted in the introductory remarks, saints are portrayed as being particularly pious individuals, then the lives of these individuals clearly fall into this schema, at least as portrayed by the missionary biographers. The biographers, in choosing the subjects for their work, also created a kind of canon of individuals that could be recommended to others as examples of a certain way of life – we could even go so far as to portray this as the establishment of an acceptable discourse on the spiritual life. The missionaries were undoubtedly extraordinary people in their time, who in various ways were models of what a particular sort of Christian should be – and this imitative process was sanctioned, enabled and promoted by the biographers.

The narrative sequences that are used to portray the lives of the missionaries serve to elevate the subject, whether this is something they want or not (bear in

---

[17] Interestingly, Forsyth is one of the exceptions here: Livingstone says that he waited until she returned to Scotland to begin work on the biography, but "she only grew enthusiastic about her converts, and was smilingly reticent about personal details". He therefore used letters and reports and the like, as well as contact with her friends to write the book. However, "[w]hen she read the MS., Mrs. Forsyth's only remark was: 'There is too much about myself in it'" (Livingstone 1918: vi–vii).

[18] Torrance was himself aware of this geopious connection, as I discuss in Marten 2006: 79–80. My usage of the term "geopious" comes from Lester I. Vogel's work on Americans in Palestine; a fuller discussion of it in contexts such as this can be found in Marten 2006: 11 ff.

mind Forsyth's hesitation about Livingstone's focus on her person, rather than on the Africans she worked with). The biographies portray the missionary as someone to imitate, who, despite the lack of formal structures of sainthood in the Protestant tradition, is *treated* as a saint: their entire life story – researched by the biographer – serves to develop the case for what we might call a kind of "canonisation in the popular imagination". After all, the point here is not that these books were simply hagiographic accounts of a life, they were more than that: they abstracted and transmitted key values from church and society and personified them in a particular individual, who was thereby given both spiritual and societal functions.[19] The construction of particular histories and memories served to create identities that were to some extent artificial, to be sure, but – bringing to mind Livingstone's *The Master Life* – we can find a parallel for this construction in the gospel narratives. Jesus, when describing the Kingdom of God, spoke of it as being both here and yet to come, and in a similar way these missionaries were real enough for readers to want to try and emulate them, but also embodied a closeness to the divine through their piety and devotion that was seen to have narrowed the gap between earth and heaven in a way that was beyond ordinary believers. In Catholic tradition, saints act as both role models and mediators for humanity. These Scottish Protestant missionaries were not mediators for humanity in the Catholic tradition of sainthood, but these narratives did create ideal figures, role models, that pointed to ways for other Christians to approach God more easily.

They are of their time, of course, and today, relatively few Scottish Christians will know of them, and even fewer will see the missionaries as described in these biographies as individuals they might wish to model their own lives on. However, this is not so different to the Catholic tradition: skimming through the 1400 entries in an introductory text such as Farmer's *Dictionary* (1978/2004), we encounter numerous saints that play virtually no role in mainstream contemporary Catholic life. They are of their time: they were important at one stage, and were venerated for a time, but that time has passed. Similarly, these missionary biographies were important for a time, and they reflect that time. Perhaps this is one of the markers of difference between the saints and the figure of Jesus: whilst Christians may see the saints as being closer to the divine even though they are still human, Jesus is regarded as fully human and fully divine – a role model that cannot be bettered, as Livingstone's life-of-Jesus argued. In their time, the missionary biographies played a part in forming a particular discourse about the Christian life, but as with

---

[19] Of course, this is closely related to the kind of criticism Schweitzer made of life-of-Jesus narratives: that they were too dependent upon their context, and therefore reflected the values of the society and the time in which they had been written. This also explains why they fell from favour as society moved away from a Christianity that can be characterised as an embodiment of muscular, masculinised heteronormativity.

so many texts, they now tell us almost more about their authors and their intentions than they do about their subjects.

This paper was presented in an early form at a workshop organised in the School of Languages, Cultures and Religions at the University of Stirling in May 2010. I am grateful to other participants for their comments.

Bibliography

Bebbington, David
1989   Evangelicalism in Modern Britain. A history from the 1730s to the 1980s. London: Routledge.

Bonk, Jonathan
2004   Ecclesiastical Cartography and the Invisible Continent. *IBMR* vol. 28 no. 4 October: 153–158.

de Waal, Esther (ed.)
1988   The Celtic Vision: Prayers and Blessings from the Outer Hebrides. Selections from the Carmina Gadelica. London: Darton, Longman & Todd.

Ewing, William
1930? Paterson of Hebron. "The Hakim" Missionary Life in the Mountain of Judah. London: James Clarke & Co. (possibly 1925).

Farmer, David Hugh
1978, 2004   Oxford Dictionary of Saints. Oxford / New York: Oxford University Press (fifth edition).

Ghabra, Gawdat [with **Tim Vivian**]
2002   Coptic Monasteries: Egypt's Monastic Art and Architecture, Cairo / New York: American University Press.

Griffiths, Gareth
2005   "Trained to Tell the Truth": Missionaries, Converts and Narration. In: Norman Eherington (ed.), Missions and Empire, series: The Oxford History of the British Empire; Companion Series; pp. 153–172. Oxford: Oxford University Press.

Kernohan, R. D.
1979   Scotland's Life and Work. A Scottish view of God's world through Life and Work: 1879–1979. Edinburgh: Saint Andrew Press.

Kirk, David
1998   Schooling Bodies: School Practice and Public Discourse, 1880–1950. London/ Washington: Leicester University Press.

Livingstone, William Pringle
1912? Laws of Livingstonia: A Narrative of Missionary Adventure and Achievement. London: Hodder and Stoughton.
1915   Mary Slessor of Calabar: Pioneer Missionary. London: Hodder and Stoughton.

1916? Mary Slessor: the White Queen of Okoyong – a True Story of Adventure, Heroism, and Faith. London: Hodder and Stoughton.

1918 Christina Forsyth of Fingoland: The Story of the Loneliest Woman in Africa. London / New York / Toronto: Hodder and Stoughton.

1923 A Galilee Doctor. Being a Sketch of the Career of Dr D. W. Torrance of Tiberias. London: Hodder and Stoughton.

1925 The Master Life – the Story of Jesus for Today. London: James Clarke & Co.

Marshall, T. W. M.
1863 Christian Missions: their Agents and their Results. London: Longman, Green, Longman, Roberts & Green (second edition).

Marten, Michael
2006 Attempting to Bring the Gospel Home: Scottish Missions to Palestine 1839–1917. London: I. B. Tauris.

Mouton, Michelle
2007 From Nurturing the Nation to Purifying the Volk: Weimar and Nazi Family Policy, 1918–1945. Cambridge / New York: Cambridge University Press.

Padwick, Constance E.
1929, 1930 Temple Gairdner of Cairo. London: S. P. C. K.

Ritchie, James McLaren
2006 The Church of Scotland South Arabia Mission 1885–1978. Stoke-on-Trent: Tentmaker Publications.

Ross, Andrew C.
1972 Scottish Missionary Concern 1874–1914. A golden era? In: *Scottish Historical Review* vol. LI/I, no. 151, April: 52–72.

Said Edward W
1993 Culture and Imperialism. London: Chatto & Windus.

Wells, James
1909 Stewart of Lovedale: The Life of James Stewart. London: Hodder & Stoughton.

Forgotten Plurality

A Cultural Analysis of Representations of St. Sebastian in the West

Jason Hartford

Abstract. – This article examines the changing focus of representation in the iconic figure of St. Sebastian. Since the Renaissance, St. Sebastian has been an outlet in Western art for expressing orthodox Christian concepts, but also discourses of sexual minority or sexual queerness. While it is generally agreed that the orthodox religious and the homoerotic form two principal streams of representation, there is some disagreement as to whether the eroticism lies in the subject or in the onlooker, who would project their desire onto the saint. There are also arguments over whether queer Sebastian is the product of new discourses of sexuality or a reflection of an ongoing tradition.

This article will address these questions, but will focus mainly on an anomaly of greater cultural studies interest. What is not commonly discussed with regard to St. Sebastian is that in France during the earlier 19th century, this paired discourse was itself destabilized. The formal experimentation of this period in art coincided with a thematic innovation for the figure of this saint, which came to be used as a foil for experimentation, departing from both previous discourses. Sebastians of the period sometimes co-opted his dual heritage in a critical way, articulating messages very different from either the doctrinal or the erotic.

In contrast, Western Sebastian representations after about 1865 are paradoxically conservative. They might be controversial in their homoeroticism, but do not show the nihilistic trauma or knowing satire of earlier 19th century pieces. The queer Sebastian discourse can now appropriate others in hostile ways. I corroborate this through analysing works taken from 20th century fiction, including a graphic novel, again with a particular but not exclusive focus on material from France.

Jason Hartford, received his BA from Yale University and did his postgraduate training at Oxford. He focuses on unifying topics: iconography, theory and aesthetics of horror, cognitive analysis, interpretations of science, and queer masculinities. He works in the long modern period from 1850 to the present, engaging with critical theory and psychoanalysis, fiction after Flaubert in France and Belgium, cinema since the 1950s, and queer theory. He is currently Lecturer in French and Global Cinema at the University of Stirling.

This article examines the changing focus of representation in the iconic figure of St. Sebastian. Since the Renaissance, and more recently in other forms of cultural production, St. Sebastian has been an outlet in Western art for expressing orthodox Christian concepts, but also discourses of sexual minority or sexual queerness.[1] Both roles are reasonably familiar among both scholarly and popular audiences

---

[1] In this article I am using "queer" to mean, "pertaining to minority sexuality and its discourses". For a fuller discussion of the term and its potential consequences, see S Cooper 2000: 11–21.

(see Darwent 2008: N. pag.). While it is generally agreed that the orthodox religious and the homoerotic constitute two principal streams of representation, there is some disagreement as to whether the eroticism lies in the subject or in the onlooker, who projects desire onto the saint. There have also been arguments over whether Sebastian as a proposed modern queer icon is the product of new discourses of sexuality, or a reflection of an ongoing tradition.

This article will address these discussions initially, but will later focus on an anomaly of arguably greater cultural studies interest. What is not commonly discussed with regard to St. Sebastian is that in one situation, namely in France during the earlier 19th century, the paired discourse was itself destabilized. I suggest that the formal experimentation of earlier 19th century French art coincided with a thematic innovation for this figure. Different representations of Sebastian within the period acknowledged his dual heritage and even co-opted it, to a degree, while articulating messages very different from either the oldest traditions that emphasized the martyr's pain, or the Renaissance focus on erotic homage to male beauty.

In contrast with the divergent and sometimes critical spirit of the French early to mid-19th century, modern Western Sebastian representations after about 1865, be they visual or ecphrastic, tend to be paradoxically conservative. They might be controversial in their homoeroticism, but they do not show the nihilistic trauma or knowing satire of earlier 19th century pieces. In terms of cultural history, I would argue that the growing discursive familiarity of a queer Sebastian is such that this particular discourse has become strong enough to appropriate other attempted figurations in hostile ways within contemporary Western culture. I will corroborate this through analysing works taken from 20th century fiction, including a graphic novel, again with a particular but not exclusive focus on material from France.

This discussion is inherently interdisciplinary and speaks to the fields of history of art, French literature, comparative literature, sexuality studies, and European cultural studies. In proposing it as an example of the latter, I want to underline its nature primarily as a work of discourse analysis. The phenomena described herein first appeared in religious art, but their influence spread beyond it. At the same time, while French art and culture obviously interact with those of neighbouring nations, especially in the modern era, there does seem to be a particular cultural change with regard to this discourse during the early to mid-19th century. In discussing this change, which does not seem to have travelled while other concepts did, I would like to ask some speculative questions about its causes and its later history.

Icons and Iconography: Early Developments

Painters and sculptors working for the Church needed to satisfy specific conventions of subject matter and iconography. Although these requirements varied and were applied with unequal weight throughout history, they did establish a general method in religious representation.

Hippolyte Delehaye explains in his *Cinq Leçons* (1934) how religious artists convey the salient features of a saint's life and nature in a single representation. The artist, whether Byzantine or Occidental and regardless of period, needed to communicate the individual's identity in a manner suitable for a potentially illiterate audience. Especially important are the basic elements still recognizable in art of more recent periods, when conformity to Church doctrine in general began to decline. These elements provide a point of recognition and contact for the ordinary Christian, helping the saint to function more easily and intelligibly as an intercessor. This would require distinguishing the saint in a systematic manner, according to three orders of scale: saint from ordinary person, category of saint and individual.

The distinction of saint from ordinary person is achieved simply, with a nimbus or halo. On the level of the three categories of apostle, martyr and confessor, apostles can be made distinct by number (twelve), or combination with or direct proximity to Christ. Martyrs and confessors can be marked by attitude; being slain, in study, etc. Individuals will be made known by tokens of their career, or perhaps the device of their martyrdom: St. Francis of Assisi with his animals, St. Lawrence on the gridiron, and so on. Such tokens are elegant in that they can sometimes indicate category and identity simultaneously.

Very close to the distillation of a saint's life into an image is the concept of the icon (literally, "image"). In ecclesiastical discourse, icons are "sacred both in themselves, and on account of their representation of God through, variously, the incarnate Christ, a Biblical narrative, or the created world or figure in which God is apparent" (Martin 1989: n. pag.). The icon in this sense is "a transparent window through which is revealed the artist's view of the nature and person of God, through the individual shown", namely Christ, the Virgin, a saint. Rupert Martin specifies that this description holds true in the Western tradition of Christianity as well as in Eastern Orthodoxy.

When the term "icon" is used more generally, to label an individual, it is understood to indicate them as a key example of a certain idea, style or period in either religious or secular contexts. In the case of a secular or pop icon, although we are dealing with rhetorical license, one can still assume that the person in question will not be seen as authentic unless they themselves are "holy" in some way. They must refer to a revered concept or ideal, which by analogy would assume God's role for an orthodox icon. It follows that the concept itself should either be well-known and obvious to the audience already, or else be shown in a very strong fashion.

The pertinence of this here is that there is an abundant queer iconography of one particular religious figure. From the late 15th century, artists in several European countries, France being one of the first, have consistently portrayed St. Sebastian with an aim to explore the beauty of the male body. This practice has developed into a cross-cultural tendency to figure a given martyred saint as a known, and in time conventional locus of homoerotic desire. Following the logic described above, St. Sebastian is made into both a religious and a sexual icon.

Other Christian figures have been portrayed in various queer contexts. The Apostle John is typically portrayed as very young and often androgynous, as in Leonardo's painting *Last Supper* (1495–1498).[2] These characteristics have been proposed as signs of minority sexuality. John the Baptist has also been painted in what have been described as homoerotic ways, notably by Caravaggio (1602: Olga). Whether or not such interpretations may be accurate is not directly in question here. The point is that the Apostle John is only sometimes shown in a homoerotic manner in modern art,[3] and John the Baptist rarely so,[4] whereas St. Sebastian is sufficiently well-known as a gay icon to have appeared as such consistently in international art, then literature, and latterly in film as well. This predictable association is both strong and unusual enough, I would argue, for considering Sebastian as a special case, notwithstanding the occasional appearance of comparable phenomena anent other figures.

Sebastian's sagittation is by far the best-known episode of his life, and easily the most popular for figurations of him ever since the 13th century. Even in the thematically experimental 19th century the vast majority of paintings of him refer to it. Sebastian's identifying token or sign, the arrow, carries two strong meanings, the one being gradually eclipsed by the other. The arrow is an ancient symbol of the plague, and Sebastian, alongside St. Giles and St. Roch, has long been revered as a protector against it. On the other hand, as Le Targat and many others point out, the arrow is also both an instrument of love (the weapon of Eros) and a phallic symbol.

Older Renaissance St. Sebastians, of which Piero della Francesca's painting (ca. 1444–1466: Olga) is a typical example, show him as an ordinary man tied to a stake, wearing a loincloth, bleeding from a few large arrows in his side and often one in his groin. (St. Roch, patron saint of the plague, is typically shown revealing or pointing to a bubo in his groin.) His limbs are not otherwise overly detailed.

---

[2] Visible online as of 20 June 2012 at Olga's Gallery <http://www.abcgallery.com>. Citations from this major collection shall henceforth appear as (Artist date: Olga). Items from small online collections shall be marked as (Artist date: online), with details in the bibliography. Images of many works cited here can be found at several addresses, including Wikipedia.

[3] Unless otherwise noted, "modern" shall be given to mean post-1789 in France, and roughly post-1800 overall. A prime example of a homoerotic Apostle John appears in the Belgian Jean Delville's painting L'École de Platon (1898: online), a spectacular, neon-hued vision of Jesus and his disciples in Paradise.

[4] There are plenty of portrayals of John the Baptist that are eroticized, without being specifically homoerotic.

He wears either a stern or, as in della Francesca's piece, a serene expression and either confronts the viewer or looks upward to the right, towards God. There is little attempt to idealize his features. Similar characteristics prevail in known older Sebastians in both painting and sculpture, all across Catholic Europe.

In Italy, however, religious art was at this time about to change in character, presenting more realistic detail and developing a style that was more affective, in the semiological sense. Louis Bréhier notes (1918: 355), in the 14th to 15th centuries, an increasingly sentimental cult of tearful faces, citing two paintings, an anonymous *Vierge de pitié* of the Avignon school (in Bréhier, *ibid.*) and Bartolomeo Bermejo's *Holy Face* (15th century, online). It is worth underlining that this approach implies a greater emotional appeal to the viewer, in tandem with a possible shift in emphasis away from the doctrinal story, in which they did not personally take part.

The specific difference for Sebastian figurations grew out of an increasingly aesthetic focus. Colin Thompson remarks that in contrast with northern artists, the Italian approach to this saint was firmly decorative in its intentions:

By the latter 15th century in Italy, however, the theme of the naked young man tied to a tree or a stake became an acknowledged vehicle for artists to present their notion of idealized manhood. So the tradition has its roots in pagan statues of antiquity like the Apollo Belvedere, it runs through Perugino, Sodoma and Titian ...[5] (Thompson 1975: 2, *sic*).

François Le Targat notes the inherent instability of the nude as a symbol, between innocence and carnality. "Ce n'est pas une exécution sordide ... c'est une mort debout que celle du beau jeune homme attaché au plus beau laurier, les bras levés, liés au-dessus de la tête, le corps offert" (Le Targat 1979: 8).[6] Within this artistic blending of sacred and profane ecstasy, "... la douleur endurée pour la cause de Dieu amène à l'extase et la beauté physique s'illumine d'une beauté divine ... Les représentations de saint Sébastien sont donc toujours un mélange de charnel et de divin" (*ibid.*, 10).[7] Ghislaine Wood, with reference to Georges Bataille, also remarks on the well-known interconnection of religion and the erotic in Western art generally (Wood 2000: 72).

There are many interrelated motives served by the iconic arrow motif, some yielding primacy to others over time. Le Targat suggests that the sheer spectacle of being shot through with arrows is in itself too tempting to pass up. He also notes two political considerations. One is the ignominy of the actual means of Sebastian's execution. By having him appear to die from bowshots instead, the

---

[5] Perugino 1493: Olga. Sodoma 1525: online. Titian 1575: Olga.

[6] "This is not a sordid execution ... this is an upright death for the handsome young man attached to the finest laurel, arms raised, tied above the head, the body on offer." All translations from French are my own.

[7] "Pain endured for the cause of God leads to ecstasy and physical beauty lights up with divine beauty ... Representations of St. Sebastian are thus always a blend of carnal and divine."

artist could be understood to hold him above the rank of common criminal. Le Targat touches on this class issue *en passant*, while dwelling longer on the second, more important problem of gender. "Admettre que le martyr fut sauvé par une femme, Sainte Irène ... pour finir par une vulgaire lapidation, c'était introduire le rôle important de la femme salvatrice dans un univers particulièrement misogyne" (1979: 6).[8] Here "univers", as Le Targat uses it, encompasses the Roman army, the cult of Classical male beauty, and the Christian tradition all at once, the three being condensed in Early Modern figurations of St. Sebastian.

To summarise, the trend towards æstheticization and sexualization of religious art was progressively making possible the articulation, and presently the establishment, of Sebastian as an outlet for homages to male beauty, by other men. There are many famous examples of this trend in painting. They include Botticelli's (1474: Olga), whose moue-cum-smile seems to anticipate the Mona Lisa's (Leonardo ca. 1503–1504: Olga); Perugino's (1493: Olga); and Raphael's, a longhaired blond youth delicately wielding an arrow, like a quill (1502–1503: Olga). Viewed together, these create an uncertain register. As Wood observes, the technique cannot ever be separated entirely from homoerotic reference in the case of male nudes (2000: 56).

Richard Dyer notes that, in attempts at representing sexuality, gender and gender roles are often conflated with it, as they are easier to convey visually (1993: 18–24). Margaret Walters goes further:

The martyr is often no more than an excuse to [portray] a luscious classic nude; he also provides an outlet for usually suppressed homosexual fantasies. The arrows signify pleasure *and* punishment, the nude saint is a focus for growing delight in the flesh, *and* for guilt at being seduced by the grace of the body (1979: 82, *sic*).

In terms of content, therefore, the visual discourse of the beautiful saint is both doctrinal and pornographic. However, not all Sebastian paintings of the Renaissance portrayed him as having yet been struck with the arrows – Raphael's, for example. The suggestion of his martyrdom is therefore more oblique and less accessible to the original, naïve onlooker, potentially to the advantage of other discourses. Timon Screech says that both artist and patron are now known to have intended their paintings to be received as pornographic vehicles, in the case of Guido Reni's as well as of other (unspecified) Sebastians (Screech 2009: 108).[9] With specific regard to the work of Reni (1600–1610 and 1617–1619: in Darwent), and in a vein reminiscent of Le Targat's idea of *le corps offert* (1979: 8, see above), Maria Wyke writes,

---

[8] "To admit that the martyr was saved by a woman, St. Irene ... to end with a vulgar stoning, would be to introduce the significant role of the soteriac woman into a particularly misogynistic universe".

[9] Screech reports how Yukio Mishima, in a fictionalized autobiography, felt shame at having masturbated to a Reni St. Sebastian. Such a response was in fact the correct one, says Screech.

Masculine penetrators do not need to be present in a painting for Sebastian's martyrdom to be rendered sexually suggestive and homoerotic ... [Here,] his uplifted face is transfixed by an ecstasy that speaks of loss of self, erotic abandon, the desire to be penetrated (1998: 253–255).

Sebastian would, therefore, be a male equivalent of Bernini's celebrated statue of St. Teresa in Ecstasy (1647–1652: WGA)[10]. The doctrinal would be superseded by the erotic. I would temper this by saying that the two messages would at least become equivocal: Sebastian effectively becomes a kind of semantic field, with the ecclesiastical and the erotic as its poles. One can imagine instances of differing proportion in their messages falling between these poles. This is a generalization that should be considered when looking at any beautiful St. Sebastian from the Renaissance onwards.

Art and Literature I: Two Beautiful Soldiers

The gradual transfer of a queer St. Sebastian from visual into literary art seems to have begun in the early 19th century. The first queer saint as such in French literature to my knowledge is Flaubert's St. Julien, in the second of his *Trois Contes* from 1876 (Hartford 2007: 434, 438, 442–446); but there are earlier hints of eroticism pertaining to a treatment of St. Sebastian in Stendhal. The first texts are from his travel diaries, concerning his two viewings in 1814 and 1837 of Puget's statue of the saint (ca. 1663: WGA). This is a flamboyant piece akin to Bernini's St. Sebastian (also a statue, 1617: online), with a beautiful face, arms flung wide in a quasi-crucifixion pose, and body arched toward the viewer. Despite being a soldierly subject, with sword and helm clearly displayed, it has a less than ideal physique. The body is not overly muscular and the abdomen is a bit flabby. This is a realistic and sensuous touch, as well as a hint of what was to come in later art.

The piece seems to have impressed a jaded Stendhal. On his first viewing, he remarked that "La sculpture ne me donne guère de plaisir. Le saint Sébastien de Puget à l'Église de Carignan de Gênes m'a paru ... moins mauvais que les statues ordinaires d'église" (Stendhal 1981: "Pisa, 22 sep 1814").[11] The second time, he elaborated:

Le saint Sébastien n'est nullement un brillant jeune homme, un ange de beauté ... Cette figure est admirable et d'une virilité qui, depuis longtemps, il me semble, a disparu de la sculpture. Aussi cet art est-il bien sujet à faire bâiller, comme tout ce qui est trop noble. Le

---

[10] This style indicates images visible online at another large collection, wga.hu (see bibliography for details).

[11] "Sculpture gives me hardly any pleasure. Puget's St. Sebastian at the Church of Carignano in Genoa seemed to me ... less bad than ordinary church statues."

Puget a osé donner du ventre à son St. Sébastien, c'est un tort, il a outré une bonne idée, par excès de mépris pour les *nobilifieurs*[12] (Stendhal 1992: 537, *sic*).

Curiously, Puget's Sebastian manages to be admirable and virile for Stendhal despite having conventionally fine, small, somewhat weak features, especially the chin, and long, luxurious ringlets. His face is one of a kind with those of the prettier 17th century *terre cuite de Maine* (soft paste porcelain) Sebastians, with Mérillon and Préhoust giving examples,[13] as well as Giorgetti's statue, a gisant (1660–1670, after a design by his master, Bernini: WGA).

Even in this kind of Church statuary, which was often produced in group workshops where copying of earlier models and of one another was routine, there was more than one accepted type or "model" for St. Sebastian. Other French church terracottas by Leclerc (mid-17th century: online) and Lemaire[14] have a strong, angular jawline, rather a stout neck, a beard, and pronounced musculature. A piece by Biardeau (1606–1651: online) is mediary in style: the body is heavily muscled, and while the face is pretty and young it also sports a dark-painted goatee. For that matter Bernini's Sebastian, although fine-featured, has a detailed beard. None of these attributes appear in Puget's piece. Indeed it is hard to imagine a church statue from either period, that of Puget or of Stendhal, that is less a model of "virilité disparue". Even a Rococo painting by Ménageot (1744–1816: WGA), which is close to Puget's statue in pose, decorative setting and accessories, and soft facial features, gives Sebastian a leaner torso and clearly masculine legs.

Given Puget's statue's physical attributes, one must conclude that either Stendhal's idea of manliness was unusual, or that the passage in this aspect is satirical. It is worth recalling that satire is a convenient means of disavowal, of self-distancing from a subject, especially a subject with an affective component – affective in both psychological and semiological senses. Whatever the statue's gender significance, it certainly seems to have been appealing to him.

Stendhal's reaction seems to resonate on a cultural level with Sebastian's semiological heritage as a soldier. Paul Fussell notes the wealth of documents attesting to the popularity of soldierly homoerotics since the early 19th century in England, and since the latter portion of that century internationally. "What makes

---

[12] "The St. Sebastian is not at all a brilliant young man, an angel of beauty … This face is admirable and of a manliness which, since long ago, it seems to me, has disappeared from sculpture. Also this art is truly something to make one yawn, like all that is too noble. Puget has dared to give a belly to his St. Sebastian. That's a mistake. He took a good idea too far, out of too much contempt for the *nobilifiers*."

[13] These works and their makers are treated in general at the French government cultural site <www. sculpturesdumaine.culture.fr>. The images are changed periodically, and I am no longer able to find all of these pieces on the site, although it does discuss Mérillon's.

[14] Another image formerly available on the site.

them so [attractive] is their youth, their athleticism, their relative cleanliness, their uniforms, and their heroic readiness, like Adonis or St. Sebastian, for 'sacrifice'" (Fussell 1975: 278). It is a commonplace that gay pornography worldwide devotes much attention to soldiers. One could consider a possible early contribution to this discourse in the parade sequence from Stendhal's novel *Le Rouge et le noir* (1830). Here Julien Sorel appears as the "fort joli garçon"[15] heading the ninth column.

Il [Julien] voyait dans les yeux des femmes qu'il était question de lui.
    Ses épaulettes étaient plus brillantes, parce qu'elles étaient neuves. Son cheval se cabrait à chaque instant, il était au comble de sa joie[16] (Stendhal 1972: 111).

The rearing horse is a familiar symbol of male sexuality; *le comble de la joie, c'est la jouissance*.[17] Julien rides the one and experiences the other, thus literally feeling both. In doing so he becomes a metonymic crossroads for them, for the reader. Is the desiring perspective on the beautiful boy strictly limited to his female onlookers within the fictional world?

Even in the case of a satire, it seems that Stendhal was sincere in his dislike of Puget's Sebastian's having a more sedentary physique. The diary passage suggests an underlying expectation that the soldier-saint should first and foremost be a commendable example of a male body. Sebastian should be an alluring soldier, of the same order of being as lovely Julien on parade.

Divisions from the Divide: Established Discourse and Variations

Camille Paglia, in a discussion of the beautiful boy as a motif in Western art, goes even further than Wyke with regard to St. Sebastian's primarily erotic role. She draws an analogy between this particular saint and Pagan erotic models:

The beautiful boy is homosexuality's greatest contribution to Western culture. Un-Christian and anti-Christian, he is an iconic formalization of the relation between the eye and reality … he is St. Sebastian, the Christian Adonis (Paglia 1990: 148).

In terms of doctrine this is true, but to expect this to hold true in terms of cultural practice and cultural signification would make one risk ignoring more complex interactions. Rhetorically, the phrase "un-Christian and anti-Christian" seems to

---

[15] "most pretty boy."

[16] "He saw in the womens' eyes that it was all about him. His epaulets were shinier, because they were new. His horse reared at every instant, he was at the peak of his joy."

[17] "The peak of joy is orgasm." *Jouissance* can mean, variously, rapture, orgasm, or simply "pleasure-taking". This lexical equivalence in French is commonplace and widely manipulated.

identify a basic divide and, perhaps, an unbridgeable gap between ecclesiastical and homoerotic discourses.

I would like to underline that these eroticized, erotic Sebastians still abide within an orthodox Christian discourse and are assimilable to it. Indeed, they still partake in the tradition of the icon in many ways. As Wyke notes, today's Church maintains St. Sebastian's place in official Church art while keeping absolutely quiet about his *Nachleben* as a gay icon, "even though its souvenir pieces contain examples of it" (1998: 257). Wyke reports that a Sodoma Sebastian appears on a postcard, uncredited, from the Basilica of St. Sebastian without the Walls in Rome. She is surely right in suggesting that this lack of credit is a deliberate attempt by the Church to conceal any link between this saint and sodomy, Sodoma of course being notorious for his homosexual proclivities. This would support the impression of a contest between the two poles, and even an expectation that a given Sebastian might be intended as an example of "one or the other".

On the other hand, the frequency and consistency with which Sebastian arises in this fashion bespeaks a tacit acceptance, an ambiguous wilful blindness on the part of the Church authorities. The paradoxical harmony that Walters had described presages a "cold peace", visible from the example of Wyke's anecdote. This peace in turn allowed these two discourses, the religious and the erotic, effectively to share the figure of Sebastian between them, to varying degrees, to the exclusion of other discourses. It is the question of excluding other discourses that I want to raise.

Sebastian as a figure is an agent both partly for, and partly against a series of power discourses manifest in visual culture. He creates tension between the religious and the erotic as much as he resolves it. This means that, as a cultural figure, he is particularly susceptible to attracting meta-discourses of power and sexuality. It is for this reason that I want particularly to investigate pieces from a part of his career in which both of these discourses were under critical review, at the very least, in contemporary art. Early to mid-19th century French painting shows a variety of discourse in St. Sebastian that is thematically broader than work from any period previously, and arguably since. I would like to recontextualize the familiar sacred / homoerotic binary by comparing it with a more pluralistic milieu, in which iconic Sebastian took on new and disparate meanings and uses.

Plurality: to Be Forgotten?

19th century French paintings of St. Sebastian demonstrate the dynamic pluralism of French art overall during that time. They reflect several Romantic trends, many of which are peripheral here.[18] What is of most interest for this study is the harmony between the well-established decorative branch of Sebastian figuration and a more self-consciously queer artistic movement, *in contrast with* a distinct, conceptually plural and innovative stream. Instead of reference to doctrinal concepts and homoeroticism, in varying measures but in non-ironic ways, these newer portrayals of Sebastian either suppress or undermine both the religious reference and the eroticism.

One way of introducing this is to consider two very different Sebastians from the mid-19th century in France, a painting by Corot and a caricature by Daumier. In Corot's painting (1850–1860: Olga), a rather coarse-featured man of indeterminate age stands trussed, but with no arrows in him. His body is generally well-developed and powerful without being outstanding, and his limbs are out of focus relative to his torso. His loincloth is an unremarkable piece of improvised clothing, the tree he is tied to verdant but again unremarkable. His eyes are closed and tilted away from the viewer, making for no affective appeal, heavenwards or otherwise. One is asked to consider an ordinary torso for its own sake. This is a good late Romantic example of rejecting an ideal subject, with only some trappings of traditional iconography.

Meanwhile, Daumier's first Sebastian (1849: online), a newspaper caricature for the Christmas holiday season, keeps the signs of his martyrdom but mocks them. Sebastian becomes an obese bourgeois, his eyes hidden by his helmet's oversized faceplate, with a blizzard's worth of satirical poison pens-cum-arrows to make a bloodless, cartoon pincushion out of his gut. The archer wears the name of the journal, *Charivari*. The original target was Dr. Louis Véron, the very wealthy and portly owner of the rival paper *Le Constitutionnel*, and a supporter of the staid and somewhat corrupt government of Adolphe Thiers (1797–1877).[19] *Charivari* was well-known in general for sending up the *grande bourgeoisie*, whom Daumier is here portraying as self-satisfied and prone to unjustified complaint. The comparison of course targets Daumier's contemporaries, instead of the religious story; but if we are to think in terms of associations it is still an undignified context for the soldier-saint.

Daumier's and Corot's Sebastians occur in sharply different media, and divergent social contexts: the high-prestige salon versus the mass market newspaper. One shows no satirical elements at all while the other is a comic grotesque. However, for what little these two figures have in common in terms of reception, neither shows any traditional signs of sexuality, neither seems to have come from anywhere other than a land of plenty, and neither makes a strong, stable religious reference.

Ribot, in another painting (1865: online), chooses for his subject a less popular

---

[18] In Bréhier's opinion (1918: 399), the late Baroque and Classicist / Enlightenment periods marked a nadir of intellectual and imaginative rigour in religious art; the Romantic one, a pronounced upswing.

[19] This period was, however, much freer from censorship than the following Second Empire (1852–1870).

portion of the Sebastian story. In the original legend, after the sagittation, St. Irene and her followers came to Sebastian's rescue and nursed him. Shortly afterwards they were all discovered by the authorities and bludgeoned to death. There have been periodic treatments of the rescue, especially the initial deposition. Sometimes these Sebastians in particular can recall pictures of Christ being taken from the Cross. In Ribot's version the young man, athletic and charismatic but not beautiful, lies moribund after his martyrdom.[20] The wounds are gruesomely realistic, rather than either æstheticized or schematic (say, with little detail other than eye-catching streams of blood, as with Sodoma's work from 1525). His body itself is shown in exquisite, merciless detail, particularly on the dusty soles of his feet. Ribot's saint, jaw lolling, shows no sign of pain, faith, or even consciousness as an older *man* carefully removes an arrow.

This departure from the legend merits a return to some of Le Targat's remarks concerning misogyny. By having a man appropriate St. Irene's role, Ribot certainly shows a misogynistic streak. This is an aggressive homosocialization, arguably more aggressive than the simple suggestion that Sebastian died from being shot. However, this is also an aggressive secularization. With the drab but sordidly clear lighting, Sebastian's closed eyes, and the intense attention to detail, the affect tends towards a grim matter-of-factness about the scene, rather than an engagement with either the viewer's libido or with God.

Le Targat had identified the Catholic church and the cult of male beauty as two elements of Sebastian's potentially misogynistic universe. One might expect a misogynistic work to quote other discourses supportive of misogyny. In Ribot's painting, neither the church nor the homoerotic seems to figure. Instead, this looks like a homosocial but also homophobic environment, as described by Eve Sedgwick and others after her.[21] Abigail Solomon-Godeau explains thoroughly (1997) that in late 18th Century and early Romantic French art, male subjects were consistently used in situations traditionally occupied by female ones, in a process of hostile appropriation. This was a pro-patriarchal discourse that easily survived the Revolution. I would propose Ribot's Sebastian as, among other things, a continuation of this. Like most patriarchal discourses it suppresses the homoerotic.

In order to outline what is at stake, culturally, in divergent Sebastians such as these, one must pause to discuss certain aspects of the historical discourse of sexuality, which is known (after Michel Foucault, 1976) to have undergone considerable change and expansion from the 17th century onwards. Richard Kaye describes how Sebastian's original appeal as a plague saint enjoyed a rebirth of sorts in the

---

[20] In Catholicism, martyrdom is the act of witnessing to one's faith, even under the threat of death. It follows that the experience may very well be horrific, but need not necessarily be fatal.

[21] Sedgwick's book *Between Men* explores this problem in detail. See for example her discussion of the homophobic double bind (1985: 89–90).

19th century, with the advent of psychology and the then-current conceptions of homosexuality as a disease (1996: 89), eventually to provide a precedent itself for what he calls the queering of the plague-saint, in the peri- and post-AIDS period (*ibid.*, 60). This pertains to the meta-discourse of queer sexuality in which Sebastian becomes increasingly implicated, a topic to be returned to presently.

Richard Dyer charts the generalized outgrowth, in later 19th century art, of what he calls "the cadaverously beautiful young man" (2002: 119), which would have developed from the popular image of the Romantic poet.[22] Dyer's prime example is Henry Wallis's painting *Chatterton* (1856: online), of the young poet moribund, which itself owes much to Giorgetti's Sebastian (again, after Bernini). This subtype, the alluring patrician æsthete, was itself undergoing assimilation to existing cultural signs for homosexuality.[23] Dyer says that this figure served to claim cultural prestige while incorporating signs of ambivalent gender and sexuality.[24]

The several Sebastian paintings by Gustave Moreau (1826–1898: online and in Damase), who can reasonably be judged to have been homosexual (E Cooper 1994: 70–72), conform to the "beautiful cadaver" type. These are frail, pallid martyrs, redolent of ill omen and ambivalence, quite unlike the haughty adolescents and robust young men of the Renaissance and Baroque. Graham Robb calls them "swooning hermaphrodites ... eerily passive and consumed by an unknown disease" (2003: 250). They do fit Paglia's description (after Colette) of the Androgyne as "eternally sad, sex-repelling, glorying in the abstract and mentalized suffering" (1990: 489) – an attenuation, an æstheticization of what she has already identified as an exercise in oppressing the viewer's sexuality with abstraction. However, although Moreau's Sebastians, with their huge gilded haloes and plaintive, confronting stare, seem quite different in affect from their unapologetic Renaissance forebears, they blend the (homo)sexual and the spiritual in comparable ways. The tone might be different, but the referential relationship in both is straightforward, regardless of the referential proportion. In contrast with these, the pieces by Daumier, Corot and Ribot show a reassessment of *both* of these established discourses. It seems fair to conclude that in approaches to St. Sebastian in France in the mid-19th century, there was a new pluralism in reference.

Daumier's second Sebastian, a shattering painting from 1852 (Olga), exemplifies this new critical spirit. I suggest that this piece articulates a critique of religion comparable with its critique of homosexuality. It claims an ethical position quite different from a straightforwardly orthodox rejection of that sexuality. It is a

---

[22] Mario Praz (1951) discusses these issues in depth, notably with regard to Byron.

[23] This hero became a cliché of the literature of homosexuality. See both Wood (2000) and Christopher Robinson (1995) for extended discussions.

[24] It is worth underlining that gender and sexuality are not the same thing. See Sedgwick 1991: 27–35, esp. 27, 31.

sombre work, mostly monochromatic but with violent colour contrast on certain features. Sebastian's attributes are distorted: thin arms; a bizarrely flattened and protrusive lower ribcage; a stomach with a layer of fat laid over large muscles. One has the impression of a healthy if idle body subjected to sudden wasting. His face, on the other hand, is of a beautiful and well-proportioned youth, albeit haggard with pain. His sunken eyes bear a vacant, delirious expression. He is not bleeding much, but the two arrows in his torso are skewed and gruesomely large. The loin-cloth – placed so low as to be only just effective – is an intense shade of blood red, expressing the violence he has suffered while also compounding the suggestion of its sexual nature. At Sebastian's ear, a large cherub floats in the upper midground, apparently whispering to him; a drape fluttering behind it glows electric blue. Two women are wandering in the background.

This work combines a number of traditional and innovative elements, to clash-ing effect. It shares some features with an earlier painting by Suvée (1743–1807), in which Sebastian is figured with hands clasped above his head, praying intensely, his glorious musculature on full show and his head tilted so far back as to make eye contact impossible. Two cherubs are high in the foreground, looking on. Another clear historic inspiration, a work by Van Dyck (1599–1641: online), shows an an-gelic messenger of a scale and age comparable to the saint, in a naturalistic pose. In Luca Giordano's first St. Sebastian, another possible inspiration (1650–1653: online), St. Irene and a handmaiden are attending to Sebastian while tiny cherubs watch from on high. In Daumier's piece the positioning is inverted even though the characters' attitudes are very similar. The single cherub carries what looks like a pale-coloured palm frond, but in fact is a quill, a token of Daumier's satiri-cal trade, and a signature familiar from his cartooning. This feature, the cherub's huge size, and the lurid colours around it cast doubt on the plausibility of the di-vine and miraculous.[25] Still, this does nothing to lessen the painting's impact. The women, preserved from the original tale (as St. Irene had minions), stand against a hopeful-looking sunset but are looking in the wrong place; Sebastian's rescue would seem doubtful. In any case, he is truly to be pitied as the victim of a mortal delirium, mortal in both senses.

While Daumier's interpretation may be a sophisticated version of what Paglia called the "pagan spectacle" of St. Sebastian (1990: 33), the unæstheticized suf-fering in the young man's face, when coupled with its *lack* of engagement with the viewer, make it difficult to consider it as a vehicle of Sadistic pleasure.[26] It is more likely that we are looking at another case where respect for the Christian martyr

---

[25] Adrianne Tooke notes that in mid-19th century France, bright colour in general was often viewed and figured as subversive (2000: 32).

[26] Probably the best-known teary moment (of many) from Sade's *Justine* (1791) is just before the hero-ine begins her tale: "Des pleurs coulèrent alors avec abondance des yeux de cette intéressante fille …" {"Tears then poured abundantly from the eyes of this interesting girl …"} (Sade 1995: 141). My im-

coexists more or less peacefully with disbelief in his religion. However, the martyr's beautiful face begs the question of Daumier's approach to the other aspect of the Sebastian tradition.[27]

In the light of Paglia's interpretation, I would suggest that Daumier intended to convey the threat, or perhaps even confess the anxiety, of a pornographic motive in producing such a well-known homoerotic vehicle. Sebastian's body is explicitly unnatural and unappealing. The torso is masculine, but the buttocks and haunches are feminine. The disproportion shown in Sebastian's abs, coupled with an equally exaggerated layer of subcutaneous fat (whereas his face and neck are slim), amounts to a raunchy mock offering for the visual consumer. These departures from the *beau idéal* sharpen the painting's moral drama for its viewer. They speak to an awareness of the painting's homoerotic referents, while doing so with a corrective message.

Daumier's technique is comparable with that of Flaubert's novella "La Légende de saint Julien l'Hospitalier" (1876), in which Flaubert negotiates a respectful distance from Christian doctrine while endorsing its ethics of hospitality (Hartford 2007: 434 *passim*). The novella communicates this by having its title character sexually embrace a leper, who transforms into Christ, in a violent rejection of conventional norms and, by extension, conventional religion. Flaubert had little time for organized religion, which he viewed as another outlet for conventional, shallow-minded human nature, and laughed at the thought that fools might take his story as a straightforward parable. At one point he even proposed it to be illustrated in polychrome, which usually gives garish effects (Tooke 2000: 63). At the same time, part of the tale's subversive agenda is to demonstrate just how shocking and rare ethical commitment truly is (Hartford 2007, *ibid.*). Daumier's piece, I would argue, dramatizes Sebastian's suffering sincerely while at the same time rejecting both the belief it had traditionally been used to promote, and the libidinal consumerism it had traditionally been used to serve.

At this point it would help to recall some questions with which this discussion began, now that there is some context. Hopefully it will be clear that the coding of Sebastian as sexually desirable for a male audience is too consistent to support the claim that he has only been *read* as a homoerotic vehicle by a projecting audience. By the same token, it should be fairly clear, even from the given sample of works, that a pattern of back-reference has been functioning consistently enough for one to be able to talk of a homoerotic tradition predating the modern era of sexuality with this saint, notwithstanding the massive upheavals in Western art and culture in the 19th century, and particularly in France. At the same time, it bears repeating

---

plied parallel in art is with the tearful faces of the Avignon school, and their successors. In Daumier's painting Sebastian's eyes are dry.

[27] Even Solomon-Godeau, a fiercely agnostic critic in terms of sexuality, acknowledges that in and since the 19th century beautiful Sebastians "… have been variously coded (or received) as homoerotic figures" (1997: 26).

that these questions are arguably less important than what happened in addition to this story of continuity. I hope to have shown that the earlier 19th century in France saw the emergence of numerous conceptual innovations in its Sebastian figures, which manifested itself variously as departure from the established themes or as a critical reflectiveness in their regard.

It would be easy to suggest that this innovation was only to be expected from that time and place, given that it saw such innovation in the visual arts generally. However, this innovation, unlike many others of the time, does not seem to have "caught on". Indeed, the late 19th century and successive years in general saw the decline of thematic variation in Sebastian treatments, and a coalescence around the familiar and at times cohabiting alternatives of the religious and the homoerotic. I shall turn now towards detailing this return to the familiar, as it were, in figures of St. Sebastian from both art and literature. The intent behind this is twofold. The first motive is to show how resilient the dual discourse of Sebastian is – so much so that it can be described as dominant and, in discursive terms, even aggressive. The second motive is to prepare the ground for a speculative answer as to what change in culture made possible a challenge to this discourse: in other words, why this innovation, now unrecognized, took place when it did.

Enter the Icon

The general breakdown of consensus in Western art during the late 19th and 20th centuries did little to change St. Sebastian's role as a focus for by then rather derivative cross-references between two streams of queer figurations. These were the established tradition in visual art and the emergent one in literature. In the course of a fairly orderly transfer process, the icon appeared in growing numbers of texts in increasingly explicit ways. With time Sebastian became only one of several options for authors increasingly free of official and unofficial censorship. However, at the same time, Sebastian seems to have been increasingly popular as a ready vehicle, a first line of resort as it were.

Prior to the fin-de-siècle no queer St. Sebastians had appeared in literature (Le Targat 1979: 8). In 1889 the British magazine *The Artist*, a Uranian publication (the Uranians being one of the oldest homophile organizations), proposed a number of subjects for homoerotic paintings. These included Apollo and Hyacinthus, the ritual whipping of the Spartan boys, and St. Sebastian, prompting many verses on the saint, both in that publication and elsewhere (Fussell 1975: 285; see also Showalter 1992: 205).[28] Since then, the conceptual link has grown strong enough

---

[28] Showalter mentions other observations to this effect made *en passant* in mainstream criticism, by Richard Ellman and Gregory Woods as well as by Fussell.

for Sebastian to function alternatively as a sign of homosexuality, and a symbolic focus which can be used as an associative bridge between queer characters and texts and the wider cultural milieu.

Queer literary references to Sebastian tend in general to emphasize his origins in art. When they do not, the reference is still normally brief and refers to an acknowledged, visually-inspired type. In probably the earliest example in French, from Belgium, not France, Georges Eekhoud briefly likens the hero of his "Quadrille du lancier" (1892) to Sebastian in a scene during which he is "martyred" for his sexuality, by being stabbed by many different women wielding miscellaneous small sharp objects (Eekhoud 1987: 250). In a later novel by the same author, *Escal-Vigor* (1901), another character who eventually identifies himself as a "martyr to love" is fatally shot with arrows, in what looks like a clear Sebastian reference (Eekhoud 1901: 249–251).

Given the cultural origins of the queer St. Sebastian in strictly visual art, as well as the internationalism of modern avant-garde literature, it seems fitting that his first explicit literary appearance in France was in a stage play written by an Italian. Gabriele d'Annunzio's masque *Le Martyre de saint Sébastien*, with music by Debussy, was first performed at the Théâtre du Châtelet in 1911. The piece offers numerous points of interest, including its use of cross-gender casting. Its subtlety lies in its weaving of numerous queer signs of different order around Sebastian, associating them with him without actually ascribing them to him.

Although D'Annunzio's casting already constitutes a queering of gender, Le Targat is more taken with the piece's queerings of sexuality. In the first scene, "La Cour des lys," "Les Jumeaux" (sung by two contralti),[29] whose connection with Sebastian is not explained, apostrophize each other longingly.

Frère, que sera-t-il le monde, allégé de tout notre amour!
Dans mon âme ton cœur est lourd, comme la pierre dans la fronde!
Je le pèse, au-delà de l'ombre, je le jette vers le grand jour!
J'étais plus doux que la colombe, tu es plus fauve que l'autour. [*sic*]
Beau Christ, que sera-t-il le monde, allégé de notre amour![30] (D'Annunzio 1911: 5–8)

Sebastian (a soprano) then replies, in speech: "Et que je serai digne de demander à Dieu des signes plus éclatants"[31] (*ibid.*, 9, unpunctuated) and the archers (chorus) hail him by name, also in speech.

---

[29] "The Court of the Lilies" and "The Twins".

[30] "Brother, what will become of the world, unweighted by our love! Within your soul your heart is heavy, like the stone in the sling! I weigh it, beyond the shadow, I throw it to the broad daylight! I was gentler than the dove, you are wilder than the vulture. {*autour* = *arch.* "vulture", but also "around".} Fair Christ, what will become of the world, unweighted by our love!"

[31] "And will I be worthy to ask of God more striking signs" {*éclat* = "burst", "shock"; *éclatant* "striking"}

D'Annunzio's work is a good example of how Sebastian can be blended with several homoeroticized pagan figures, as described by both Paglia and Fussell. After Sebastian calls upon God as "light of the world" in scene ii, a Pagan court sings a pæan to Apollo and performs a ritual deploration and celebration of Adonis (scene iii). This association of Apollo and Adonis provides another link between Apollo and St. Sebastian, although the link relies partly on a contrast. Apollo shoots whereas Adonis bleeds. Moreover, although the two were linked by virtue of their shared masculine beauty and homoeroticism, Apollo and Adonis do not traditionally exist in the same myth or myths, even though Adonis does share much with Hyacinthus, who was Apollo's lover, and whom he accidentally killed.

Perhaps this inexact, metonymic association between the three figures is precisely to the point: the only elements to be taken seriously would be the ones they incontrovertibly share; namely, cultural origin, masculinity, beauty, "arrows", and homoeroticism. As though to confirm this superficially comedic approach, an irreverent Sebastian is then tied to a laurel and shot (scene iv, "Le Laurier blessé")[32], and then mournfully reflects, "Toutes les fleurs sont flétries"[33] (l. 81–84). The affect overall is therefore either variable or unstable. In the fifth scene, "Le Paradis," he is hailed by the awaiting martyrs as the "lys de la cohorte"[34] (l. 89).

D'Annunzio's sobriquet for Sebastian sounds Biblical, evoking as it does the lilies of the field (cp. Matthew 6: 28). At the same time, the lily is an emblem of the decadents, while the wilted, ruined or crushed flower is a familiar sign for homosexuality, known as such at least since Edmond de Goncourt's 1882 novel *La Faustin* (Robb 2003: 213–214). Sebastian thus is carrying three potential discourses already. The queering works in the mythical realm also. It is said of Adonis that "il renaît dieu, vierge et jeune homme, le florissant!… La mort est immortelle, dieu, par ton sang"[35] (D'Annunzio 1911: 61). Immortal Apollo shoots, mortal Sebastian is shot; demigod Adonis is penetrated and dies beautifully, albeit not by arrows. (Adonis was stabbed by a boar; wherever he bled, anemones sprang.)

One can imagine a continuum of penetrative acts in association with masculine beauty, a system of exchanges whereby one is invited to view the mortal, yet exalted penetrated victim as a portmanteau of both the participants and the acts themselves. The succession of subjects invites comparison between them: the masque becomes a montage, or at least a phantasmagoria, which fosters the blurring and slippage of individual significations within it. Recalling Paglia's reading of Adonis as Sebastian's true identity, we can see the phantasmagoria as being religiously

---

[32] "The Wounded Laurel."

[33] "All the flowers are withered."

[34] "Lily of the Cohort."

[35] "He is reborn, god, virgin and young man, the blooming one! … Death is immortal, o God, by your blood."

syncretist, usurpatory of Christianity, or both. Queering uncertainty here is rein-forced by the always-existing possibility of viewing the lily simply as a token of Sebastian's purity, itself bolstered by his devotion to the Light of the World. Sym-bolically and religiously speaking, the result is deliberately, provocatively open: queer.

D'Annunzio manages to combine this all within his woman-Sebastian in a scan-dalous assertion of male passivity; or rather, he portrays them together in such a way as to prompt his audience to construct the link. The Twins' discourse can now clearly be seen, in context, as speaking of more than fraternal or Christan love. This caused no little scandal. The spectacle of the famous Russian dancer Ida Ru-binstein in the title role crying "Encore, encore" to the archers attracted sufficient attention to be condemned by the Bishop of Paris (Kaye 1996: 88). The implied view of homosexuality as a sort of androgyny is not new for this era. However, from a psychological point of view, one could suggest the confusion, or equivo-cation, of archer (Apollo) and target (Sebastian) as a hint of a process of projec-tion. By identifying the passive participant in an exchange with the active one, it is possible to reverse the polarity of violence. Just who is the real perpetrator of violence and who is the real victim is not entirely clear here, but it is worth specu-lating that this might be the first attempt at using Sebastian to signify an *aggressive* queer sexuality. In discursive, symbolic terms, D'Annunzio's system of metony-mies is bringing Sebastian closer to the archers, which is only a few steps away from turning him into an archer himself, as we will see happens in later literature.

It is notable that an author such as D'Annunzio, who from all evidence was heterosexual and very probably "straight" as well,[36] should explore autonomous variations on the theme of queerness in such a direct and compact way.[37] It is also notable that the references that sustain this derive essentially from the Classical period of culture, and are not taken up in ways that destabilize those sources them-selves. However, the critical spirit that obtains in 19th century art with regard to the cult of the beautiful boy is lacking. Despite the hint of a willingness to engage aggressively with church doctrine and, with it, conventional morality in terms of sexuality, Sebastian's homoeroticism is be taken, in D'Anninzio's masque, at face value.

---

[36] It is possible to be both heterosexual and of minority sexuality Sedgwick (1993: 13). See Calvin Thomas (2000) for a full discussion.

[37] On the subject of Modernist queer experiments, it is interesting that D'Annunzio seems to have worked primarily with gender, whereas James Joyce (also heterosexual) did so with sexuality, includ-ing homosexuality, through the character of Cranly in his *Portrait of the Artist as a Young Man* (1916).

Art and Literature II: Surreal Sebastian

Sebastian's "homo-associative" potential comes to the fore in both plastic and literary works from the Surrealist period. By this time, literary Sebastians began to acquire a depth of commentary and intertextuality comparable with that of the visual realm. At the same time, their attitude towards that blended heritage remains largely uncritical. The Classical cult of beauty is, for these 20th century texts, a reliable source of iconic propaganda. In this context, queer Saint Sebastian's desired referent – homosexuality – is as unproblematically self-evident as the Christian referent would be for orthodox religious art. In context with earlier cultural history, then, Sebastian's more recent role as a queer icon is as much a return in culture as a renewal. The semantic field is the same as it was in Renaissance painting; it no longer shows the critical and digressive approaches seen in 19th century art.

One early queer Sebastian in French fiction appears in René Crevel's *Mon corps et moi* (1925).[38] The narrator describes at length a working-class youth in a gay bar, advertising himself while trying desperately to be fabulous. The passage is dense with cultural references:

Il y a deux ans, il était ouvrier plombier. Le voici coquette. Ses bras sont blancs, ses aisselles épilées. Le malheur vient de ce qu'il n'avait pas de santé. [...]
  Dame aux camélias des faubourgs, il crache le sang.
  [...]
  Ce jeune saint Sébastien de la zone, habillé en rat d'hôtel, désigne son entrejambe!
  Voici la fleur de volupté ...
  Quand il est ivre, il montre sous des bracelets de cuivre doré deux cicatrices aux poignets. Il a essayé de s'ouvrir les veines. Petit Pétrone anachronique de beuglant, il n'a pas su mourir, mais depuis cet essai manqué, des bouquets, les plus mauves, les plus tristes, sous ses yeux, se fanent.
  Qu'il reprenne son refrain: «Voici la fleur de volupté», et je songe à ces longues fleurs pourpres dont se couronna Ophélie et que, nous dit Shakespeare, les bergers appellent d'un nom licencieux et les jeunes filles réservées, doigts d'homme mort.
  Un jour sans doute, le Pétrone raté deviendra l'Ophélie réussie du canal Saint-Martin.[39]
(Crevel 1974: 62–64).

---

[38] Whatever his exact sexuality may have been, Crevel certainly was attracted to men (Gauthier 1971: 230–240).

[39] Two years ago, he was a plumber's labourer. Here he is now as a tease. His arms are white, his armpits plucked. The downfall comes from his not having had good health. [...]
  A Dame aux Camélias from the precinct, he spits blood.
  [...]
  This young Saint Sebastian from the Zone, dressed like a lounge lizard, points out his groin!
  Here is the flower of passion ...
  When he is drunk, he shows under his gilded copper bracelets two scars on his wrists. He tried to open his veins. Little anachronistic baying Petronius, he didn't manage to die; but since this failed attempt the bouquets, the purplest, the saddest, under his eyes, have been fading.
  Let him take up his refrain again: "Here is the flower of passion", and I'm dreaming of these long purple flowers

This passage creates layers of equivalences between and among different successive tragic archetypes, by exploiting different semiotic levels and techniques across a series of comparisons. Alexandre Dumas *fils*'s Marguerite Gautier, St. Sebastian, Petronius and Shakespeare's Ophelia are all linked together by means of each one being applied interpellatively to the boy. Doing this justice requires a close reading of the different associations.

To prepare the ground for its strategy, the narrative puts the whole passage in a "visual context." It confirms the boy's queering of himself through transvestism by combining and, in time, multiplying binary contrasts that depend on various symbols. It introduces first his intentions (*it était plombier, le voici coquette*), next his appearance, which is then commented on. The accumulating pathos and intertextual references, again linked through shared symbols, come to demonstrate how this character is in his own way iconic.

The first step in building the complex analogy lies in linking the first two archetypes, Marguerite and Sebastian, in three steps. First it compares the boy with Dumas *fils*'s beleaguered heroine, who had made a sexual spectacle of herself at the opera. Marguerite wore red or white camellias, according to whether or not she was menstruating; hence, whether or not she was sexually available. There is a convenient symbolic parallel with homosexuality here, in the "stained" flower as a token of sexual imperfection. *La Dame aux camélias*, especially in her incarnation as Verdi's Traviata, is an established gay icon in her own right (Koestenbaum 1993: 205–206).

Second, the passage invokes the boy's martyrdom, apparently in the cause of his sexuality rather than his faith, through a comparison with St. Sebastian. What is shown is actually a dense metonymy. Like Sebastian, the boy points to his groin. Now, the saint better known for showing his groin is St. Roch. He too is a plague saint, but unlike Sebastian, we are led to suspect, he has no other reasons for showing what is between his legs.

Third, the use of rhythmically parallel phrases to associate the two archetypes to "questionable" working-class space, *Dame des faubourgs*, *Sébastien de la zone*, reinforced with the reminder that this Sebastian is dressed like a *rat d'hôtel*, invites one to consider St. Sebastian and the real-life Traviata, the "working girl" Marguerite Gautier, as being of a single type. As a Prætorian guard, Sebastian might well have been of humble origins, as was Marguerite. Both died in painful, yet heroic and authentically Christian martyrdom. Marguerite sacrifices her own happiness for her lover's future and career in respectable society, and at the novel's close leaves the world in a dramatic scene of extreme unction. Her confessor says,

---

Ophelia crowned herself with and which, Shakespeare tells us, the shepherds call a raunchy name and ladylike young girls call dead man's fingers.

One day doubtless, the failed Petronius will become the successful Ophelia of St. Martin's Canal.

"Elle a vécu comme une pécheresse, mais elle mourra comme une chrétienne"[40] (Dumas 1950: 169–170). The whole is presented as a quasi-martyrdom. Furthermore, she and Sebastian can each chase their demise to having been penetrated by many different men: she, a prostitute, winds up ruined and diseased while he, of course, was shot with arrows. (This parallel itself might lend strength to the common misconception that the original saint actually died from that experience.) Each is thus an appropriate and equivalent figure of apotheosis for Crevel's young gay prostitute.

The innuendoes only accumulate in light of the second pair of binary interpellations. After two martyrs, Crevel presents us with two suicides, also of opposite sex. The male in this case, Petronius, was both author of a celebrated novel laden with homosexual revelry (the *Satyricon*) and in his life an aficionado of the same, and would have been instantly recognizable as such to an educated French audience. Ophelia and Marguerite, both women, are scorned lovers of the main man in their stories. Sebastian and Petronius are both legendary Roman men. Petronius, we can be fairly certain, was homosexual. Following Crevel's reciprocal binaries, in order to complete the pattern established by Ophelia and Marguerite, we are invited to perceive a similar equivalence in the "sex lives" of the two men as well (setting aside, of course, that in the original Sebastian's case there is no evidence he had one), and conclude that Sebastian too was homosexual.

To consider another angle, Marguerite and Petronius are known to have had a historical existence, whereas Ophelia and Sebastian are, for Crevel, strictly fictional.[41] The first two were ultimately destroyed through the consequences of their social dynamic: Marguerite, a prostitute among men of station, and Petronius, one courtier among many to a cruel and fickle emperor. With regard to the other pair, Ophelia, an innocent, loved a man, Hamlet, but died after he had treated her as a disposable sex object. The implication, again reinforced by the phallic symbolism of the arrow, is that much the same is true of St. Sebastian.

The weight of discursive evidence points towards an assumption that the reader realizes St. Sebastian to be a queer icon, assuming that they had not already presumed he was one. The comparison above strongly suggests equivalence, while the referential system of the surrounding narrative is too coherent to assume that Sebastian is being included solely for the sake of emphasis. The literature creates an equivalent overdetermination to that visible in earlier art.

The theme of homosexuality apparent in Crevel's writing is reflected in Sebastian paintings by Alfred Courmes, from about a decade later. In his first *Saint Sébastien* (1934: online), the saint is wearing a sailor's striped jersey and pomponned

---

[40] "She has lived as a sinner, but she will die as a Christian."

[41] Paul Cooke, in his study of Crevel's developing atheism, traces the writer's "Deist" approach to, and respectful distance from, Biblical figures and faith throughout *Mon corps et moi* (Cooke 2000: 96–98).

hat, with a full moon "halo" in the background. A wire mast behind him doubles as a cross. From the waist down he is naked, his realistic genitals exhibited right in the centre of the painting, and he holds his arms high in an inverted A, like a photo model flexing his chest. His legs, which bear all the arrows, are distractingly mis-shapen, the barbs hanging in them like javelins from a bull, but there is no blood. Incongruously, he wears long formal socks and fashionable shoes.

Masculine legs drew much attention in queer literature of the early 20th century. Georges Eekhoud's *Voyous* (1904, repr. 1926) fetishizes them frequently, especially when they belong to fit young dockers and sailors. "Je sens mes reins se bomber, mes jambes s'allonger et se rétracter en étroite sympathie avec les mouvements des athlètes"[42] (Eekhoud 1991: 67). Jean Cocteau, in a longing ecphrastic passage from *Les Enfants terribles* (1929), evokes a pair of photos to show the appeal of Dargelos, the *coq du collège*. In one of them, "comme un joueur de football il ex-hibe avec orgueil ses jambes robustes, un des attributs de son règne"[43] (Cocteau 1974: 34) – a token, by which he might be known. In the case of Courmes's first painting, which in its own way is more explicit, we are looking at a visual pun on cruising. The weird outfit's components would betoken different social classes, mingling in the anonymous homo-activity symbolized by this un-bloodied, un-miraculously haloed "saint". Anonymity is reinforced in that this Sebastian's face is distinctly ordinary. The juxtaposition of bourgeois business dress with "sailor kit" and the saint's prominent genitalia reinforces the impression of disorderly, camp sexuality.

Michel Remy-Bieth was later (ca. 1976: in Damase) to create a similar piece, with an unfettered, trim, dreamily handsome Sebastian with "Farrah hair", thus associating the saint with the female pinup du jour (Fawcett *perf.* 1976: n. p.). We recall again Dyer's comment, to the effect that signs of gender often stand in for signs of sexuality because they are easier to portray. However, this saint is also sexually unambiguous and available, being nude from the waist down. He gazes calmly at the onlooker from what looks like a park fence. Synecdoche and me-tonymy connect the subject with his referent: the fence is part of a park, which is where anonymous gay sex happens. Perhaps the park fence has even become a new career token for this Sebastian, with homosexual passion as the reality to which he testifies and for which he might suffer.

Courmes returned to the general topic with his later painting *Saint Sébastien de dos à l'écluse Saint-Martin* (1974: online). That Crevel's hero threw himself into the same canal is likely to be a coincidence, although the possibility of a tribute by Courmes is intriguing. In any case this painting is very similar to Courmes's

---

[42] "I feel my hips arching, my legs stretching out and drawing back in tight sympathy with the ath-letes' movements."

[43] "Like a footballer he displays pridefully his robust legs, one of the attributes of his reign."

earlier pieces. Again we have a shapely sailor-saint, a few arrows jutting from his unbleeding hip, his naked buttocks in the centre. The piece quotes the visual metaphor of spilling water from Dalí's *William Tell* (1930: in Moorhouse). It is likely here that, in keeping with Surrealist technique in general, the object was to make explicit what had previously been implicit (Hughes 1991: 225).[44] In the original, the water signifies castration (Moorhouse 1990: 53), but in Courmes it could also indicate ejaculation. A few handsome, similarly muscular men are visible in the background. While of a type with Sebastian, they also look like figures from tough-guy pornography – such as Klaus Bodanza's drawing *Saint Sébastien en cuir* (ca. 1977: in Damase). This Sebastian sports two arrows shot into his pubic hair, itself exposed by his open fly. His beard is trimmed in the classic "clone" style, making him a lovely man rather than a lovely boy.

In both this and Courmes's work, Sebastian is thus to be recognized as the apotheosis of that most abject and degraded of beings, the male who enjoys being penetrated. That statement synthesizes observations by Leo Bersani and others on contempt for the penetrated male, and its socio-cultural genealogy. This prejudice occurs in a society with a profoundly misogynistic gender system, the founder-example usually being ancient Greece. Homosexuality *per se* was not stigmatized. However, as Bersani explains in his uncompromising language, "… to be fucked was a sign of social inferiority (the fate of women and slaves); the adult male citizen who allowed himself to be penetrated was *politically* disgraced" (1995: 28, *sic*; cf. Dover 1978: 104). The arrow symbol appears in order to prevent any escape for the audience through denial. Courmes's painting, especially if we suspect an "unmanned" Sebastian, is a homosexual variation of the typically confrontational Surrealist approach, only superficially subversive of surrealist misogyny, combined with the familiar figure of this saint.

Discursive Innovation: Sebastian Shoots Back

The next major appearance of St. Sebastian in French literature occurs in 1955, in Julien Green's *Le Malfaiteur*. This tightly-plotted piece holds intertextual connections with works as diverse as *Trois Contes*, *L'Immoraliste*, the Book of Revelation and anecdotes by Oscar Wilde. Its interest here is in the way it uses St. Sebastian as an indicator of queerness in its protagonist, Jean, and especially as a sign of his tastes and activities. Although lacking the element of satire, *Le Malfaiteur* uses Sebastian in a manner very close to that of Courmes's paintings.

Jean is an intellectual and a dilettante, if a frugal one, who lives with his wealthy

---

[44] Hughes explains that the Surrealists viewed beauty, fear and sexual desire as entities of equivalent order, to be found in "chance" associations and released mediumistically through art.

cousins. He is gentle but distant and obsessively private. Hints as to the nature of Jean's preoccupations come early in the novel, when we see him writing, then tearing apart successive attempts at expressing how he has lived a "vie tragiquement faussée"[45] (Green 1995: 11–12). There are strong clues at Jean's taste for cruising, as it would now be called, surfacing every twenty-five pages or so. Publicly, he shows emotion most openly when negotiating with his cousin, Mme. Vasseur, for monies to fund a journey to Italy to research his current and much-cherished project, an iconography of St. Sebastian. It is later revealed (*ibid.*, 91) that Jean privately longs specifically to visit Naples, by then a notorious, almost passé destination for men seeking boys, to examine several vital pieces for his iconography, he says.

This association with a prime destination for gay sex tourism is the first of St. Sebastian's four appearances in the novel. The most apposite one for this discussion is the second, when Mme. Pauque, Mme. Vasseur's sister, considers two postcards Jean keeps in his room. One is of a Last Judgment, the other an unconventional Sebastian. Although he is holding an archer's pose,

il n'avait point d'arc, mais sur son visage renfrogné se lisait l'attention du guerrier qui entend bien ne pas manquer son but. De longs cheveux bouclés encadraient son visage. Pas un fil ne couvrait ses membres robustes.[46] Au-dessous de cette image se lisait le nom de Michel-Ange que suivait celui de saint Sébastien[47] (Green 1995: 99).

The original painting, from the Sistine Chapel (Michelangelo, 1537–1541), shows a burly Sebastian holding a bundle of arrows in his left hand, his right elbow bent and his index finger hooked as though he were actually cocking a bow. Mme. Pauque, who might as well personify establishment philistinism, decides that Jean has chosen the picture for its curiosity value, given that Sebastian should be shown as a "vivante pelote d'épingles."[48] A few moments later, however, she overhears a threatening conversation outside between the concierge and the baker and his son ("[qui] semblait presque un gamin"),[49] who have unexpectedly arrived at the house. They demand to speak with Jean, who has already left for Naples. Mme. Pauque satisfies herself that the conversation is going nowhere and turns back to her work, but not before wondering:

Pourquoi le boulanger et son fils voulaient-ils parler à Jean? Entre ce monsieur studieux, réservé, tranquille et ces deux hommes rudes et bruyants, quel rapport y avait-il donc? N'était-

---

[45] "a life tragically belied."

[46] Compare this passage with the selection from Cocteau's *Enfants terribles*, above.

[47] "… he had no bow at all, but in his scowling face one read the attention of a warrior who knows just how not to miss his mark. Long ringlets framed his face. Not a thread covered his robust limbs. Above this image there appeared the name of Michelangelo, followed by that of Saint Sebastian."

[48] "a living pincushion."

[49] "who seemed almost a kid."

ce pas absurde? Son grand œil inquiet se posa sur le saint Sébastien qui l'avait fait rire, un instant plus tôt, mais elle ne riait plus, à cet instant, elle ne voyait même plus l'archer vengeur qui semblait la viser[50] (Green 1995: 100–101).

All the while the novel has been building its balance of inarticulacy and innuendo, its *kairos*, around Jean's homosexuality, culminating in his confession, a document which Mme. Pauque, who is not the intended reader, has just discovered and is about to read. Mme. Pauque's anxieties now focus *in denial* on Sebastian figured as an *archer*. She looks to him as though he were somehow to reveal the true motives of her cousin.

The dramatic inversion is, I think, a veiled allusion to Green's own defiance in mounting a gay apologia. The fear Mme. Pauque feels represents that of society in general. One can see within it her repressed recognition of the psychosexual hunter, *inversion* incarnate. In borrowing Michelangelo's figure and adding to it a recognized, if implicit cultural threat, Green has projected violence in ways that D'Annunzio's masque had only barely suggested were possible. Recalling that Green's text originally dated from the mid-1950s, the inkling of violence to come might even have marked a kind of high water mark for Sebastian, just before gays and queers lost their patience with the limitations of iconic passivity.

Facing the arrows from the viewing perspective is an innovation in the iconography. Derek Jarman's film *Sebastiane* (1976) has been said to show an iconographic innovation in its final scene, in which the audience shares Sebastian's dying view of his executioners through a fish-eye lens (see Wyke 1998: 263). In a more recent interpretation, the Belgian Bavo Defurne's featurette, *Saint* (1996), uses fast intercutting to achieve the same effect. Not only does Green seem to anticipate this, he also brilliantly compresses the threat to normativity inherent in queer sexuality into this suddenly deadly Sebastian.[51] However, from the potentially rejecting straight viewer's perspective, Green's representation projects the fear and the resulting attack on queer Sebastian back at the viewer, whereas Jarman's and, after him, Defurne's only concretize and reiterate them.

It seems clear that Green wishes for us to perceive within his Sebastian an assertive homosexuality. It is possible to suggest that Michelangelo *might* have had a similar intention, but for a host of cultural and historical reasons this idea looks problematic. However, one can assert confidently that Green's projected marksmanship is striking precisely because it refers so closely to the religious story and

---

[50] "Why did the baker and his son want to talk to Jean? Between this studious, retiring, peaceable gentleman and these two rude and noisy men, whatever connection could there be? Wasn't it absurd? Her great, disquieted eye fixed on the Saint Sebastian who had made her laugh, a moment ago, but she was not laughing any more, at this moment; she no longer even saw the vengeful archer who seemed to take aim at her."

[51] Cf. Dollimore 1999: 222.

its themes, hence relying on them strongly. The motif is all the more effective because it is newly scandalous, given the fact that the other privileged cultural discourse behind Sebastian, the Church, was finding itself increasingly obliged to voice publicly its hostility to a now-manifest(ing) homosexuality. It seems ironic that cultural memory should be so short: "Sebastian's lost his appropriateness as the official gay patron after the Stonewall riots. Modern Sebastians, after all, shoot back" (Greif 1982: 26–27, *sic*).

Modern Sexualities, Familiar Discourse

It is worth discussing the meta-discourse over the cultural logic behind Sebastian's alleged emergence (coming-out?), actually a return, as a homosexual symbol. The present consensus seems to be that this development in Sebastian's career was a natural result of the developing Foucauldian discourse of sexuality, or *sexualities*. Wyke, elaborating on Kaye's reflections, says that as the legendary Sebastian was punished for his candour in revealing his true self, "[he] could thus stand for homosexual self-revelation as opposed to homosexual affection, and as such he was a splendid vehicle for a new conception of same-sex desire … [showing] a shift from a stress on homosexual *acts* to an emphasis on homosexual *identity*" (Wyke 1998: 255, *sic*; cf. Kaye 1996: 91). The underlying argument here would be that in the past, signs of gender would have been used to denote gender-*practice*, *à la rigueur* gender roles, instead of sexuality. This differs from Dyer's analysis, according to which the one would have been shown instead of the other simply because it was easier to convey. While Dyer's position seems on the face of it simpler, it bespeaks a more cautious sensitivity to the plurality of motives, and conceptual models, that potentially underlie this material.[52]

Regardless of the iconic referent, when we are shown a St. Sebastian we are asked to recognize both what he is, and what he does. This is clear from a pre-existing iconographic tradition. Queer Sebastian turns his powers of propaganda from an ecclesiastical purpose to a homoerotic one. The referent changes, but it is still a transcendental reality, albeit a different one. The critical materialism suggested in Corot's and in Daumier's Sebastians has no role to play in works such as Green's and Jarman's. These phenomena confirm a general cultural process, as described by Jonathan Dollimore:

the indebtedness of sexual radicalism to religion remains apparent in the way it imagines sexuality as a powerful force. Only now it is the medium not of evil but of freedom. … The religious antecedents are also apparent in the sexual radical's idea of sexual desire being

---

[52] Here I am implicitly following comments by Sedgwick, in her critical reading of new histories of homosexuality with which Wyke and Kaye agree (Sedgwick 1991: 46–47).

an identity, *the source of an authentic selfhood* for which we must be prepared to fight and suffer (Dollimore 1999: 226, my emphasis).

Nowadays St. Sebastian functions reliably as a sign of homosexuality in European culture, and several lively disputes as to what he represents with regard to "homoculture" seem set only to increase his popularity. Pieces by the Belgian Pierre Demard (painting, n. d.; late 20th century) and, more subtly, the American Matthew Kelly (mixed media sculpture, 2003) incorporate possible sexual and purely æsthetic references with religious sensibility and clear signs of martyrdom. These more modern Sebastians are more than exercises in style, or essentially pornographic vehicles. In print as well as in paint, they propagate complex references along recognized lines. Dominique Fernandez's novel *L'Étoile rose* (1978) likens its characters' sufferings to a "martyrology of the [homosexual] cause" (Fernandez 1994: 130). The Grasset paperback reprint features a detail of Guido Reni's second Sebastian on its cover. Apparently St. Sebastian's queer subtext has by now grown so powerful as to be effective in marketing.[53]

Sebastian's homo-associations are now sufficiently well-grounded for gay pop culture sometimes to appropriate him in an arguably hostile fashion. In (the British) Howard Hardiman's semi-autobiographical graphic novel, *The Lengths* (2010), the protagonist sees a reprint of a work by Egon Schiele in a gay brothel where he is considering working. The poster is a self-portrait of Schiele as St. Sebastian (1915: online). It is hardly homoerotic, drawing instead on the early 20th century trope of the starving artist, martyred to his vocation. Indeed it might be another, rare example of a non-homoerotic Sebastian without a doctrinal primary reference. However, it seems the brothel management's idea was to make the customers feel more "at home" on seeing a Sebastian, any Sebastian, regardless of the original intent behind it. The fact that the narrator himself "gets the joke" reinforces this impression.

The present day, Kaye says, has witnessed yet another avatar of the plague-saint, with Sebastian now an icon of the AIDS victim (1996: 98). This meaning would not speak solely to gays, as the drug addict's needle tracks approximate Sebastian's marks of sagittation, according to Kaye. Sebastian is not the only saint to have served this new purpose, in fiction at least. In Vincent Borel's novel *Un ruban noir* (1995), the infected hero André, sunbathing, guiltily thinks of having kissed his ex-lover while his own gums were bleeding. He considers himself as a bit like St. Lawrence roasting on the grill, writhing "dans un tourbillon où la culpabilité traîne ses griffes"[54] (Borel 1995: 143). However, the basis of comparison with St. Lawrence, the (moral) burning, is a step removed from the illness itself.

As presented by Borel at least, St. Lawrence is not comparable with Sebastian

---

[53] Darwent gives one of many possible examples, a magazine cover from 2007.

[54] "in a whirlwind where guilt drags its claws."

in terms of the directness, the clarity of his tokens and their references. Moreover, the paucity of examples of non-queered AIDS Sebastians would speak to a competitive double bind, in terms of the discourse. There is competition for the role of plague saints without other attributes, whereas Sebastian is uniquely qualified to out-compete any other saint who might otherwise represent a sexual minority.

At the same time, Kaye's recognition of an undeniable self-referentiality in more recent sexually queer Sebastian portraits points towards a possible hermeneutic instability, perhaps a different kind of queerness. There are a few modern and contemporary Sebastians with no apparent sexual queerness to them, paintings by Jaff Seijas (2002: online) and William Cash (2005) furnishing examples. Matthew Kelly's sculpture, of a white-painted cello shot through with sharpened steel girders, seems to play on the concept of lovemaking as music while also being open to orthodox readings. The music a doctrinal Sebastian is built to make would be the voice of his spirit, which can communicate even when his body is broken by martyrdom. This is at least a possibly harmonious, rapturous combination of the two familiar discourses, rather than an oppressive one like Moreau's. Still, it remains the case that the cultural discourse has returned to the familiar binary field known since the Renaissance, only now it is being discussed and contested openly.

Parting Shot

This discussion has sought to establish that the cultural iconography of St. Sebastian, once it had incorporated an erotic element during the Renaissance, has maintained its dual character in a fairly stable fashion. The Western discourse of sexuality emergent in the modern era has not affected this; arguably, it has only noticed it. What seems to have gone unnoticed is a temporary disruption in this discourse, aided at times by a critical attitude, in the early and mid-19th century.

It would seem fairly uncontroversial to suggest that, given the emergence and consolidation of sexual minority movements within various Christian communities, it would be only natural that a more self-conscious "friendly blending" of the two main discourses should appear in recent figurations of Sebastian, of which I have proposed Kelly's as an example. What is less clear, and more tempting grounds for speculation, is the cultural logic behind the much earlier disruption in the dual discourse in 19th century France, and its relatively short half-life and limited dispersion into other Western cultures.

I speculate that this disruption occurred in the early 19th century in France because this was the first milieu in which an artistic revolution, in the wake of a political one, coincided with a sustained secularization in *general* cultural discourse. This coincidence made it possible for Saint Sebastian to be used as a foil for experimentation, independent of any discourse previously found in religious art. Egon Schiele's self-portrait as a martyr to art still relies on an iconic paradigm of reference, and so is more traditional than Ribot's radical materialism or Daumier's satire. Once the discourse of sexual identities had begun to develop in France, however, the homoerotic propaganda that marks Sebastian's career became self-evidently useful, and French Sebastians quickly became more like those of the country's cultural neighbours again.

The paradigm of the icon has withstood today's controversies over homosexuality. Judging from Saint Sebastian's career in Western art and literature, nothing short of a second Age of Revolution could even trouble patterns of belief and signification set by religion.[55]

References

Primary Works (literature)

Borel, Vincent
1995   Un ruban noir. [Arles]: Actes Sud.

Cocteau, Jean
1974   Les Enfants terribles [1929]. Paris: Grasset.

Crevel, René
1974   Mon corps et moi [1925]. Paris: Jean-Jacques Pauvert.

D'Annunzio, Gabriele
1911   Le Martyre de saint Sébastien: mystère en cinq actes. Libretto with original music by Claude Debussy. Paris: Durand.

Dumas, Alexandre, *fils*
1950   La Dame aux camellias [1848]. [Montréal]: Petit Format.

Eekhoud, Georges
1991   Voyous de velours ou l'autre vue. 1904, 1926 [version définitive]. Bruxelles: Labor.
1977   Cycle patibulaire [1892]. Bruxelles: Jacques Antoine.
1901   Escal-Vigor. Paris: Mercure de France.

Fernandez, Dominique
1994   L'Étoile rose [1978]. Paris: Grasset.

Flaubert, Gustave
1973   "La Légende de saint Julien l'Hospitalier". Trois contes [1877]. Éd. Samuel de Sacy. Intr. Michel Tournier. Paris: Gallimard.

Green, Julien
1995   Le Malfaiteur [1973]. Censored original 1955. Paris: Arthème Fayard.

[55] In addition to the anonymous reviewer, I thank Madelon Hartford, Michael Marten, Christopher Milligan, Katja Neumann, and Gal Ventura for their assistance with this piece.

Joyce, James
1977   A Portrait of the Artist as a Young Man [1916]. Ed. Chester Anderson. New York: Penguin.

National Council of the Churches of Christ in the United States of America
1989   The Bible NRSV. New York: Oxford University Press.

Petronius Arbiter ca. 61 AD
1986   Satyricon. Trans. J. P. Sullivan. Harmondsworth: Penguin.

Sade, Donatien Alphonse François, Marquis de
1995   Justine ou les malheurs de la vertu [1791]. Éd. Michel Delon. Paris: Pléiade-Gallimard.

Stendhal [né Henri Beyle].
1972   Le Rouge et le noir: chronique du XIXᵉ siècle [1830]. Paris: Gallimard.
1992   Voyage en France. Voyages en France. Éd. Victor del Litto. Paris: Pléiade-Gallimard.
1981   Œuvres intimes. Éd. Victor del Litto. Paris: Pléiade-Gallimard.

Primary Works (art, film and music)

Unless another (earlier) date is given, all references to internet sites were valid as of 20 June 2012.

Bermejo, Bartolomé (1430–1496/98)
Not dated   Santa Faz. Painting. Museo de Vich (Catalonia). <http://www.capillarealgranada.com/es/vn/afvn_4sacristia_4pinturas_0226.html>

Bernini, Giovanni Lorenzo
1647–1652   The Ecstasy of Saint Teresa. Marble. Santa Maria della Vittoria, Roma. WGA: <http://www. wga.hu/>
1617   St. Sebastian. Marble. Thyssen Collection, Lugano.   <http://www.cityandguildsartschool.ac.uk/news/conservation_news/bernini_marble_sculpture>

Biardeau, René II
1606–1651   St. Sebastian. Sculpture en terre cuite du Maine. Notre-Dame, Sillé-le-Guillaume. <http://www.sculpturesdumaine.culture.fr/>

Bodanza, Klaus
1977   Saint Sébastien en cuir. Cartoon. In Damase 179.

Botticelli, Sandro
1474   St. Sebastian. Oil. Staatliches Museum, Berlin. Olga: <http://www.abcgallery.com/>

Caravaggio
1602   Saint John the Baptist. Oil on canvas. Galleria Capitolina, Roma. Olga: <http://www.abcgallery.com/>

Cash, William
2005   Self-portrait as St. Sebastian. Acrylic canvas.

Corot, Jean-Baptiste
1850–1860   St. Sébastien. Oil on canvas. Olga: <http://www.abcgallery.com/>

Courmes, Alfred
1974	St. Sébastien de dos à l'écluse St.-Martin. Oil on canvas. Coll. Claude Bouquignault. <http://www.courmes.org/>
1934	St. Sébastien. Oil on canvas. Centre Pompidou, Paris. <http://www.courmes.org/>

Dalí, Salvador
1930	William Tell. Oil and collage on canvas. Moorhouse 52.

Daumier, Honoré
1852	Le Martyre de St. Sébastien. Oil on canvas. Musée Municipal, Soissons. Olga: <http://www.abcgallery.com/>
1849	St. Sébastien. Lithograph. Dresden. Brandeis Institutional Repository. <https://bir. brandeis.edu/handle/10192/2278>

Defurne, Bavo (dir.)
1996	Saint. Perf. Olaf Nollen. Silent. 10 min. Belgium.

della Francesca, Piero
c. 1444–1466	Saint Sebastian. Mixed media on wood. Pinacoteca Communale, Sancepulcro. Olga: <http://www.abcgallery.com/>

Delville, Jean
1898	The School of Plato. Oil on canvas. In: Sébastien Clerbois, In Search of the Forme-Pensée: The Influence of Theosophy on Belgian Artists, Between Symbolism and the Avant-Garde (1890–1910); n. pag. *Nineteenth-Century Art Worldwide: a Journal of Nineteenth-Century Visual Culture* 2.2 (2002): Online.

Demard, Philippe
Late 20th c.	St. Sébastien. Triptych. Oil, acrylic and gold leaf on canvas. <http://bode.diee. unica.it/~giua/SEBASTIAN/PICS/demard.jpg (Apr 2006).

Fawcett, Farrah (perf.)
1976	Farrah in "Target: Angels". Anonymous television still of Farrah Fawcett. In: *Charlie's Angels* 1: 5 (27 Oct 1976). <http://www.charliesangels.com/gallery.html>

Giordano, Luca
Ca. 1650–1653	St. Sebastian Healed by Irene. Oil. Gemäldegalerie Alte Meister, Dresden. <http://en.wikipedia.org/wiki/File:Luca_giordano,_san_sebastiano_curato_da_ irene,_1653_circa.JPG>

Giorgetti, Antonio
Ca. 1660–1670	The Martyrdom of St. Sebastian. Marble. After a design by Bernini. San Sebastiano fuori le Mure, Rome. WGA: <http://www. wga.hu/>

Hardiman, Howard
2010	The Lengths. Serialized graphic novel. Issue 1. N. pag.

Jarman, Derek and **Paul Humfress** (dirs.)
1976	Sebastiane. Perf. Leonardo Treviglio, Barney James. 90 min. UK.

Kelly, Matthew
2003	St. Sebastian. Encaustic and mixed media on musical instrument. Fort Wayne, IN. <http://bode.diee.unica.it/~giua/SEBASTIAN/PICS/kelly.jpg> (Apr 2006).

Leclerc, Pierre
Mid-17th c.	St. Sébastien. Sculpture en terre cuite du Maine. Saint-Martin, Yvré-le-Pôlin (France). <http://www.sculpturesdumaine. culture.fr/>.

Lemaire, Jean-Jacques
Mid-17th c.   St. Sébastien. Sculpture en terre cuite du Maine. Saint-Pierre, Bouër (France).
<http://www.sculpturesdumaine.culture.fr/> (Apr 2006).

Leonardo Da Vinci
1503–1506   La Gioconda [alias Mona Lisa]. Oil on canvas. Louvre, Paris. Olga:
<http://www.abcgallery.com/>
c. 1493–1498   Last Supper. Oil and tempera on plaster. Refectory of Santa Maria delle
Grazie, Milano. Olga: <http://www.abcgallery.com/>

Ménageot, François
1744–1816   Le Martyre de St. Sébastien. Oil on canvas. Haggerty Museum of Art, Mil-
waukee. WGA: <http://www.wga.hu/>

Mérillon, Noël
Mid-17th c.   St. Sébastien. Sculpture en terre cuite du Maine. Notre-Dame de l'Assomp-
tion, Congé-sur-Orne. <http://www.sculpturesdumaine.culture.fr/> (Apr 2006).

Michaelangelo Buonarroti
1537–1541   Last Judgment. Fresco. Sistine Chapel, Città del Vaticano.

Moreau, Gustave (1826–1898)
Not dated   St. Sebastian. Painting. Louvre, Paris.   <http://www.bc.edu/bc_org/avp/cas/
fnart/moreau.html/> (30 Jun 2005).
Not dated   St. Sebastian and Angel. Sanguine drawing. Louvre, Paris. In Damase 148.

Perugino, Pietro
1493   St. Sebastian (detail). Oil on wood. Galleria degli Uffizi, Firenze. Olga:
<http://www.abcgallery.com/>

Préhoust, Julien
Mid-17th c.   St. Sébastien. Sculpture en terre cuite du Maine. Saint-Rémy, Saint-Rémy-
des-Monts (France). <http://www.sculpturesdumaine.culture.fr/> (Apr 2006).

Puget, Pierre
Ca. 1663   St. Sebastian. Marble. Sta. Maria Assunta di Carignano, Genova. WGA:
<http://www.wga.hu/>

Raphael
1502–1503   St. Sebastian. Oil on wood. Accademia Carrara, Bergamo. Olga: <http://www.
abcgallery.com/>

Remy-Bieth, Michel
c. 1976   Saint Sébastien horizontal. Stained glass with mixed media. In Damase 181.

Reni, Guido
1617–1619   St. Sebastian (second painting). Oil on canvas. Prado, Madrid. In Darwent.
Ca. 1600–1610   St. Sebastian (first painting). Oil on canvas. In Darwent.

Ribot, Théodule-Augustin
1865   The Martyr Saint Sebastian. Oil on canvas. Musée d'Orsay, Paris.   <http://www.
musee-orsay.fr/>

Schiele, Egon
1915   Self-Portrait as Saint Sebastian. Poster. <http://www.egon-schiele.net>

Seijas, Jaff
2002   Self-Portrait as St. Sebastian. Ink and gouache on paper. Santa Fe. <http://bode.diee.
        unica.it/~giua/SEBASTIAN/PICS/seijas1.jpg> (Apr 2006).

Sodoma (né Giovanni Barzi)
1525   Saint Sebastian. Oil. Galleria degli Uffizi, Firenze.   <http://en.wikipedia.org/wiki/
        Sodoma/>

Suvée, Joseph-Benoît (1743–1807)
Not dated   Saint Sebastian. Oil on canvas.

Titian
1575   Saint Sebastian. Oil on canvas. The Hermitage, St. Petersburg. Olga: <http://www.
        abcgallery.com/>

Van Dyck, Sir Anthony (1599–1641)
Not dated   Saint Sebastian and the Angel. Oil. <http://www.art.co.uk/gallery/id--a40393/
        sir-anthony-van-dyck-prints.htm?ui=5BD212036D8649B5BFC44B45C5071F3C>

Verdi, Giuseppe
1849   La Traviata. Perf. Ainhoa Arteta. Cond. Alessandro Siciliani. Cincinnati Music Hall,
        Cincinnati. 25 June 1998.

Wallis, Henry
1856   Chatterton. Oil on canvas. Tate Gallery, London. Internet: http://www.tate.org.uk

Secondary, Theoretical and Critical Works

Bersani, Leo
1995   Foucault, Freud, Fantasy, and Power. *GLQ* 2.1: 11–33.

Bréhier, Louis
1918   L'Art chrétien: son développement iconographique des origines à nos jours. Paris:
        Laurens.

Cooke, Paul
2000   René Crevel's Road to Atheism. In: Paul Cook and Jane Lee (eds.), (Un)faithful
        Texts? Religion in French and Francophone Literature, from the 1780s to the 1980s;
        pp. 93–105. New Orleans: University of the South Press.

Cooper, Emmanuel
1994   The Sexual Perspective: Homosexuality and Art in the Last Hundred Years in the
        West [1986]. 2nd ed. London: Routledge.

Cooper, Sarah
2000   Relating to Queer Theory: Rereading Sexual Self-Definition with Irigaray, Kristeva,
        Wittig and Cixous. Bern: Peter Lang.

Damase, Jacques
1979   Saint Sébastien dans l'histoire de l'art depuis le XVe siècle. Intr. François Le Tar-
        gat. Paris: Jacques Damase.

Darwent, Charles
2008   Arrows of Desire: How Did St. Sebastian Become an Enduring, Homo-erotic Icon?

Independent. Newspaper. 10 Feb 2008.   <http://www.independent.co.uk/arts-entertainment/art/features/arrows-of-desire-how-did-st-sebastian-become-an-enduring-homoerotic-icon-779388.html

Delehaye, Hippolyte
1934   Cinq leçons sur la méthode hagiographique. Bruxelles: Bollandistes.

Dollimore, Jonathan
1999   Post/Modern: on the Gay Sensibility, or the Pervert's Revenge on Authenticity. In: Fabio Cleto (ed.), Camp: Queer Æsthetics and the Performing Subject: a Reader; pp. 221–236. Edinburgh: Edinburgh University Press.

Dover, K[enneth] J[ames]
1978   Greek Homosexuality. London: Duckworth.

Dyer, Richard
2002   The Culture of Queers. London: Routledge.
1993   The Matter of Images: Essays on Representations. London: Routledge.

Foucault, Michel
1976   Histoire de la sexualité I: la volonté de savoir. Paris: Gallimard.

Fussell, Paul
1975   The Great War and Modern Memory. Oxford: Oxford University Press.

Gauthier, Xavière
1971   Surréalisme et sexualité. [Paris:] Gallimard.

Greif, Martin
1982   The Gay Book of Days. New York: Lyle Stuart.

Hartford, Jason
2007   Flaubert, Ethics, and Queer Religious Art: "La Légende de saint Julien l'Hospitalier". *French Studies* 61.4 (Oct): 434–446.

Hughes, Robert
1991   The Shock of the New. rev. ed. New York: Knopf.

Kaye, Richard
1996   Losing His Religion: Saint Sebastian as Contemporary Gay Martyr. In: Peter Horne and Reina Lewis (eds.), Outlooks: Lesbian and Gay Sexualities and Visual Cultures; pp. 139–143. London: Routledge.

Koestenbaum, Wayne
1993   The Queen's Throat: Opera, Homosexuality and the Mystery of Desire. New York: Poseidon.

Le Targat, François
1979   Saint Sébastien. In Damase.

Martin, Rupert
1989   The Icon. In: Martin Rupert, New Icons: Christian Iconography in Contemporary Art; N. pag. [Coventry:] Warwick University Press.

Moorhouse, Paul
1990   Dalí. London: Bison.

Paglia, Camille
1990   Sexual Personæ: Art and Decadence from Nefertiti to Emily Dickinson. New Haven
        CT: Yale University Press.

Praz, Mario
1951   The Romantic Agony [1942]. 2nd ed. Trans. Angus Davidson. London: Oxford University Press.

Robb, Graham
2003   Strangers: Homosexual Love in the Nineteenth Century. London: Pan Macmillan.

Robinson, Christopher
1995   Scandal in the Ink: Male and Female Homosexuality in Twentieth-Century French
        Literature. London: Cassell.

Screech, Timon
2009   Sex and the Floating World: Erotic Images in Japan 1700–1820. 2nd ed. London:
        Reaktion.

Sedgwick, Eve Kosofsky
1993   Queer Performativity: Henry James's "The Art of the Novel." *GLQ* 1.1: 1–16.
1991   Epistemology of the Closet [1990]. Hemel Hempstead: Harvester Wheatsheaf.
1985   Between Men: English Literature and Male Homosocial Desire. New York: Columbia University Press.

Showalter, Elaine
1992   Sexual Anarchy: Gender and Culture in the Fin-de-Siècle. London: Virago.

Solomon-Godeau, Abigail
1997   Male Trouble: a Crisis in Representation. London: Thames & Hudson.

Thomas, Calvin
2000   Straight with a Twist: Queer Theory and the Subject of Heterosexuality. In: Thomas
        Calvin, Joseph Aimone and Catherine MacGillivray (eds.), Straight with a Twist:
        Queer Theory and the Subject of Heterosexuality; pp. 11–44. Urbana: University of
        Illinois Press.

Thompson, Colin
1975   Van Dyck: Variations on the Theme of St. Sebastian. Edinburgh: National Gallery
        of Scotland.

Tooke, Adrianne
2000   Flaubert and the Pictorial Arts: from Image to Text. Oxford: Oxford University
        Press.

Walters, Margaret
1979   The Nude Male: a New Perspective [1978]. Harmondsworth: Penguin.

Wood, Ghislaine
2000   Art Nouveau and the Erotic. London: Victoria & Albert Museum.

Wyke, Maria
1998   Playing Roman Soldiers: the Martyred Body, Derek Jarman's Sebastiane, and the
        Representation of Male Homosexuality. In: Maria Wyke (ed.), Parchments of Gender: Deciphering the Bodies of Antiquity; pp. 243–266. Oxford: Clarendon.

Whose Bones Are They Anyway?

Lindy Richardson

Abstract. – Through the creation of a series of paper artefacts comprising of skulls and printed paper bones, "Whose bones are they anyway?", attempts to move away from the age old obsession of the verification of the human bone mosaic on the walls of Saint Ursula's chapel in Cologne presented as those of 5ᵗʰ century Saint Ursula's martyred companions. Symbolically reconnecting skeletons from the jumbled bones, the aim is not to question their origins but to re-humanise this decorative wall covering. *[Saint Ursula, Cologne, art, relics, textiles]*

Artist and lecturer **Lindy Richardson**, Programme director of Textiles at Edinburgh College of Art / Edinburgh University has exhibited widely nationally and internationally.

An Unusual Activity

I am sitting in my studio making 11 skulls and the associated bones of their skeletons, threading these paper creations together with cotton. Each skull symbolically represents one of the virgin companions for every thousand appearing in the legend of Ursula, a 4ᵗʰ century Christian Saint. Of the 11,000 individuals mentioned in Saint Ursula's story and her martyred virgin companions almost all but a handful are un-named. Through these artefacts I am creating, it is my intention to validate the bones of these nameless souls which have been presented in the Church of Saint Ursula's for more than 850 years.

The skulls are crafted from printed papers, pieced together to create fragile 3 dimensional forms. Components are literally stitched together at their seams, each skull's individual pattern distinguishing it from the others. These un-named skulls are decorated treasures, beautiful artefacts, and precious riches.

Fig. 1: Paper skulls in progress

A wallpaper collage pattern is created from the decorated paper bones associated with each of the skulls, 11 pelvises, 22 tibias, and the bones necessary to complete 110 digits. Intricate designs are collaged into panels with these patterned bones placed decoratively side by side; a bone patterned wallpaper, with each and every bone relating to one of the 11 skulls.

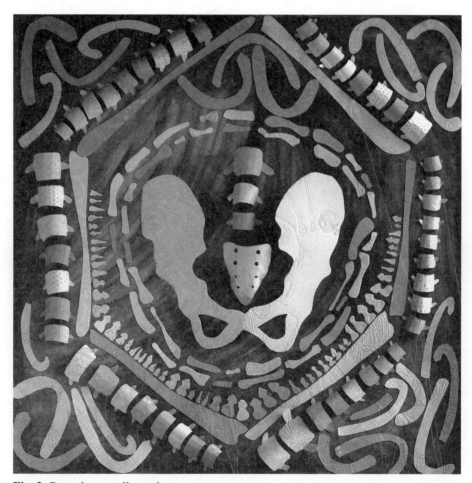

Fig. 2: Paper bone wall panel

Defined by the pattern printed onto them, which codifies the bones' relationship, the individual bones can be associated and repatriated with their skull.

Fig. 3: 11 beautiful paper skulls

Highlighting this relationship are fine cotton threads of communication, attaching the bones to their skeleton partners.

Fig. 4: Individual threads tied to each bone

Every body is sacred. In life each person is born, grows and dies as a single whole body. In death the bodies in this particular story have been disjointed, jumbled and presented as bone units of a huge spectacle. Identifying each of the skeletons and the bones which make it up as unique is vital to this project.

With a specific pattern for each of the skeletons imprinted onto the paper almost akin to an all-over tattoo of unique identification, a personal barcode, a paper skeleton visual DNA is assigned. The pattern identity is subtle yet unique.

Fig. 5: Printed recycled paper

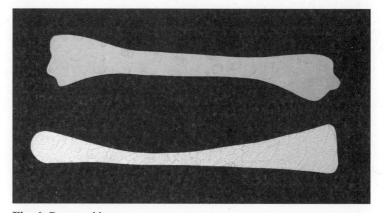

Fig. 6: Patterned bones

By branding each of the components in this project at the beginning with specific patterns accorded to each of the 11 skeletons I am identifying the bones from
the outset. Each skull and its bones are harvested from one sheet of recycled paper.
The skulls are cut and assembled, the bones cut and sorted.

Fig. 7: Skull and hand components

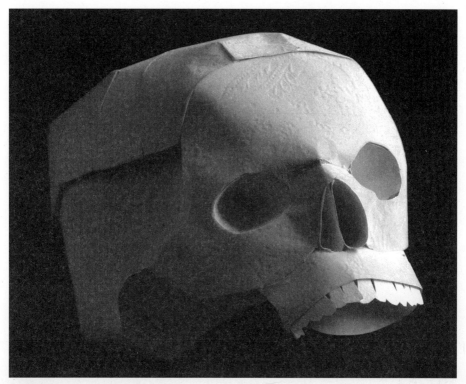

Fig. 8: Flower printed skull profile

Who am I, and what qualifies me to tell the story of Saint Ursula and the virgin martyrs of Cologne? I see myself as neither a historian, nor a hagiographer but as an artist and storyteller highlighting the bone spectacle as opposed to seeking validation for them. I am an artist who crafts eyes from stones and wool, embroiders breasts emblazoned with beautiful flowers, and pieces together shrouds from cast off sheets and old alter cloths. These artefacts tell stories of the Christian saints, presenting them in new media for a 21st century audience who may lack the religious fervour to understand and venerate the women behind these stories, but none the less are fascinated by their tales as stories. I am not making them for religious reasons; I have no idea whether I even truly believe in these people's existence. I am however bringing their stories to the fore, to a new audience. I am exposing their tales through new media. I may even be considered to have become a hagiographer, by default rather than by design.

Why am I recreating these artificial relic skulls and bones from what may appear inaccurate and inappropriate materials? The fragility and impermanence of paper has for me as an artist always held a particular poignancy. The transient nature of these artefacts in this media is at odds with the permanence of the bones they strive to represent, human bones which have graced the wall of a chapel in a European city for many hundreds of years. The significance of stitching the skulls together with thread emphasises the reconfiguration of a whole. Attaching the bones to the skulls with threads highlights the relationship between the components of each skeleton, linking them back together as a unit by attaching them to each other with a tenuous thread. The threads cross and tangle with one another drawing attention to the confusion, the criss-crossing of cottons striving to delineate the link between each of the bones with its skull.

Fig. 9: Coloured threads defining each bone

I am using my skills as a maker, as a tool, to inspire people to engage with old stories in a new way. Rather than attempting to validate the truth of these tales I am bringing them to the fore as they are, but presenting them in unexpected ways for a new audience. Recreating a myth with paper and thread for a new audience, my motivation is to raise awareness and in doing so to find a relevance in the 21st century for a huge pile of human bones as something other than simply a spectacle.

Ursula's Story

If a myth is a traditional story about a heroine, attempting to explain aspects of human behaviour, I am illustrating a myth. If a legend can be described as an old story passed down for generations but unlikely to be true, I am perpetuating a legend. If a fable can be defined as an imaginative tale, I am creating my own fable derived from an embellishment of the pieces of the story I have inherited and patchworked together through my interpretation of stories passed on through historians, hagiographers, artists and illustrators. However the nub of this artistic adventure into history and hagiography is the physical evidence which has inspired this research, that is the bones presented as those of Ursula's martyr companions in the church in Cologne. The truth behind the story pertaining to these bones is largely irrelevant. For me it is the bones in this particular story which are real as opposed to the story itself.

The Chapel in Cologne is unquestionably real. However, the focus and driver of this project is the contents of this grand church with stained glass windows, statues and religious artefacts scattered around its interior, reminding 21st century tourists of the intended purpose of this impressive building. In a far flung corner is a more intimate chapel, the golden chamber, a safe haven for treasures. Within, are arranged the busts of beautiful women, carved and sculpted, tinted and glowing with gold in parts, encasing the precious bones of those recognised as especially religious. These metal and wooden containers of bones are inscribed to identify the bone origins e.g., Cordula, Artimia and Benedicta.

Fig. 10: Reliquaries in the golden chamber

Fig. 11: Interior of the Golden Chapel, Saint Ursula's, Cologne

Above them fixed to the wall with wood and wire are sewn more and more human bones, tibias, fibulas, sacrum, digits, all arranged in beautiful decorative patterns, a visual spectacle of disjointed skeletons.

Fig. 12: Bone wall of the Golden Chamber, Saint Ursula's, Cologne

My making takes the focus away from the beautiful women, and places the spotlight onto the bones denied boxes and special cases for their presentation to the world, but instead fixed to the walls with nails and wire.

Ursula's story has been told many times in many ways. Theories of the origins of her tale, the identities of those associated with her and the truths and untruths interwoven into her story have been constructed, embellished and deconstructed for the past 1,700 years with the large bone repository of the Church of Saint Ursula's in Cologne featuring centre stage.

There are many versions of the legend of Ursula, the daughter of a King of Brittany named Notus or Maurus, however the central themes of this 4th century heroine's journey on her pilgrimage from England towards Rome and subsequently via the Rhine, with a group of companions (most versions suggesting this to be 11,000) all of whom were slain by the Hun, hold true in most tellings. Her virginity is a central theme to the story, along with her martyrdom. The people of Cologne are said to have buried the remains of Ursula and her companions, and approximately 300 years after their death the church of Saint Ursula was built over the tomb. Subsequently in 1155 a huge haul of bones were exhumed from surrounding area and claimed to be those of Ursula's companions.

Today the Golden Chamber within Saint Ursula's Church houses many of the

bones believed at the time to be these excess bones of Ursula's companions, spectacular in their numbers and display. Amongst them are the heads of Christina,
Aetherius, Pantalus, Artimia, Cordula and Benedicta. Of Ursula herself, are displayed the relics of her arm, her foot, a piece of her hairnet and a part of the garment she was wrapped in, all presented with care in reliquaries. The other bones
in the chamber are simply affixed to the walls of the chapel.

The Authenticity of the Bones in Question

The recurring preoccupation with each generation presenting or discussing this
story appears to be in their desire to authenticate the bones placed within the church
in Cologne purported to be the relics of Saint Ursula and her virgin companions.

Relics can be considered to be the material evidence of Saints and martyrs
earthly lives. In the 10th and 11th century the cult of female Saints re-emerged with
renewed interest fuelling the desire for relics. Fortuitously when in 1155 the huge
numbers of bones uncovered around the original chapel in Cologne were uncovered, a rich source of relics was pronounced. This treasure trove of bones in Saint
Ursula's in Cologne are presented as first class relics of Saint Ursula herself and
her martyr companions in both Saint Ursula's in Cologne and providing many
other skulls and bones attributed to this story to churches around Europe. Christian
Pilgrims made their way to the Holy place of The Saint or Martyrs burial and some
would occasionally manage to bring a relic back with them, almost like a souvenir. The relics were venerated with the faithful believing they could come close to
God through the relic without having to travel on long pilgrimages to Holy sites.
The wealthy bought and transported relics and over the centuries devotion to relics increased, and accordingly their value rose, the most precious being stored in
reliquaries. Originally simple boxes, over the centuries containers for these bones,
hair, pieces of wood and fragments of cloth became increasingly elaborate and rich
with precious metals and stones. Monstrances were also used to display both private and public collections, enabling the viewer to see the relic within its precious
casing. Possibly one of the most zealous holy relic collectors was King Phillip II
of Spain (1527–1598) whose collection was estimated to include 7,421 relics from
across the world, including Saint Margaret of Scotland (minus her skull),and her
husband King Malcolm. King Phillip II's collection would have been encased in
reliquaries and the items labelled with care, the various body parts and associated
saints' patronages focussing his prayers. Economically and socially it is therefore
not particularly surprising that the discovery of bones in 1155 in the vicinity of this
holy site were claimed to be those of the virgin martyrs. 12th century Christians
had no desire to doubt the validity of the "relic haul" of Cologne.

In the 19th century academic Reverend H. T. Armfield cast his doubts on the authenticity of the bone relics on display in Saint Ursula's chapel, albeit in a subtle way, in his book, *In the Legend of Christian Art*:

The legend is of great account in the modern city of Cologne, where a chapel is shown whose walls are entirely formed of bones laid one upon another-bones which affect to be those of Saint Ursula's retinue (Armfield 1869: 113).

This pattern of doubting the historic significance of the huge bone collection continued with a contemporary of Rev. H. T. Armfield, Albert Gereon Stein writing in Cologne itself. Rather than simply denouncing the authenticity of the bones, he gives his interpretation and explanation of Ursula and her companions, suggesting that Ursula and her companions may well have other identities and reasons for being in Cologne. He lays down his theory as follows:

During the 5th Century the invading Anglo Saxons may have driven the Christians of Southern Britain to the continent to Holland and Gaul as asylum seekers. Amongst this group of people were many virgins whose fathers and brothers had been slain by the Anglo Saxons, one of these being Ursula. On reaching Cologne she was honoured and popularised for her royalty and personal qualities and had many admirers and followers, particularly in young women. At this time the Huns were invading and marauding Belgium, Italy and Germany, and in October 451 advanced on the City of Cologne. The men were massacred, and the women and young maidens were led up to the north of the city. Ursula implored the women to die rather than consent to the Huns.

The Huns enraged by such constancy fell like wild beast on these Christian heroines and murdered them in the field where they were assembled (Stein, 1882: 7).

Besides these females many men and children who would probably have been slaves to the Huns were also murdered. The Huns crossed the Rhine and the remaining citizens were left with the devastation, burying the bodies in the same field where they were slain. Ursula was therefore buried alongside her British companions and the citizens of Cologne killed by the Huns.

As the greater part of those martyred were virgins and as the Church was built on the place of their martyrdom was called "The Church of The Virgins", the whole company of 11,000 persons came to be taken as a company of virgins (Stein, 1882: 9).

Stein neatly explains how this large number of people came to be buried in such huge numbers in the same site. He maintains their martyrdom as they were killed for their faith, regardless of gender or virginity.

In the *Oxford Dictionary of Saints* David Farmer cast doubt on the genuineness of the haul of relics, again drawing attention to the possibility that men and children were amongst the skeletons presented as "The virgin companions" of Saint Ursula.

In 1155 a vast collection of bones was found at Cologne, which was unhesitatingly identified with those of Ursula and her followers and were sent out as relics to many countries. The fact that some of these were men and children (the collection probably came from a large hitherto unknown burial-ground) only added to the legend (Farmer, 1978: 518).

The theories outlined by Stein and again suggested by Farmer presenting the bones in the Chapel in Cologne as unidentified women, men and possibly even children rather than virgin martyrs fuels my desire to focus attention not on the authenticity of the bones as those of Saint Ursula's female companions, but rather as unnamed massacred people.

Bone Sorting Regardless of Authentification

It is the anonymity of the bones as they become more and more detached from their human frame, disassembled units from a whole, which has moved me to create this body of work. I imagine those digging around for bone relics like gold diggers, the prize nuggets being the skulls.

The visual stimulus of the story in the layering of the bones within the earth, the plants, the piling of one body onto another in mass graves mixing together limbs, body parts and bones, arms becoming detached and lost from their original bodies, fingers from hands, legs from torsos, that I find so fascinating. In many of the renditions of the story the virgins are beheaded with the skulls abandoned and buried separated from their bodies. The bodies were exhumed as the original building of the Church took place firstly over the site of the cemetery, and subsequently as the Church grew and was rebuilt, bones and skulls taken from the surrounding land dug up from the earth not as whole skeletons but broken, detached and in separated pieces.

In Michele Roberts' fictional book *Impossible Saints*, the description of bones lining the upper walls of a chapel encapsulates the anonymity of these human remains, sorted by size and shape then placed together to form a beautiful bone mosaic.

the bones of the nameless ones, the women with no identities. Nobody knew to whom these scrap bones belonged. They had been sorted and classified simply according to shape and appearance, then made into a mosaic ... Only on a second glance did you realise that what you were looking at were massed tibias, fibulas and femurs (Roberts, 1997: 2).

Roberts portrays the forlorn anonymity of these bones, each bone becoming simply a part of a decorative pattern. Whilst Roberts' book is fictional there are clear parallels in her portrayal of this spectacle and the reliquary of Saint Ursula's in Cologne.

The hierarchy with which relic body parts appear to have been sorted and displayed in Christian churches across Europe over the centuries is fascinating. Whilst the complete or "incorrupt" body was always the most prized for any Christian Church Skulls remained a treasured part of any Saint or martyr. This is demonstrated particularly well in Saint Ursula's in Cologne where skulls are displayed with pride of place in the most extravagant of reliquaries . Draped in silk embroidered scarves or carefully stored in the heads of wooden busts of beautiful women they are accorded special treatment when compared to other parts of the skeleton.

The bones pinned onto boards and displayed on the high walls of the chapel as decorative mosaics, were viewed by scholars of the 19th and 20th centuries as an aid for closer communication with God. What purpose do these bone mosaics on the walls of Saint Ursula's fulfil in the 21st century? In our multi-cultural society where most visitors to Saint Ursula's in Cologne are visiting as tourists as opposed to worshippers, the bones housed within this building have lost their connection to God, and are instead individual calcium contributions to a breathtaking human collage of body parts, which has now become a visual spectacle devoid for most of its religious significance. In a modern context therefore without their spiritual relevance the presentation of these human remains in Saint Ursula's Church now viewed simply as a decorative wall covering may in some ways have de-humanised them. Contemporary society accords different values on any human remains, Saint, prince or pauper. Attitudes have altered through time and culture towards the preservation of skeletons, and more recently to holding any sort of human remains within museums and churches. In some cases descendants have requested re-burial of their dead and are at odds with scientists who demand that these remains be secured for the advancement of science and empirical knowledge. Bioarcheologists view

human remains [as] … sources of historical evidence that are key to understanding what really happened during the biological and cultural evolution of our species (Katzenberg and Rae-Saunders, 2008).

The BABAO (British Association of Biological Anthropology and Osteoarcheology) have produced a Code of Ethics and Standards in relation to human remains, amongst others, of which highlight my immediate observations
– Biological remains, particularly human remains, of any age or provenance must be treated with care and dignity.

What is to be gained from the scientific analysis of the bones contained within the Golden Chamber of Saint Ursula's? Professor Sue Black and her team at Dundee University's Centre for Human Anatomy have brought forensic anthropology to the British public in a recent BBC series where they demonstrate how modern technology can help to reveal the person behind the skeleton. Using CAD techniques they are able to reconstruct an image of the person through analysis of the skeleton and speculate about the causes of death, lifestyle and other aspects of the skeletons being analysed.

The factual evidence from the potential scientific test results of the bones them-selves risks throwing up ethical and religious quandaries by questioning the au-thenticity of sacred religious relics. Alongside this the ethical questions persist in the presentation and preservation of human remains.

If as artists it is our duty to reflect the culture we live in, as conduits like histo-rians, recording and passing on certain aspects of our generation to those who fol-low us, how do the responsibilities of 21st century knowledge and understanding weigh on contemporary interpretation and presentation of Ursula's story? Some may argue that it is necessary for the artist to acknowledge the potential scientific evidence of his/her generation in the interpretation and presentation of stories for a new audience. Whilst this approach and the scientific exploration may be applied to the remains held in Saint Ursula's in Cologne it is not factual or historical evi-dence which this work is seeking to gain, but rather an awareness-raising of these nameless providers of body parts. The works created here are made in reverence to whoever has unintentionally grown these bones which have become calcium units for this fascinating wall covering, rather than confirming their identities.

Does Hagiography Have to Be Historically Verified?

Considered as conduits to God, proof of miracles performed during their lifetime is required and verified by the Roman Catholic Church before the individual is declared a Saint. Eusibius Pamphilus (AD 263–339), Socrates Scholasticus (c. 380),Evagrius of Antioch, and additionally Dorotheus, Bishop of Tyre (AD 255–362) in the same era all wrote of the Saints' stories. It is from these scholars that in 1275, *The Golden Legend* by Jacobus de Vorgarine, considered one of the most important collections of the stories of the saints and martyrs, is largely indebted. Hagiographers have continued to expound on the lives and works of saints and martyrs over the centu-ries, their works consumed by contemporaries of their age, developed and ques-tioned by future generations, adapted, embellished and in some cases dismantled.

In 1905, Hippolyte Delehaye challenged the then current thinking about stories of the saints in his book *The Legends of The Saints*, from a slightly different per-spective. He plainly demonstrates the need to acknowledge the tales as a mixture of fact, pious fabrication and myth. In the preface to his book he warns:

The aim of this book is to briefly show the spirit in which hagiographical documents should be read, to sketch the methods of discriminating between the material that the historian can use and those that he should leave to the poets and Artists as their property, and to put readers on their guard against being lead away by formulas and preconceived ideas (Delehaye, 1962: xiii).

He warns of "the simple narrative of heroic days, written … with pens dipped in the blood of martyrs" (Delehaye, 1962: x). Delehaye explains that in his opinion hagiographical documents must be of a religious character and aim at edification. The writings of the hagiographer should be inspired by religious devotion and should aspire to increase devotion to the Saints, and whilst the hagiographer may be a historian, he/she is not necessarily so. It appears that Delehaye is sanctioning historical inaccuracies in the accounts of the saints, rather than correcting earlier accounts through modern interpretation. He sees the hagiographer's main role as an agent to inspire religious devotion rather than to record and impart accurate historical information and its interpretation.

What is the Relationship Between Contemporary Hagiography and the Contemporary Artist?

Considering Delehaye's theory, should the responsibility of any modern hagiographer be to build a story through a 21st century interpretation: the truth as it is seen in our own age, in our own culture, with our own technology and through our own knowledge and understanding?

Perhaps as an incidental and entirely unintentional sideline I may in turn regard myself in Delehaye's eyes as some sort of hagiographer, since the works created aspire to refocus attention on the bones presented in Saint Ursula's as something other than a visual spectacle. As an artist I consider myself an unqualified interloper in the specialised area of hagiography, an academic world of words. However, if hagiographical information looks to art as well as literature to provide the substance for its development, then perhaps historical verification and validation is not the primary justification required to make works which can be presented as hagiographic. Does the privilege of presenting this work as an artist, as opposed to a historian validate the creation of a new myth as opposed to opening up this research for scrutiny and revision by the subsequent generations who appear fixated on the true provenance and authentification of the bone mosaic gracing the walls of Saint Ursula's in Cologne?

Art and hagiography are inextricably linked throughout history, interdependency peaking in the medieval period when they functioned as the messengers for telling the stories of the Saints.

The earliest artistic evidence of visual representations of the saints largely relied on symbolism for interpretation by a mainly illiterate society and therefore artists had a prominent role in keeping their stories alive. Gregory The Great (540 AD – 604 AD) pope and legendary writer, wrote that painting was to the illiterate what writing was to readers.

Particularly in mediaeval art each saint is identified through costume, objects and animals. Each of the saints had particular patronages which accorded them specific care of certain members of society. Ursula as patroness of young females became a conduit to God for young women. Her symbols include royal garments and/or a crown identifying her regal status, an arrow which is what killed her, a white banner with red cross signifying victory over death, a palm of martyrdom, a boat representing her pilgrim's journey, and a cape sheltering her handmaidens. By using these visual keys the faithful were therefore reassured that they were indeed praying to Saint Ursula because they could identify the symbols in the painting or sculpture they knelt before. Indeed, the faithful venerating the bones of particular saints held in beautiful reliquaries were often able to identify their contents by virtue of the images on these containers of bones. During the 10th and 11th centuries with the growth in the cult of saints, art became an important addition to the relics, in some cases usurping the relics as an item for veneration. Icons, that is holy art, took on many of the characteristics and functions of the relics as a focus for prayer to aid communication with God through the saints.

The physical act of kissing or seeing a relic, of viewing an inspirational painting spoke to the faithful through their emotions rather than intellectually.

Whilst historians and writers continued to record and modify Ursula's story through the centuries, the depictions of Ursula and her entourage also adapted to the cultures who consumed them: idealistic depictions of Ursula sculpted in wood shielding young women under her cloak laden with symbolism for medieval pilgrims, or romantic illustrations of Ursula in her flowing purple cloak looking serene and beautiful delicately carrying an arrow and gazing heavenwards for the 20th century missionaries and Christian Sunday Schools and Schools. Each era created their own unique representations of Ursula appropriate to the needs of their society as consumers of these stories and artworks to portray them and venerate them.

Hans Memling (c. 1430/40–1494) working in the 15th century created a series of paintings depicting scenes of Ursula and her companions. He portrays the women in a gentle pious way.[1]

Vittore Carpaccio (b.1472) an Italian painter of the same era presents his version of an angel appearing to Ursula. The interior of the room portrayed is medieval with heavy symbolism of that era.[2]

This can be compared to a Spanish version of Saint Ursula's tale,[3] and a beautifully decorated painting by Venetian artist Niccolo di Pietro (c. 1304–1427/30).[4]

---

[1] Memling, Hans, 1489, "Saint Ursula Shrine, 1489", on *Web Gallery of Art*: http://www.wga.hu/frames-e.html?/html/m/memling/4ursula/index.html (accessed 5.1.2012).

[2] Carpaccio, Vittore, 1495, "The Dream of Saint Ursula", on *Web Gallery of Art*: http://www.wga.hu/frames-e.html?/html/c/carpacci/1ursula/2/50dream.html (accessed 5.1.2012).

[3] Lady Lever Art Gallery, 1400–1410, "'The Life of St. Ursula and the 11,000 Virgins', c. 1400–1410', by Valencian School", on *Lady Lever Art Gallery*: http://www.liverpoolmuseums.org.uk/picture-of-month/displayPicture.asp?id=49&venue=7 (accessed 5.1.2012).

[4] Pietro, Niccolò di, 1410, "Saint Ursula and Her Maidens", on *Metropolitan Museum of Art*: http://www.metmuseum.org/Collections/search-the-collections/110001670 (accessed 5.1.2012).

These artworks were illustrations of the stories of saints, used to tell the story through pictures and sculpture, the consumers, looking to art for inspiration and as a means of communication with God through a focus for their prayers. As hagiographic documents these artworks fulfilled their task of inspiring and increasing religious devotion.

The relationship between contemporary art and hagiography has never seemed more remote than it appears to be today.

We continue to study the writings and art of our predecessors to help us unravel and understand the world we inhabit, however access to information has changed dramatically over the centuries with advances in art, literacy and travel. Particularly over the past 3 decades speed and accessibility to volumes of information has transformed our relationship with knowledge and understanding. Amongst many technological advancements one of the major forces has been the advent of the worldwide web, facilitating almost instant communication across the globe. Wikipedia encourages the collective construction of information built and added to by the public. Flickr opens up the instant publication of images along with Facebook and other social networking sites. In a matter of seconds images and comments can be found, for example Thomson's photos of Saint Ursula's in Cologne.[5]

Whilst information is almost instantly accessible, the providers of that information are not always necessarily qualified to give it and therefore it is not fully verified. Forums, blogs and discussion groups abound with individuals finding a voice for their views and opinions, all of this happening almost instantly. Ursula's story is handed down through these communication streams with questionable unverified "facts" offered up akin to Chinese whispers, not unlike the oral and visual history we inherited from our predecessors who lacked literacy.

YouTube offers the facility for amateur individuals to construct and publish their own unvetted video clips, such as "Christian Martyr Economy", uploaded in 2007.[6] This video demonstrates the amateur approach to presenting a story using the tools on hand to everyone with access to a computer and the internet. Visuals, historical information and even the music of Cliff Richard (unverified) help to tell the amateur unvetted and unverified interpretation of Saint Ursula, accessible to all. Despite the rudimentary approach it could be argued that this is an example of amateur 21st century hagiography. The maker of this video has given an account of Saint Ursula's biography, described her deeds and miracles and is aspiring to increase devotion to this particular saint through words, music and images using modern tools as a means of communication.

---

[5] Thomson, Aidan McRae, 2007 "St. Ursula, Cologne", 11.6.2007, on *Flickr*; http://www.flickr.com/photos/amthomson/3201976705/ (accessed 5.1.2012).

[6] Jeremias1111, 2007, "Christian Martyr Economy", 17.10.2007, uploaded by Jeremias1111: http://www.youtube.com/watch?v=i_KiR6zai5M (accessed 5.1.2012).

In contrast, the video uploaded by madelinesweeney333 (2008)[7] takes a more academic approach to the same subject: the commentator again presents another interpretation to the story accompanied by a visual tour of the interior of Saint Ursula's Church in Cologne. This clip is presented in a historical more factual way. It may be argued that the maker is neither an artist nor a hagiographer. The presentation of the story of Ursula lacks passion and vision of faith. The piece does not inspire religious devotion. This might lead us to ask if it is a requirement of a hagiographer to show an uncritical and reverential regard for their subject?

How Has the Visual Portrayal of The Saints Stories Been Interpreted and What Influences Our Interpretation and Presentation in the 21st Century?

In contemporary society, artists talk and write about their artwork in order to aid interpretation by the spectators, as opposed to placing paintings or artefacts into galleries, homes or churches which might have been the norm in the past. Indeed with the vast array of media on tap to reach audiences, Artists increasingly produce works through social networking, film and video, as opposed to traditional paintings or sculpture. Artworks can be virtual and transient, using a myriad of materials and settings to communicate concepts and ideas with audiences which do not demand symbolic interpretations but may well require, or be aided by other forms of explanation for full interpretation and appreciation. Quick Response (QR) Codes can be attached to artworks linking the viewer straight to websites with in-depth information to aid understanding or interpretation. Complex connections can be linked with multi sensory information relating to the work, for example, music and voice, written word, film, TV. etc.

Since previous generations of artists' portraying the saints were telling their stories for religious teaching and veneration, finding relevance for Ursula's story in the 21st century with diminishing Christian belief and observation is a challenge in itself.

In both art and science each generation is challenged to review and develop the stories and material of the previous generation, utilising current thinking and technology in a relevant setting. Over the centuries writers and thinkers have challenged Ursula's story, developed it and provided what they believe to be their truth of the legend, mostly focussing on the explanation for the huge numbers of people involved in this story.

As an artist I see my role as an agent for the 21st century. I am studying a woman

---

7 madelinesweeney333, 2008, "St. Ursula", 13.10.2008, uploaded by madelinesweeney333: http://www.youtube.com/watch?v=TcSiREoP-k8 (accessed 5.1.2012).

and a group of people from hundreds of years ago. My goal, as I see it, is not to illustrate the story I have researched, but to challenge my contemporaries to take up this story on new levels. By re-engaging with physical materials and a narrative supported by the physical evidence of a room full of human bones, I aspire to re-connect contemporary audiences with the human element of this story. The intention of these works is not simply as an illustration of the story of Saint Ursula handed down from generations, but rather as a challenge to re-visit the bones on display which have caused controversy for many generations.

I do not present myself as a historian; however, as an artist my expectation might be to inspire creative and alternative approaches to the subject, by inviting people to focus on and question the human ethical presentation of this bone spectacle as opposed to questioning their authenticity as saints and martyrs. The work I have produced aspires to sanctify the bone mosaics within the chapel of Saint Ursula as those of human beings regardless of origin.

How contemporary society views and presents theories on the existence of these bones provided the initial drive for my research, however rather than authenticating the bones the aim of this project aspires to help to re-humanise them. Indeed questioning the role for this visually fascinating interior, this saint and these relics in contemporary culture has focussed the research. The contribution art has to make, and the relationship of the artist to 21st century technology, knowledge and understanding in the modern re-interpretation and presentation of this bone collection to a 21st century audience is also significant. Does the part an artist has to play in contemporary society carry with it the privilege of validating any works created in response to myths, tales and legends without scrutiny of history or science simply by presenting them as art? The making of art is not about the making of truth or verifying historical facts, it is a process of authentification in itself. Truth in art does not require the evidence and theoretical substantiation expected by historians or scientists. My endeavours to bring the story of the bones lining the walls of the golden chamber of Saint Ursula's of Cologne exist as a collection of paper artefacts which I present as an authentic trigger; their role being to encourage the viewer to engage with the story and the people whose bones have been used to illustrate this story for centuries. The bones presented in Saint Ursula's were presented as conduits to God, as objects to be venerated. The paper skulls and bones are presented as a conduit to the anonymous people behind these precious bones. As such they complete the link between God, Saint Ursula and her companions and the original anonymous bones regardless of their provenance and authentification. The paper skulls and bones have become symbolic conduits to the story, the truth or otherwise no longer relevant. By doing so I believe this may inadvertently arouse religious edification and new understanding. If this is the case then I might present myself as both an artist and a hagiographer to Saint Ursula and her companions in Cologne. This however is merely an incidental to the main ambition of

Fig. 13: Bone wallpaper

these artworks which persists to incite and inspire a new visualization of the people behind the human bones currently pinned to the walls of a chapel in the city of Cologne. One skull and 206 bones for each one thousand virgins of the legend arranged in one huge complex pattern with the roman numerals M.XI.V marked out in bones: 11 thousand virgins, a symbolic wallpaper memorial.

References Cited

Armfield H. T.
1869   The Legend of Christian Art. Salisbury: Brown & Co.

Carpaccio, Vittore
1495   "The Dream of Saint Ursula", on *Web Gallery of Art*: http://www.wga.hu/frames-e.html?/html/c/carpacci/1ursula/2/50dream.html (accessed 5. 1. 2012).

Delehaye, Hippolyte
1962   The Legend of the Saints. London: Geoffrey Chapman.

Farmer, David
1978   Oxford Dictionary of Saints. Oxford University Press: Oxford.

Jeremias1111
2007   "Christian Martyr Economy", 17. 10. 2007, uploaded by Jeremias1111: http://www.youtube.com/watch?v=i_KiR6zai5M (accessed 5. 1. 2012).

Katzenberg, Mary Ann and Shelley Rae-Saunders
2008   Biological Anthropology of the Human Skeleton. 2nd ed. Hoboken, New Jersey: Wiley & Sons.

Lady Lever Art Gallery
1400–1410   "'The Life of St. Ursula and the 11,000 Virgins', c. 1400–1410', by Valencian School", on *Lady Lever Art Gallery*:   http://www.liverpoolmuseums.org.uk/picture-of-month/displayPicture.asp?id=49&venue=7 (accessed 5. 1. 2012).

madelinesweeney333
2008   "St. Ursula", 13. 10. 2008, uploaded by madelinesweeney333: http://www.youtube.com/watch?v=TcSiREoP-k8 (accessed 5. 1. 2012).

Memling, Hans
1489   "Saint Ursula Shrine, 1489", on *Web Gallery of Art*: http://www.wga.hu/frames-e.html?/html/m/memling/4ursula/index.html (accessed 5. 1. 2012).

Pietro, Niccolò di
1410   "Saint Ursula and Her Maidens", on *Metropolitan Museum of Art*:   http://www.metmuseum.org/Collections/search-the-collections/110001670 (accessed 5. 1. 2012).

Roberts, Michelle
1997   Impossible Saints. London: Little Brown and Company.

Stein, Albert Gereon
1882   The Church of Saint Ursula and her companions in Cologne: Its memorials, monu-
       ments and curiosities. Cologne: A. Seche.

Thomson, Aidan McRae
2007   "St. Ursula, Cologne", 11.6.2007, on *Flickr*:   http://www.flickr.com/photos/
       amthomson/3201976705/ (accessed 5.1.2012).

St. Joseph as Loving Father
in Seventeenth-Century Hispanic Devotional Painting

Josefa de Óbidos and Diego Quispe Tito

Jean Andrews

Abstract. – This essay offers an overview of the changing iconography of St. Joseph as father of the child Jesus in Hispanic devotional painting during the course of the seventeenth century. These changes were driven by evolving devotional practice and new emphases introduced by the Church in Spain, Portugal and their colonies in Latin America. The essay examines works by two painters in particular: the Portuguese Josefa de Óbidos and the Inca Diego Quispe Tito, each working on the margins of the respective metropoli, and explores the uniqueness of the gloss provided by each artist on the iconography of St. Joseph in the mid-seventeenth century. *[St. Joseph, Quispe Tito, Josefa, iconography, father, St. Teresa]*

Jean Andrews, Jean Andrews is Associate Professor of Hispanic Studies at the University of Nottingham. She has published on Hispanic religious painting of the sixteenth and seventeenth centuries, baroque festal culture in Spain and Latin America and eighteenth and nineteenth-century opera on Hispanic themes. She also writes on and translates modern poetry in Spanish.

In the mid seventeenth century in Spain, Portugal and the two most important viceroyalties of Latin America, New Spain (Mexico) and Peru, the depiction of St. Joseph in pictorial devotional art underwent significant change. The evolution of the iconography of St. Joseph in Spain and Mexico from the sixteenth to the eighteenth centuries has recently been comprehensively documented by Charlotte Villaseñor Black (Villaseñor Black 2006). Building on Villaseñor Black's framework, and the work of Joseph Chorpenning (1992), this article will examine representations of St. Joseph originating somewhat further from the metropoli by two artists who probably had little direct communication with the great centres of European and Hispanic art at the time. It will be argued that their comparative isolation from these centres led to the inclusion of layers of nuance in their paintings which, while reflecting the milieu in which the work was produced, added connotations which might not have been considered either orthodox or sufficiently respectful of the persons of the Holy Family closer to the seat of church and state power.

It is important to note that the figure of St. Joseph carried political as well as religious significance in the early modern period and nowhere more so than in the Hispanic realms (Chorpenning 1992: 31–35). He was installed as patron saint of Spain in 1679, by Charles II, the last Habsburg monarch, thereby displacing St. James the Great who had been the celestial champion of Spanish Christians since the wars of Reconquest against the Moors began in the eighth century. Yet, fearful of drawing the wrath of the legendarily fiery apostle down on his kingdom, the pious, not to say superstitious, king rescinded the investiture of St. Joseph and reinstated St. James the following year. In the Americas, however, St. Joseph was more securely positioned. The patronage of the Conquest and Conversion of Mexico had been awarded to him in 1555. In 1679 this was formalised as patronage of the viceroyalty of New Spain and he would be joined in 1746 by the Virgin of Guadalupe (Villaseñor Black 2006: 157, 13). In the other great viceroyalty of the Spanish New World, Peru, St. Joseph would come to share his patronage with the first female saint of the Americas, St. Rose of Lima, in 1671.

The temporary elevation of St. Joseph to the status of full national patron of Spain was the symbolic culmination of a movement which, in the Hispanic world, had its first major impetus in the lifelong devotion of the reforming mystic, St. Teresa of Avila (1515–1582). She believed herself to have been cured of a very grave illness, as a young postulant around 1539, by St. Joseph, and ever afterwards applied herself to the promotion of the cult of this most pragmatic of saints, dedicating all her convents to him (Chorpenning 1992: 5–15). Early in her autobiography, the *Life*, she explains that Joseph was the most powerful of saints because as a child on Earth, Jesus, his step-son, had to obey him. She argues that as Jesus was a perfect son, such filial respect must therefore be expected to hold in Heaven:

this glorious Saint in my experience helps with everything and the Lord wants us to understand that just as He was subject to him on Earth, as he had the name of being His father though he was His tutor, he could demand of Him thus in Heaven anything that is asked of him (Comas 1984: 28–29)[1].

Furthermore, she suggests that Joseph's role in educating and nurturing Jesus should be given as much recognition as that of his mother, the Virgin Mary:

I don't know how anyone can think about the Queen of the Angels, about all the time she passed with the Child Jesus, and not give thanks to St. Joseph for how well he helped them along (Comas 1984: 28–29)[2].

This apprehension received powerful reinforcement over twenty years later. Shortly after a vision of St. Clare encouraged her to carry on her conventual reforms, she had a vision of the Blessed Virgin and St. Joseph, on the Feast of the Assumption (August 15th, 1561) while staying in a Dominican convent (Comas 1984: 205–

---

[1] "a este glorioso Santo tengo expiriencia que socorre en todas y que quiere el Señor darnos a entender que ansí como le fue sujeto en la tierra, que como tenía nombre de padre siendo ayo, le podia mandar ansí en el cielo hace cuanto le pide" (Comas 1984: 28–29).

All translations are the author's.

[2] "[…] no sé cómo se puede pensar en la Reina de los Ángeles, en el tiempo que tanto pasó con el Niño Jesús, que no den gracias a San Josef por lo bien que les ayudó en ellos" (Comas 1984: 28–29).

207). While this encounter bore more relevance to her personal devotional practice (in private Teresa had been going through a period of feeling overcome by her own sinfulness and of consequent reluctance to attend Mass), it also strengthened her public championing of St. Joseph. In the vision she had a sense of two figures dressing her in a pure white garment which had the effect of making her feel completely free from sin. The Blessed Virgin then took her by both hands and assured her that she was very happy that the new convent (her first foundation) was to be dedicated to St. Joseph, adding that she and St. Joseph would ensure that she was protected by the Lord and by Jesus Christ, whatever difficulties she encountered. The Virgin appeared to her in white, she was very beautiful and very young but not easily discernible as a human form. St. Joseph was even more elusive:

I did not see our glorious St. Joseph so clearly, even though I could well see that he was here, like those visions which I have said, which cannot be seen (Comas 1984: 206)[3].

By 1597 the devotion of St. Teresa's reformed order, the Discalced Carmelites, to St. Joseph was underlined by the publication of the *Summario de las excelencias del glorioso S. Ioseph Esposo de la Virgen María (Summary of the Excellencies of the Glorious St. Joseph, Husband of the Virgin Mary)*, also known as the *Iosefina*, by Fray Gerónimo Gracián de la Madre de Dios (Manero Sorolla 2001: 21; Villaseñor Black 2006: 33). Fray Gerónimo (1514–1614), who had been expelled by the Observant Carmelites in 1592, would become the first superior of the Discalced order. This compendium (initially published in Rome in Spanish and Italian) constitutes the first major work on St. Joseph. In it, Fray Gerónimo provides a summary of extant writing on Joseph, from the beginnings of Christianity to his own time, asserting, with conventional modesty, that it were better that he should summarise all these authors so that what he says is not mistaken for his own invention (Gracián 1609: paratexts "Los libros"). In the "Third Excellence of St. Joseph", Gracián maintains that Joseph is of the noblest blood within Jewish tradition and handsome as those who are noble must be. This allows him later on to beg, rather playfully, the question as to why virtue which is beautiful in itself should have been equated with physical ugliness and, specifically in the case of Joseph, why this metaphor should translate as great age. Citing Marcus Vigerius' (1446–1516) *Incarnatione Dominica* as proof, he completes his argument by asserting that, contrary to established pictorial convention, Joseph, who has to be the breadwinner for a young family and engage in manual labour, must therefore be a young man:

And if in paintings he is shown as elderly, this is because he was a wise, prudent man of mature counsel, and in order to avoid the frivolous thoughts of stupid and weak people, to whom it might seem that two persons of such youth and beauty living together might

---

[3] "A el glorioso San Josef no vi tan claro, aunque bien vi que estaba allí, como las visiones que he dicho, que no se ven" (Comas 1984: 206).

not be able to converse with such ineffable purity, not remembering that Joseph was most chaste and chastity is of more worth in the attainment of purity, than great age (Gracián 16-9: Fol. 1, 12–13)[4].

Thus, because the *Josefina* was widely read in Spain and the New World, the template was set for the Hispanic St. Joseph to become a young and handsome man in all depictions. In addition to the perennial ubiquity of the Nativity, which usually included Joseph, the Betrothal or Marriage of the Virgin and St. Joseph, and the Dream of St. Joseph were frequently commissioned topics. However, and in accordance with St. Teresa's apprehension of him as central figure in the bosom of a loving family, by far the most interesting and popular images were those of the Holy Family with Jesus as a small child. These are best exemplified by Murillo's Holy Family paintings with their emphasis on domestic felicity, relative poverty and St. Joseph as a good and loving father: for example, *The Holy Family with the Little Bird* (Prado, 1650), *The Holy Family* (National Gallery of Ireland, c. 1650 and its cognate, in St. Stephen's Cathedral, Budapest) or the later *Two Trinities* (National Gallery, London, 1682). The persons of the Holy Family are in general dressed as working-class people in inexpensive fabrics in these depictions, with Joseph usually in combinations of beige-brown and grey. He is, in the main, young, handsome and smiling, and he enjoys a very close and affectionate relationship with his son.

In the years before Murillo produced his interpretations of the Holy Family, the two great Spanish theorists of painting made significant statements on the subject on canvas and in writing. The Sevillian painter and theorist, Francisco Pacheco (1564–1644), an orthodox advocate of Council of Trent strictures on correct religious art, included an important note on the representation of St. Joseph in his posthumously published *Arte de la Pintura* (1649). Basing himself on Book 4 of the *Josefina*, where the source deployed in this instance is the visionary St. Bridget of Sweden, Pacheco discusses his own *Dream of St. Joseph* (1604), painted for the Jesuit chapel of St. Hermenegildo in Seville and now kept in the Real Academia de Bellas Artes de San Fernando in Madrid (Bassegoda i Hugas 2001: 599–602). This painting is a rendering of St. Joseph, assailed by doubt as to the virtue of his 3-months pregnant wife and having decided to leave her, receiving a vision of the Archangel Gabriel who, at the behest of the Virgin, comes to him in a dream to assuage his fears (Matthew 1: 18–250; Villaseñor Black 2006: 50–53). St. Joseph, depicted as a virile and slender man in his thirties, following Gracián, sleeps on a carpenter's bench outside his house. At Joseph's feet there is a bundle of cloth-

---

[4] "Y si en las pinturas se pinta anciano, es, porque era varon sabio, y prudente, y de maduro consejo, y para obviar la ligereza de los pensamientos de personas torpes, y flacas; que les pareciera que viviendo juntas dos personas de tanta hermosura y poca edad, no podrían conversar con tan inefable pureza: no acordándose, que Ioseph era castissimo y la castidad vale mas para la pureza, que la mucha edad" (Gracián 16-9: Fol. 1, 12–13).

ing tied with a cord with a staff lying across it. The angel points with his left hand back to the house and with his right lightly touches the back of St. Joseph's head. Pacheco highlights Joseph's trade as a carpenter by lining six of the most important of the tools of Joseph's trade up against the humble house in the background, held together by a rope, and in his description of his own painting, he cites various authorities to prove that Joseph was a carpenter. In doing so, he reinforces a key indicator of Joseph's working-class occupation and lifestyle which would be given greater visual prominence by Murillo. As if to balance this mundanity with celestial beauty, he then notes that his angel Gabriel is very handsome, "muy hermoso". Indeed, his depiction of the archangel shows a blond and androgynous being, with the idealised, soft-focussed roundness and softness of facial feature and hair reserved for women. His wings are made of real-looking dark feathers and he wears a large, scalloped triangular gold brooch set with a single large stone on his breastbone over an aubergine-coloured tunic. As the colours have faded over time, this might originally have been a more intense purple. St. Joseph, on whose physical features Pacheco does not comment, is a much more realistic figure. He is dressed in a dark pink tunic and blue cloak, a combination usually associated with the Virgin. He wears a pair of sturdy sandals, indicative of the long journey facing him, and he has big strong hands with prominent veins, typical of one engaged in manual labour. His body is draped in sleep with great elegance, nonetheless, and his head and face are reminiscent of depictions of the adult Christ in contemplation of his fate: the Man of Sorrows. While the depiction of strong family resemblances between Christ and the male members of his immediate family, such as his blood relative St. John the Baptist, and even his stepfather St. Joseph (indicative of a benign deception engineered by God to protect Christ from the stigma of illegitimacy in childhood), were the accepted norm in post-Tridentine Hispanic art, Pacheco's Joseph is perhaps too like the suffering Christ (Villaseñor Black 2006: 76). Given his palette, which is typically Sevillian and sombre, in tones of red and brown, the overall effect might be construed as pointing more strongly towards the suffering of Christ and the sorrows of the Virgin, than the dilemma and individuality of St. Joseph.

A further variation on the Holy Family theme involved portraits of father and son, without the Blessed Virgin, consonant with the emphasis placed on St. Joseph's nurturing nature in Gracián and his sources. Pacheco's Madrid-based coeval and fellow theorist of painting, the Florentine-born Vicente Carducho (1568–1638) produced an important model for the representation of St. Joseph with Christ as a little boy in 1634 (Villaseñor Black 2006: 91; Musée d'Art et d'Histoire, Narbonne). As with Pacheco, his iconography proves useful in making plain the development of such compositions. Here, a full-length St. Joseph, with long dark brown hair and beard stands with his dark-blond son, aged about three or four, seated, or rather floating in a seated position, in the crook of his left arm. As in Pacheco, the face and figure of Joseph could easily be mistaken for that of the adult Christ, if it were not for the symbols associated with Joseph included in the image. In his left hand, he holds a tall staff with a lily, for chastity, sprouting from its head. Christ's left hand also grasps the staff, above his father's. In his right hand, Joseph holds a pale rose, the symbol of God's love for mankind, by its stem, while the child's hand wraps round it, above his father's, just touching the underside of the petals. Above the two figures the dove representing the Holy Spirit hovers in a pool of golden heavenly light, surrounded by putti in a glory on either side of a simple stone arch. Joseph is clad in a luminous grey tunic and a flowing golden cloak while Jesus wears a red tunic and dark blue cloak, the combination usually associated with the Virgin. The fabrics are beautifully rendered by Carducho as the finest of silk in luxuriant folds, the emphasis still, in the 1630s, on the magnificence of the Son of God and his saintly, and simply-haloed, step-father. Joseph's mournful gaze is directed downwards towards his left and Jesus looks across Joseph's body to the right. The child's face is remarkably mature in its expression of sorrowful awareness of what is to come. Because Jesus seems to float over rather than rest in the crook of Joseph's elbow, the strongest physical link between adult and child is their joint grasp of the lily staff on the left and the pale rose on the right, a relationship rooted in theological symbolism rather than family affection.

This particular father and son iconography would undergo subtle emendations in the hands of two artists removed, by geography and circumstance, from the centres of Hispanic art in Seville and Madrid: Josefa de Óbidos (1630–1684) working in a small town north of Lisbon and the indigenous Peruvian, Diego Quispe Tito (1611–1681) in Cuzco, in the high Andes. Unlike Pacheco, Carducho and Murillo, all three highly successful painters who could call on the very best of materials and set up well-staffed and equipped workshops, Josefa worked more or less on her own, in relatively small format and often without access to the more expensive materials. While the Inca Quispe Tito in Cuzco operated a highly successful studio, he did so in an aesthetic and cultural environment which was totally different from that of metropolitan Spain.

Josefa de Óbidos, also known as Josefa de Ayala, was born in Seville in 1630, to a Portuguese painter father, Balthazar Gomes Figueira and a Spanish mother, Catarina Camacho Cabrera Romero. Her godfather was the Sevillian painter, Francisco de Herrera the Elder, a friend of the family. Josefa spent the first eleven years of her life in Seville, from 1634 in the household of her maternal grandfather, Juan Ortiz de Ayala and in close contact with Francisco de Herrera. It is assumed she returned to Portugal some time after the restoration of Portuguese independence after the 60 years of Spanish rule in 1640. From 1644, Josefa lived, probably as a boarder as opposed to a postulant, in the Benedictine convent of St. Anne in Coimbra, where she painted her first recorded works. At some point between 1647 and 1653 Josefa left the convent of St. Anne, passed a period of time in the convent of

St. Maria de Celas and then returned to her family home in Óbidos. Apart from whatever she may have learnt from her father and her godfather, Josefa was more or less self taught. While there have long been theories about a possible journey to Flanders and another to Italy, it is most likely that this singular woman, who remained unmarried and made a living as a painter in a small medieval town some distance from the seat of power, spent the entirety of her adult life, once she left the convents in Coimbra, walled up in the family home, painting and taking delight in the small blessings of a domestic existence, in the words of Vitor Serrão "a woman of solitary habits and mystical tendencies" (Serrão 1992: 19–24).

The Teresian ideal of conventual life had become embedded in Portugal over the last 20 years of the sixteenth century, due in no small part to the support of Teutonio de Braganza, the influential archbishop of Évora from 1570–1602 and Philip II's brother and viceroy, the Cardinal-Archduke Albert. Indeed, Fray Gerónimo Gracián was in Lisbon in 1585, precisely in order to play a part in the establishment of the Discalced Carmelites in the Portuguese capital, and in making peace between the Observant Order and the Discalced movement (Manero Sorolla 2001: 23–26). In the 1670s, Josefa de Óbidos undertook a couple of major commissions for the Discalced Carmelite Convent of Cascais, outside Lisbon: her series of six paintings depicting the life of St. Teresa of Avila (1672) and her *Child Jesus, the Saviour of the World* (1674), all of which are now kept at the Parish Church in Cascais. The Child Jesus, an essential image in any Discalced convent due to the emphasis placed on devotion to the Child Jesus by St. Teresa, would go on to be her most popular and frequently reproduced image (Moura Sobral 1992: 63–65). Two years later, she produced a *Holy Family* for a convent in Évora (Museu Regional, Évora) which appears in the inventory of items donated, some time after the dissolution of the convents in 1834, by the archbishop of Évora, Frei Manuel do Cenáculo Vilas-Boas Nero to Évora public library (Serrão 1992a: 196). The painting shows the Child Jesus standing on the left of a round table lit in chiaroscuro by a central candle. Wearing a red tunic, with gold trim at the neck and a dark blue sash, he blesses the repast on the table (half a melon, three uncut raw carrots, three whole fish, salt and a loaf of bread) as Mary, in the centre, and Joseph on the right pray with fine, long-fingered, steepled hands. Mary wears her traditional red tunic and dark blue mantle, as opposed to the working-class garb of many contemporary Murillo Virgins, with a touch of individuality and possibly local craftsmanship visible on a series of embroidered vertical bands sewn onto the slightly ruched sleeves of her white shift while Joseph, on the other hand, wears the dark grey tunic and beige mantle common to most seventeenth-century Iberian representations of him. The Virgin's gaze seems absorbed in her son and his precocity while Joseph's gaze is more inward, as if he does not quite belong to the mother-son telepathy at this point. Such a depiction would, of course, be utterly correct, as Mary was in the seventeenth century, and in Iberia above all, believed by a majority to have been conceived without sin (even though this doctrine would only finally be proclaimed by Pope Pius IX in 1854) while Joseph, however chaste, was a mere sin-prone mortal and not blessed with such divine insight (Moura Sobral 1998: 210–212; Bassegoda i Hugas 2001: 575–577; Stratton 1994: *passim*). This hierarchy of holiness is made explicit in the three haloes: Joseph's is a simple fine gold ring over his head, the Virgin has the same gold ring with a nodule of light with a couple of rays emanating from it while Jesus has a much larger nodule of light with several strong rays and no outer ring. In addition, Joseph's skin tone is darker than that of Mary and Jesus, befitting his mortal status, and he is not a brightly lit as they are. He is, however, quite as beautiful.

Josefa, in her relative isolation and possibly because it would have been either difficult or impossible for her to use human models, developed a language of form for human figures which renders them as soft-contoured figurines. If religious painting in the seventeenth century can be said to distinguish human children and adults from putti or cherubim, and sometimes seraphim, by softening the lines and infantilising the features of the cherubim in comparison to the realistically-depicted human beings, then this is an approach Josefa brings to her representation of humans and angels alike. At times, her modelling of the human figure is not that different from that of her slightly later contemporary, Bento Coelho (1620–1708), court painter to King Pedro II, but he, much-travelled and lionised in his lifetime, shows a much broader and more conventional range of modelling in his work (Moura Sobral 1998: 28–38). However, while it is the case that in much baroque painting, the female figures, and especially the face and figure of the Virgin, are rendered in a more soft-focussed or idealised manner than the males, Josefa does not distinguish between the genders and her male figures are every bit as soft-contoured and cherubic as her females. Moura Sobral characterises her gift as being that of transmitting, in all its bathetic innocence, the "gluttonous and sublime fine-pointed religiosity of her own time" (Serrão 1992: 45). This quality of innocence is epitomised in her attitude to male figures. Thus, the Joseph of the Évora *Holy Family*, with his beautiful and realistic tapered hands and well-rendered drapery, has a face which is unlined, doe-eyed and peach-skinned, his beard looking like the hesitant sproutings of early adolescence. What she achieves, as in all her best work, is a sense of an instant of spiritual transcendence caught in time, on this occasion, in a group of beatified beings whose purity of intention and experience could not be questioned.

Josefa's soft-texturing of the figure of St. Joseph is very well exemplified in a miniature of St. Joseph with the child Jesus, done in oils on copper, a support Josefa employed with some frequency, ten years previously, in 1661 (Private Collection, Lisbon; Serrão 1993: 135). The image is significant, not only because of its depiction of St. Joseph with his infant son on his knee, but because, given its size, it was almost certainly a commission from a private individual, not a member of the clergy or nobility, for personal devotional purposes (Brown 2002: 35–36). The representation of St. Joseph with the child Jesus on his knee was relatively rare in Hispanic painting, largely because of a concern that the Virgin's lap might be seen as evocative of the throne of wisdom or the throne of Solomon with its implication of the Virgin's role in the redemption of Mankind, a claim that should not be made for Joseph (Villaseñor Black: 106). A private commission may, however, have allowed the artist more freedom of interpretation.

The copper support lends a filminess to the depiction. It allows for extremely detailed brushwork and also confers a, predictably, warm golden hue, on the composition. St. Joseph is pictured seated with his right knee raised to provide a perch for his son and his left disappearing below the frame. He wears a soft red tunic, with a buttoned, unstructured collar and a gold brocade cloak, red on gold with gold thread detail and edging, flowing from over his left shoulder across his chest and over his right elbow, against which the child is seated. He wears a crown of flowers, wild red roses and white or mixed pink and white carnations, with some greenery, and resting against his left arm is the rod with lilies blooming from it. A halo of fine gold spokes surrounds Joseph's head with a glory of three putti on either side. The blond child sits on his father's knee, holding a single white lily, the same as those on Joseph's staff, in his right hand, while his left forearm rests just below his father's collar button. His is dressed in a very fine lace shift, trimmed with exquisite lace flowers on the neck and cuffs with a grey skirt made of fine fabric. Joseph supports his son's seated position by holding his right foot in his own left hand. Father and son have the same doe eyes, the same milky complexion (Joseph's more heightened on the cheeks), the same gesture of the head, leaning over the right shoulder, the same pensive but not tragic gaze and indeed the child Jesus shares his facial features with the six putti overhead. The impression is of a beautiful harmony tinged with melancholy. The child appears to move towards the viewer by bracing himself against his father's breast, while Joseph's gaze remains inward and his physical focus on his son.

According to sources Josefa would have been familiar with, such as Frei Isidoro Barreira's *Tractado das signifaçoens das plantas, flores, e fructos que se referem na Sagrada Escriptura*, 1622 (Treatise on the Meanings of the Plants, Flowers and Fruit Which Are Found in the Holy Scriptures) the wild red rose, usually associated with the Virgin, symbolised martyrdom. The white carnation, which Isidoro does not gloss since it does not appear in the Scriptures, is according to legend, the product of a tear the Virgin wept on her way to Calvary and therefore emblematic of maternal love; it may also refer to conjugal happiness (Hatherly 1992: 81). The mixed carnation signifies affection (Serrão 1992a: 248). Alternating in St. Joseph's crown, the flowers effect a transfer of the Virgin's maternal love to the father, and possibly the awareness of the martyrdom of Christ to come, inherent in the child's biological mother, to his adoptive father. Thus the father is feminised, not simply by the soft-focus depiction, but also by the language of flowers, and this is further intensified by the fine fabrics in which the two figures are dressed. Joseph is also raised to his step-son's level of divinity since there is no distinction in skin tone between child and man, god and mortal.

A much more common depiction of father and son, and one utterly in line with the Church-fomented emphasis in the Hispanic world in the seventeenth century on involving fathers in the upbringing of their children, with Joseph as a model, was that of Joseph leading his son by the hand as they go for a walk (Villaseñor Black: 95–97). The Museu Nacional de Arte Antiga, Lisbon, has an altar panel, painted by Josefa in 1670, showing Joseph and Jesus, as a boy of perhaps seven or eight, walking together in the countryside. In the nature of altarpieces, and secondary panels in particular, this is not the most highly finished of Josefa's output (Serrão 1992a: 172). As a piece of public art, the iconography is much more in keeping with the accepted mid-seventeenth century norm. Joseph, the same figurine as in the other two paintings, leaning slightly forward, holds Jesus by the left hand in his right while in his own left he holds a very long lily stem, with six white flowers sprouting from it. He wears the grey tunic and golden beige mantle of the mid-seventeenth century Joseph, with a golden beige undershirt and a couple of Josephine touches of detail: a soft fastened collar on his tunic and a buttoned, gathered sleeve opening to show the undershirt. Joseph and Jesus wear identical sturdy sandals in brown leather with two leather studs holding the thongs together. Joseph has a simple narrow golden halo while Jesus has a little spoked starburst, just as in the Évora *Holy Family*. The blond Jesus wears a dark pink tunic, symbolic of his impending martyrdom and his love for humanity, and an aquamarine mantle with a golden beige cummerbund, to pick up the golden beige of his father's mantle. Jesus holds a short staff with a T on the top of the stem between his thumb and index finger, symbolising the cross on which he will be crucified. Joseph's head leans forward and his gaze seems to be on the path before him, making sure of the road ahead. His gaze is also inward, as if he is concentrating not just on the physical road but on his son's future path towards Calvary. Here Jesus does not reach out to the viewer. Instead, his gaze is directed up towards his father's abstracted face. The flow of the drapery indicates that Joseph and Jesus are walking relatively quickly, as if Joseph is so absorbed in thought that he has not realised that the child is confused by his speed. Jesus looks at his father with concern, as if his preoccupation in this image is for his father's peace of mind and well-being, rather than his own or his engagement with the viewer, which would be more usual. The use of figurines blurs the boundaries between childhood and adulthood and therefore the child appears more convincingly to be the nurturer of the parent than would be the case if the representation were more realistic of the differences between a little boy and a man. They walk through a generalised landscape of trees and clouds against a blue sky. At the bottom left, at the level of Jesus' right shin, there are daisies and red anemones growing out of a clump of earth and stones: these wild flowers echo the red of the red rose of martyrdom, the white of the lily of chastity, and the mound they emerge from with its proximity to the child's staff may well be a harbinger of Calvary: orthodoxy for those with eyes to discern it. Even so, here, Josefa inverts the father son relationship, inverts the expectation that she should depict Joseph as loving, caring father of a little boy, and shows instead a concerned child worried by the inner turmoil he discerns in his preoccupied father and seemingly unaware of his own fate, so discreetly signalled by his staff and the roadside daisies and anemones. This work brings the viewer close to the human dynamic of the father-son relationship; it also demonstrates the primacy of the child Jesus over his human step-father. Thus, while this work may be considered secondary in terms of craftsmanship, it is certainly first rate in terms of ingenuity.

In the Viceroyalty of Peru and more precisely in the indigenous painters' workshops of Cuzco in the Andean highlands, there was a much greater amount of interpretive leeway than on the Iberian Peninsula, in practice if not in principle, when it came to the depiction of holy personages (Bailey 2005: 169–206). The uniformly European clergy ministering in the High Andes accepted that the persons of God, the saints and the Holy Family had to be sumptuously arrayed in pictorial representations, contrary to evolving seventeenth-century Peninsular practice, or they would not be taken for divine figures by an Andean audience. In effect, this licence led to a deepening of the Cuzco style such that, towards the end of the seventeenth century, it would involve:

hieratism, planiform figures, painted [..] as if they were sculptures, gold brocade and the predominance of the colour red.
These compositions [...] represent certain essential elements of fourteenth and fifteenth century painting, with a manifest pre-Colombian influence. [..] "the pantheism of the Incas influencing Catholic mysticism" (Pastor de la Torre 1999: 121–122)[5].

In this School, the persons of God, the Virgin and the saints were usually depicted wearing very costly raiment, embroidered and bedecked with gold to indicate beyond all doubt that these were holy personages of the highest order. The secondary effect of the sculptural, almost two dimensional nature of the figures was to return the religious art of Cuzco to the Byzantine aesthetic of hieratic mysticism which underlies Medieval northern Italian religious pictorial art and indeed that of Renaissance Siena. The anonymous indigenous painters of Cuzco's many collaborative workshops would therefore depict the Virgin, St. Joseph and the child Jesus clothed in mantles and tunics emblazoned in gold filigree detail, this gilding being,

---

[5] "el hieratismo, la figura planiforme, tratada [...] en la forma de escultura, el brocateado en oro y la preminencia del color rojo.
Estas composiciones [..] representan [..] ciertas esencias de la pintura cuatrocentista y del quinientos, con un manifiesto influjo precolombino. [...] 'el panteísmo de los incas influyendo en el misticismo católico'" (Pastor de la Torre 1999: 121–122).

as far as the indigenous aesthetic was concerned, correct attire for the persons of god and the saints (Pastor de la Torre 1999: 122). Pastor de la Torre provides an interesting comparison, from his own extensive collection of paintings from the Cuzco School. He shows a *Holy Family* painted in Cuzco in the late seventeenth century, depicting a very conventional Virgin in red robe and blue mantle on the left, with a youthful Joseph behind her, in grey tunic and beige cloak, holding his lily-topped staff, a glory of putti holding a banner with *Gloria en excelsis Deo* in the centre and two seraphim guiding the first of the shepherds in to see the baby Jesus uncovered by the Virgin. The image is consonant with Pacheco, Carducho, Josefa et al as regards composition, and there is no gilding. The angels look like Pachecho's Gabriel while the Holy Family, particularly Joseph, are closer to Josefa's figurines than to her Spanish counterparts' modelling of form. On the facing page, Pastor de la Torre shows an eighteenth-century depiction of the Holy Family returning from exile in Egypt. It displays the two Trinities, with Joseph, Mary and Jesus in the lower half of the painting and God the Father and the Holy Spirit in the upper half. The faces, hands and necks of the figures are painted conventionally in oils, but each garment is over painted with a filigree of gold detail and each person has a very elaborate spiked gold halo which looks as solid as those on the monstrance used to display the host in procession (Pastor de la Torre 1999: 120–121). While it is entirely possible that the anonymous, conventional *Holy Family* was commissioned by a *criollo* (Peruvian of Spanish descent) or *peninsular* (native Spanish) patron from a *criollo* workshop, demonstrating the palpable difference in taste and custom between indigenous and non-indigenous patrons, the comparison serves to demonstrate just how far indigenous practice had diverged by the early eighteenth century from European norms.

Diego Quispe Tito was one of relatively few Peruvian painters to have the independent means and societal status (he was a descendent of Inca royalty and entitled to style himself "Inca" or nobleman) to enable him to maintain a workshop in his own name and sign his own work (Bailey 2005: 194; Pastor de la Torre 1999: 57–73). Several documented indigenous painters trained in his workshop in San Sebastián, outside Cuzco, and he mixed easily with Inca and Spanish nobility, so much so that he was awarded membership of the Order of Calatrava by the Viceroy, an unusual honour for a non-*peninsular*. While there are theories, inevitably, that he undertook a long voyage to Europe in order to learn his craft, possibly at the instigation of the archbishop of Cuzco, Manuel de Mollinedo y Ángulo, he did indisputably become the protégé of this influential churchman, credited with much of the reconstruction of Lima after the earthquake of 1650. Whether he went to Europe or not, however, Quispe Tito did develop his own style. Like all painters of the period, he used engravings and paintings by other artists as references, but he did not fear to innovate or indeed to domesticate Bible stories for an indigenous audience. Indeed, Pastor de la Torre credits him with single-handedly changing the convention of depicting St. Joseph as an elderly man, still the norm in Peru, in a painting depicting the Holy Family on the Flight into Egypt, kept in his own collection, which Quispe Tito executed between 1660 and 1670 to a private commission (Pastor de la Torre 1999: 60–67). This composition is typical of the eclecticism, born of necessity, of the Cuzco School. In it a young Joseph, wearing dress more redolent of early sixteenth-century Flanders than Biblical Judea but a broad-brimmed hat more akin to those worn in seventeenth-century Cuzco, leads Mary on a white donkey. She is coiffed in a straw hat with broad ribbons woven into the brim which is, in the view of Pastor de la Torre, very similar to that worn by Luis de Morales' Virgin in his *Virgin with a Straw Hat* (Carmelite Convent, Alba de Tormes, c. 1570) and chosen to allude to Andean headwear. The baby Jesus is swaddled in the indigenous manner. The journey takes them across a conventional Flemish landscape which includes however, between the heads of the two adults, a *pisonay* tree (a kind of palm) native to Cuzco and unknown in Flanders.

For the purposes of this argument, the most relevant of Quispe Tito's depictions of Joseph may not be his at all and is certainly not unadulterated by other hands. Pastor de la Torre's collection contains a head and shoulders portrait of St. Joseph and the baby Jesus, framed by a garland of flowers and gilded in high Cuzco indigenous style (Pastor de la Torre 1999: 58; see also Chorpenning 1992: 14; 35). Compositionally, it is, in effect, a Byzantine Madonna and Child in which the Madonna has been substituted by a soft-featured St. Joseph, accentuated by the probable use of *sfumato* (layering of many fine coats of varnish) to produce the very delicate skin tones. St. Joseph, whose head and facial features are modelled in Byzantine style, with a large crown and forehead, large prominent eyes and eye sockets in a face tapering down to a very slender nose, narrow rosebud mouth and pointed chin, looks lovingly towards his son. Christ's head is modelled according to Western Renaissance convention, a rounded, well-proportioned baby's head. He leans the left side of his head, with cheeks touching, against his father's right cheek. Joseph's right hand supports the baby's neck and shoulders and his left hand holds Jesus' waist. Jesus' arms are clasped around Joseph's neck, with his two linked hands shown on the left of Joseph's neck. Jesus looks out at the viewer with large brown eyes, confident and comfortable in the paternal embrace. Each figure is decked in gilded fabrics and both heads framed in solid-looking golden haloes. Beneath the gilding, Joseph wears a simple grey tunic and red mantle; Christ, though it becomes difficult to discern, may have been wrapped in a white swaddling cloth. Joseph holds his lily in his right hand and they appear to be framed by a garland of alternating lilies and wild roses. The overall effect is, naturally, to feminise Joseph.

Villaseñor Black argues that in Colonial Mexico, the feminisation of St. Joseph derives from two different influences: the fact that in indigenous Mesoamerican culture the nurturing of children was an activity seen as proper to both parents in comparison with the seventeenth century European norm with its strong division of labour

on gender lines; and the increased emphasis in Spain and the New World on pro-
moting the dogma of the Immaculate Conception. In order to convey the concept of
the Virgin conceived without original sin pictorially, it was necessary to portray her
on her own, in an idealised and ethereal manner, a representation which went counter to the fashion for placing her as a loving, working-class mother within the Holy
Family compositions of domestic felicity of the mid-seventeenth century. To make
up the deficit as it were, the role of nurturing parent fell more frequently on the
shoulders of the wholly earthly figure of St. Joseph (Villaseñor Black 2006: 109–
110). There is no reason why this analysis should not also apply to the Cuzco context.
In the case of this particular painting, if, as seems likely, an original by Diego Quispe
Tito was subsequently gilded and garlanded to bring it into line with the indigenous
aesthetic of the very late seventeenth and early eighteenth centuries in Cuzco, it
would seem that it was chosen precisely because the feminised Joseph conformed
to the more androgynous norm established, for example, in the Joseph of the gilded
Holy Family Returning from Egypt already cited, in the output of indigenous workshops. It may further be argued that the feminisation of Joseph in this style brings
him closer to the androgynous figure of the angel, and this then, congruent with the
indigenous viewpoint, locates him amongst heavenly rather than earthly beings.

In Portugal and Peru, therefore, two artists working away from the metropolitan centres, one in a small town north of Lisbon, the other in Cuzco in the High
Andes, both probably untravelled beyond their native environments and therefore
reliant on engravings and paintings, both originals and copies, imported from the
metropoli or already present in their surroundings, each with an individual style
and vision which no amount of travel or painterly influence could have spontane-
ously induced, added their own codicils to the representation of St. Joseph, patron
of Peru and the Conversion of the Indigenous, and champion, by virtue of Teresa
of Avila's devotion to him, of post-Tridentine reform of conventual practice, in the
mid-seventeenth century Hispanic world: a feminised, angelic, innocent, even in-
fantilised, Joseph, more redolent of the beings of heaven than the mundane earthly
realm which both artists, in their different ways, eschewed in an age of hyper-re-
alism and disillusionment.

References

Bailey, Gauvin Alexander
2005 [1995]   Art of Colonial Latin America. London: Phaidon.

Barreira, Frei Isidoro
1622   Tractado das significaçoens das plantas, flores, e fructos que se referem na Sagrada
       Escriptura: tiradas de divinas, & humanas letras, cõ suas breves consideraçoes. Lis-
       bon: por Pedro Craesbeeck.

Bassegoda i Hugas, Bonaventura (ed.)
2001   Francisco Pacheco, El arte de la pintura. Madrid: Cátedra.

Brown, Jonathan
2002   The Devotional Paintings of Murillo. In: Suzanne L. Stratton-Pruitt (ed.), Bartolomé Esteban Murillo: Paintings from American Collections; pp. 31–45. New York: Harry N. Abrams Inc.

Chorpenning, Joseph
1992   Patron Saint of the New World: Spanish American Colonial Images of St. Joseph. Philadelphia: St. Joseph's University Press.

Comas, Antonio (ed.)
1984   Santa Teresa de Jesús: La Vida, Las moradas. Barcelona: Planeta.

Gracián de la Madre de Dios, Fray Gerónimo
1597 [1609]   Sumario de las excelencias del glorioso San Ioseph esposo de la Virgen Maria, recopilado de diversos autores. Rome: Antonio Zannetti; Brussels: Ivan Momarte.

Hatherly, Ana
1992   As Misteriosas Portas da Ilusão: A Próposito do imaginário Piedoso em Sóror Maria do Céu e Josefa d'Óbidos. In: Vitor Serrão (ed.), Josefa de Óbidos e o tempo barroco; pp. 71–85. Lisbon: Instituto Português do Património Cultural.

Manero Sorolla, María Pilar
2001   La peregrinación autobiográfica de Anastasio-Gerónimo (Gracián de la Madre de Dios). *Revista de literatura* (CSIC), LXIII, 125, pp. 21–37.

Moura Sobral, Luís de
1992   Josefa d'Óbidos e as Gravuras: Problemas de Estilo e de Iconografia. In: Vitor Serrão (ed.), Josefa de Óbidos e o tempo barroco; pp. 51–67. Lisbon: Instituto Português do Património Cultural.
1998   Bento Coelho e a Cultura do seu Tempo. Lisbon: Instituto Português do Património Arquitectónico.

Pastor de la Torre, Celso
1999   Perú: Fe y Arte en el Virreynato. Córdoba: Publicaciones Obra Social y Cultural Cajasur.

Serrão, Vitor
1992a   Josefa de Óbidos e o tempo barroco. (ed.), Lisbon: Instituto Português do Património Cultural.
1992b   Josefa de Ayala, pintora, ou o elogio da inocência. In: Josefa de Óbidos e o tempo barroco; pp. 13–49. Lisbon: Instituto Português do Património Cultural.

Stratton, Suzanne L.
1994   The Immaculate Conception in Spanish Art. Cambridge: Cambridge University Press.
2002   Bartolomé Esteban Murillo: Paintings from American Collections. (ed. as Suzanne L. Stratton-Pruitt), New York: Harry N. Abrams Inc.

Villaseñor Black, Charlene
2006   Creating the Cult of St. Joseph: Art and Gender in the Spanish Empire. Princeton and Oxford: Princeton University Press.

Pachamama and the Virgin Revisited

Coincidences and Convergences

Sabine Dedenbach-Salazar Sáenz

Abstract. – This article examines the Virgin's and Pachamama's representations by studying evidence from Spain and the Andes in order to approach the question if a combination of Andean and European traits might have caused a "blend" or "fusion". European and Andean intellectual-theological and folk-popular conceptions show that pre-existing coincidences could be projected onto each other and often lead to convergence. The outcome is a religious tradition and practice influenced by the indigenous population as well as Christian priests. It developed in a cultural space and climate in which both approaches could blend into each other and thus converge. *[Andes, Christianisation, Colonial era, Syncretism, Virgin Mary, Pachamama]*

Sabine Dedenbach-Salazar Sáenz is Senior Lecturer in Latin American and Amerindian Studies at the University of Stirling (Great Britain). Her research focuses on the Andes, combining ethnohistory, cultural anthropology and ethnolinguistics (see http://www.dedenbachsalazar.stir.ac.uk/). Recent projects include the direction of the documentation of the endangered Bolivian Chipaya language and the Christianisation of the Andean peoples in the colonial Quechua language. Her publications include "'Our grandparents used to say that we are certainly ancient people, we come from the *chullpas*': The Bolivian Chipayas' mythistory", *Oral Tradition* 27/1 (2012): 187–230, http://journal.oraltradition.org/issues/27i/dedenbach-salazar_saenz, and *Die Stimmen von Huarochirí* (Aachen: Shaker Verlag 2003), http://hss.ulb.uni-bonn.de/2003/0253/0253.htm. She is currently preparing a book on *Entrelazando dos mundos: Experimentos y experiencias con el quechua cristiano en el Perú colonial* (Quito: Abya-yala) and an edited volume on *La transmisión de conceptos cristianos a las lenguas amerindias: Estudios sobre textos y contextos de los siglos XVI y XVII* (Collectanea Instituti Anthropos, Sankt Augustin: Anthropos Institut 2014).

1 Introduction

Pachamama,[1]	Pachamama,
kay derechosniykitan qanman haywarimushayki, kay wata lloqsisqanchis agostopi.	this is your due I serve you as our new year has dawned in August.
Chaskiykukuy uywaqniy kay despachota.	You, the one who nurtures me, receive this offering.
Tuta p'unchaw,	Day and night,

---

[1] I use the Quechua spelling as it is employed in each of the sources I quote. When explaining the origin of a term I follow the official Peruvian Quechua alphabet.

ñuñuqniy unkaqniy.	you [are] the one who feeds me as a mother giving me the breast, as a bird that feeds its young.
Sumaqllataña chaskiyukuy,	Receive this kindly
tukuymanta defendiway,	and from all things defend me,
onqoytapas karunchachay,	cause all illness to be removed far from me,
ama ima llakikunapas qhawasunchu,	and may I be free from all trouble,
hasta watakama sumaqllaña kawsakusun.	may I live happily for another year.

Text 1: Prayer from the highlands of Southern Peru, 1966[2]

In the academic literature on the Andean republics, formerly Spanish colonies, the "deity" Pachamama and the Virgin Mary, both belong to what one could call supernatural beings. They have been closely related, explicitly or implicitly supposing a kind of "syncretism",[3] a "fusion",[4] "blending"[5] or even "substitution" of European and Amerindian religious phenomena.

For example, Hall (2004: ch. 6) writes that "Andean ceremonies … were wrapped into Christian ones" (*ib.* p. 151), when she adduces colonial evidence[6] to what for her and other authors are the Andeanising features of the Virgin: she appears on rocks, uses a combination of Andean and Spanish clothing elements and spinning implements, and a candlestick which reminds the viewer of the Andean lightning deity Illapa.[7] Damian's varying terminology for this phenomenon – "disguise" (1995: 10), "combination" and "fusion" (50, 90) – show quite well the

---

[2] Hoggarth (2004: 163, translation SDS). He (*ib.*) comments the prayer which he collected from a man named Anacleto in June 1966 as follows: "In the highland regions of Southern Peru the month of August signals the beginning of a new year, the beginning of the agricultural cycle. At this time the Earth Mother (Pachamama) is considered as being alive (**kawsashanña**), ready and in condition for the new season of sowing the seed and production of new crops of food. During the first weeks of August, offerings and libations are made with the appropriate prayers to the various nature deities, especially the Earth Mother." (Bold in original.)

[3] syncretism: "… integrating foreign and/or suspending one's own elements when religions meet" (Berner 2007: 49, translation SDS; German original: "… das Integrieren fremder und/oder das Suspendieren eigener Elemente in der Begegnung der Religionen".)

[4] My own understanding would be as joined by melting together (see Webster 1989: 548, *s. v.* fusion).

[5] In my opinion a very similar concept to "fusion". The merging together can make a new indistinct mixture (*cf.* Webster 1989: 148, *s. v.* blend).

[6] Mostly based on Damian. See also footnote 37.

[7] We meet Illapa as a deity in the form of lightning and thunder in pre-European times. In the colonial era there is the – rather bewildering – association/connection of Santiago Matamoros and Mataindios [Saint James the Moor-slayer and the Slayer of the Indians] with the indigenous deity of lightning (Illapa) and animal fertility rites. The connection is probably due to the light of the gunfire with meteorological lightning, and to the date of the year (early July) respectively. (For literature see Domínguez García 2008, esp. 99–116.)

Illustration 1: La Virgen del Cerro Rico de Potosí (The Virgin of the Rich Mountain of Potosí) (Potosí, Bolivia, 18th century) (source see Ref. Cited).

dilemma we encounter as researchers. How can we, for example, know that the triangular shape of the Virgin in paintings represents an Andean mountain (Rishel and Stratton Pruitt 2006: 447, *Illustration 1*) if we don't know whether and how these were presented in pre-colonial times? How can we suppose that a spinning device is typical especially of Pachamama and not just as well of the Spanish Virgin? Therefore, does the visual (and textual) combination of certain European and Andean traits really imply a "blend" or "fusion" or a convergence of coincidences?

The argument I proceed from is that many of the interpretations of these features are only suppositions,[8] therefore I will examine closely both the Virgin and Pachamama, by studying available evidence from Spain *and* from the Andes, mostly in textual form. I do this in order to see if, where and how European and Andean intellectual-theological and/or folk-popular conceptions[9] are responsible for similarities which would make "syncretism" a plausible scenario, or whether it is more probable that we deal with pre-existing coincidences[10] which can easily be projected onto each other and often lead to convergence.[11]

2   The Framework

2.1   Pachamama

It is necessary to specify that, in the present, there is a number of different conceptions of Pachamama. Across the Andes (Ecuador, Peru, Bolivia, Argentina, Chile), Pachamama is a "deity", a being to be revered and prayed to in rituals which are carried out by the members of rural communities, but also of highland cities, above all on special occasions such as the beginning of August. However, Pachamama worship is nowadays also often performed in a tourist context. In parts of Argentina, where this ritual is much publicised in the press, it seems, nonetheless, to

---

[8] As indicated in the previous paragraph, it has to be conceded that the source situation, especially as far as the colonial era is concerned, is less than satisfactory: all the information we have for the Andes stems from a time (and from quills) which already post-date non-European influenced Amerindian cultures (which themselves were, of course, not static). But also with respect to early manifestations of the Virgin or her supposed predecessors do we have to recognize that often all we have is material archaeological evidence and what secondary sources say.

[9] With the words "folk" and "popular" I refer to the majority of the people who are often also called "common", not so much in the sense of "less educated", but as the large part of a people. Society is multi-layered, with people of different social opportunities and privileges, which makes it possible for them to access different kinds of education and training, health and wealth etc. – or hinders them from doing so. Regional variations have to be added to different "popular" beliefs (e.g. Christian 1998: 328). In 16th/17th century Spain such a society is clearly recognisable. The same kind of difference between theological and folk/regional customs existed in the Andes. However, here the differences seem to manifest themselves mostly in the scale of the rituals. It is also evident that the Incas partly respected and even took over regional deities, whereas the Spanish elite's concept of Christian religion was that of clear dominance and eradication (although in the early Middle Ages Christianity built on pre-Christian belief practices; *cf.* footnote 44).

[10] I take my working definition from Webster (1989: 272, *s. v.* coincidence): "an accidental and remarkable occurrence of events or ideas at the same time, suggesting but lacking a causal relationship".

[11] Webster's (1989: 304, *s. v.* convergence) definition for biology is apt here as well: "the development of similarities in unrelated organisms living in the same environment". "Fusion" and "blending" could be seen as forms of convergence.

be a "genuine" concern of rural and urban citizens to worship Pachamama (e.g. Sehringer et al. 2008; Madre Pachamama 2006).

The communication with Pachamama which we find especially in the southern central Peruvian Andes is normally carried out by farmers (see e.g. Hoggarth 2004: 163, at the beginning of this section), an activity which is difficult to describe in detail and understand because the public is not included. However, during what I would like to call a kind of "indigenismo" movement, local politicians have been using or can be even said to have taken over Pachamama for the purpose of making themselves "part of the people" (Ofrendas a la Pachamama 2009). The study of the linkage between these different dimensions would constitute a work on its own. Here I will centre on the "traditional" or "ethnographic" understanding of Pachamama (being well aware of the traps these terms and their applications present).

A review of the 17th century ethnohistorical sources shows a broad spectrum of names, almost all of which include the element *pacha*, "time, space, world" (or *allpa*, "earth, ground") and *mama*, "mother". Therefore the name Pachamama indicates that she is more than an "Earth Mother", tied to the soil or ground, but rather a "World Mother", which I interpret as a principle of life.

There are few images or ideas of what she looks like, but she seems to be an old, small woman when visualised at all (Mariscotti de Görlitz 1978: 32). According to contemporary sources she lives inside the earth (*ib.* 33). The high mountain peak spirits, called *apu*, are also ambivalent beings (see section "Pachamama today") who sometimes seem to be part of Pachamama, in other instances complementary to her. Mariscotti de Görlitz (1978: 193–229) studies how difficult it is to relate Pachamama to any of the other "supernatural" beings, female or male.[12]

2.2   Saint or Deity?

When writing about the "Virgin Mary" and "Pachamama" we need to clarify our concepts – which, of course, is a difficult task because the term "saint" as well as "deity" are characteristic of the Christian culture(s), and they have more than one meaning. It is therefore only a working definition I can offer. In order to understand which concepts colonial and modern authors relate(d) with "god" and "saint", it is necessary to look at Christian explanations and definitions first.[13]

---

[12] The most comprehensive study on Pachamama Santa Tierra ("Holy Earth", as she is frequently called) was written by Mariscotti de Görlitz (1978) and gives a concise description of the whole phenomenon: the name, its archeological evidence, its ethnohistorical occurrence, the places she comes from, other deities related with her, the functionaries or mediators who bring her offerings for economic well-being, including the composition of those offerings.

[13] Of course, there is no framework-less observation of these concepts (as, for example, the Christian vs. Hindu explanations and differentiations of God and saint show). Interestingly enough, the rather

According to Bonwetsch ([1911] 1953, X, 175–177) the Christian saints' most important characteristic is that of being especially pious; they are always human beings whose foremost role was to intercede before God with a human being's wishes. The Nicene Council sanctioned the veneration of saints officially in 787, and even the Council of Trent almost 800 years later kept to the guideline of "intercessors" from whom nothing could be obtained directly and who could only be asked for the help of God (Council of Trent 1848: 25th session [1563]: On the invocation, veneration, and relics, of saints, and on sacred images).

Around the same time, which in the Americas was that of colonialisation, the general concept of God would have been, on the one hand, that of a mystic God who is present in everything, and, on the other, as a certain reaction to this, God as a strict autocrat and judge.[14] We find both concepts expressed in the Peruvian Third Lima Council's sermons, where, for example, it is made clear that Godliness transpires all human work and every being, and also that God is almighty and fearsome (Tercer Concilio Provincial de Lima, e.g., in sermon 18 and 24).

With respect to this Christian image of God as a spiritual being full of will and power, it is clear that, from the point of view of the Andean people, it would have coincided well with the characteristics of a deity like Pachamama. However, the native concept of a deity in the Andes is that of a *huaca*. S/he is not, like the Christian God, a unique deity, but there are many *huacas*. Other traits are that a *huaca* can be any element or feature found in nature and is considered to have particular force and power. *Huaca* refers to both the physical manifestation of the supernatural force (e.g. a mountain peak, a stone), and to the force or being itself, either as an abstract concept of a numinous being located in these features of nature, or a man-made object representing it (e.g. a statue). An important characteristic of the Andean conceptualization of "deities" is that they can transform themselves into human beings, animals, stones etc.[15] However, the *huacas'* power is not permanent (although they hardly ever die or disappear completely): it can increase or diminish over time, especially as a *huaca* is closely related to a community or region, and the prosperity or decline of the *huaca* and the community are closely interrelated. As among human beings, power between the *huacas* can shift, often associ-

---

dated edition of the New Schaff-Herzog Encyclopedia of Religious Knowledge (English edition 1908–1914, reprint 1953; German original second half of the 19th century) gives, although, of course, slightly evolutionary in tone, good and comprehensive explanations.

[14] Köstlin ([1909] 1953, V, 5). The Council of Trent itself ([1562–1564] 1848: *passim*) talks of the almighty, wrathful, powerful, but also clement and merciful God, and human beings are his servants who praise and glorify him.

[15] In the Huarochirí myths of a central Andean region (ca. 1608) it also becomes clear that so-called *huacas*, "supernatural" beings, often the culture heroes of certain ethnic groups, can transform themselves into all kinds of beings at will, such as beggars, attractive young men, fast animals etc. (e.g. *Huarochirí Manuscript* [ca. 1608] 1991: ch. 5, 6). The Christian coincidence is, of course, Christ's appearance as the human being Jesus (and we can also think of the Holy Spirit in the form of a dove).

ated with a change in the status of the corresponding community (e.g. *Huarochirí Manuscript* [ca. 1608] 1991: ch. 8, 26).[16] In (pre-)colonial times some *huacas* were important oracles. An important aspect of a *huaca* was (and still is) the reciprocal relationship which exists between him/her and human beings and which reflects such relations among humans themselves.

Nonetheless we cannot apply all features of a *huaca* to Pachamama. To my knowledge, she is never called a *huaca* and just because of this she seems to be slightly different from a *huaca*. Whilst she maintains a reciprocal relationship with her human worshippers and may be represented in female *huacas*, her power does not enter into any kind of competitive relationship with other such beings. She is always present and her power will not diminish. Therefore Pachamama seems to be what we might call a spiritual being of "higher order" or, how I understand her, an underlying principle of life.

The Christian colonial missionaries would have made a distinction between the (highest) saint, i.e. the Virgin Mary, and God. And the indigenous *huacas* were seen as creations of the Devil (e.g. *Tercero cathecismo* 1585: sermon 19). But would the Andean indigenous[17] population therefore have made the same distinction? I maintain that they would not, because none of the powerful beings in their world, whom we would call "supernatural" or "spiritual", qualifies as intermediary (see section "Pachamama today"). Therefore the Andean population would not – neither in the colonial era nor in the present – venerate a Christian saint as intermediary ("douleia") to contact a supremely powerful being ("latreia") (*cf.* Bonwetsch [1911] 1953, X, 176). Rather we have to imagine all "supernatural" beings as "deities" (also the Christian saints) – and this is why I will refer to them as such. I will use "supernatural" (being conscious of the fact that the supernatural cannot really be separated from the natural in the Andes), "deity" or "spirit" interchangeably, but the term "saint" will be limited to its explicit Catholic meaning.

---

[16] See Pillsbury (ed. 2008, especially vols. 2 and 3) for bio-bibliographical summaries of most of the colonial authors mentioned here.

[17] "Indigenous" is a highly complex term. When I use it with respect to the colonial era, it mostly refers to those who were of Andean roots and descent. But already at that time, the mixture of races, and more than that, of cultures, became evident in the so-called "mestizo". I also call "indigenous" those who nowadays live in rural areas and through their habits, such as music, eating, clothing and/or descent are not conceived of as European (although with heavily influenced European features since colonial times).

3   Pachamama Today

Chaymi kay Pacha Tierra, Pacha mamaqa tumpan roygada,	This is why this Pacha Tierra, Pacha Mama is requested a little,
tiempullanpi llank'ana,	she has to be worked just in her time,
tiempullampi [sic] unuwampas churana,	she also has to be given her water just in her time,
tiempullampi qarpa kaqtinpas llank'ana.	she also has to be worked just in her time if she is irrigated.

Text 2: On Pachamama, Southern Peru, 1997[18]

I would first like to look at how 20th century indigenous people from Southern Peru themselves describe Pachamama (in Quechua) and thereby show the importance of her for human being and society, and then discuss anthropological interpretations.

Mariano Phuturi Suni, an elderly man from Southern Peru at the time he narrates his (hi)story in the 1990's, calls her Pachamama and Pachatierra (*tierra*, from Spanish "earth, world") and says that she is part of the universe created by God the Sun (after the era of the Incas, identified as that of the Father) (Phuturi Suni 1997: 282 ff.). This Pachamama is closely related to humans: "wawankunatan khuyupay[a]wanchis," "she always loves us, her children" (*ib.* 282). We are alive because of her. Only together with her husband, *para*, "the rain", can she fertilise the ground.[19] People work her with hands and feet, and she gives them their food, their livelihood. In return they have to make well-smelling burnt-offerings to her, including coca leaves[20] (*ib.* 284–285). Pachamama, for example, receives prayers and offerings at the marking of the animals at carnival, for a good birth of the sheep, a sprinkled liquid offering when maize is sown or at the festival of the lambs (several authors, in Frommeyer 2007: 63–72).

Also in the second half of the 20th century a North American and a Peruvian anthropologist collected stories in an area (Gow y Condori eds. 1976: Intr., followed by texts) not far from Phuturi's. The narrator of one of the stories about Pachamama ("Pachamama", *ib.* 10–12) emphasises her productive force by using terms such as "kuyda", "to take care of", "uywa-", "to nurture small children and

---

[18] Southern Peru, Phuturi Suni (1997: 282, translation SDS).

[19] This is not a commonly found connection. Be it European or Andean in origin, it points to the importance of having a male-female couple who is responsible for fertility. Normally there is no mention of any kind of partner Pachamama would have.

[20] Chewing coca leaves helps to overcome the stress from hard, physical labour. They are also a very important part of Andean social (chewing as part of the greeting ceremony and in the company of others) and religious life (especially in divination and offerings). (For a study on the use of coca see Allen [1988] 2002).

animals". She is alive: she has hair, which is the pasture, and blood and milk inside her (see *Text 9* for the literal quotation). He adds that she is really like our mother. It is important to respect her and work her at the times due to her (but not around Christmas and August), otherwise her sadness and wrath may cause harm. The same consultant makes it clear that she is not personally the one who brings bad luck over the people, but she warns them.

Pachamama (Mariscotti de Görlitz 1978: 31–35, 57–84) is located beneath the earth in certain places, as the rituals carried out for her show. She lives in particular mountains, close to mines, the salt-providing places for the animals, in stones of certain forms. She is often related to irrigation systems and springs, lakes and rivers as well as to mysterious grottoes, geographically precarious sites; she is also said to reside in *pacarinas* (from *paqari-*, "to be born"), which people also imagine to be the ancestors' and herding animals' origins.

It is possible to address her directly, but there is a long tradition of asking indigenous "priests", who are powerful intermediaries, to communicate with her through offerings.

Although the narratives of Pachamama are varied, their essence is always the same, and even people in the cities respect her. So Gregorio Condori Mamani (1977) who lived in Cuzco most of his lifetime said: "Out there no one can miss even a single day of working the fields – you just can't do it. You can neglect your wife and even forget all about her, but never the land, never Earth Mother. If you forget about Earth Mother, she'll forget about you too."[21] The respect shown to her especially in August and even in towns is illustrated by offerings of incense municipal workers make to Pachamama (*Illustration 2*).

Even the Catholic priests who at the same time were/are anthropologists and studied indigenous religion in the Peruvian highlands, saw Pachamama as a "deity". Núñez del Prado (1970: 73) emphasises her role as spiritual equivalent of the high and powerful *apus*, the mountain peaks. He suggests that, as the feminine factor in the genesis of everything, she is of a general importance in the conception of the whole world.[22]

Pachamama is hardly ever explicitly related to the Catholic patron saints whose festivals are carried out in a very similar way to those in Spain, with dressing up the saint, taking her through the village, organising masses and several social activities, especially through the Spanish-derived system of social functions (*cargos*) and organised in brotherhoods (*cofradías*). It is made clear that the *cholos*

---

[21] Translation of Gregorio Condori Mamani's passage from Mamani and Quispe (1996: 41). Quechua original: "Haqaypeqa manan pipas ni huk p'unchaypas mana chakrata llank'aspaqa kanmanchu; manan chayqa atikunchu. Quizas warmiykitapas manapas atendenkichu otaq qonankípas, pero chakrataqa mana atikunchu, pachamamata" (Mamani and Quispe 1982: 36).

[22] Neither he nor his contemporary Marzal (1971: 253–254) suggests that Pachamama and the Virgin are somehow related or associated.

Illustration 2: Sahumerio: Incense offer on the day of Pachamama, 1 August 1997, in Puno, Peru (photograph A. Salazar).

and *mestizos* (townspeople) are responsible for these festivals (e.g. descriptions by Marzal 1971: 153–190).

On the other hand, for example with reference to a more Southern area where Aymara farmers live, van den Berg (1990: 238) found in the late nineteen-seventies what he called the "Aymarisation of the Christian supernatural beings". He was told that "at Candelaria [the Virgin of the Candlestick festival] Pachamama is kind-hearted because she gives us the first potatoes" (*ib.*, 245). The litter the Virgin is carried in is decorated with big potatoes which were selected at harvest, and the accompanying dances are associated with agriculture (*ib.*, 245). Here Pachamama's and the Virgin's protection of crops coincide. Van den Berg (*ib.*, 245) calls this phenomenon the "closeness" of both the Virgin and Pachamama.[23]

On the basis of my discussion there is little to suggest that an earlier fusion, in colonial times, occurred between Pachamama and the Virgin Mary.

---

[23] Translations by SDS, original passages: "La aymarización de los seres sobrenaturales cristianos" (238); "En Candelaria, la *pachamama* es bondadosa, porque nos da las primeras papas" (p. 245), "cercanía" (245).

4   Pachamama and the Virgin in Colonial Peru

4.1   Pachamama

Es cosa comun entre Indios adorar a la tierra fertil, que es la tierra que llaman Pachamama, o Camac pacha, derramando chicha en ella, o coca o otras cosas, para que les haga bien.	It is common among the Indians to adore the fertile earth, which is the earth they call Pachamama, or Camac[24] pacha, sprinkling maize-beer on her, or coca leaves or other things, so that she may do them well.
Y para el mismo effecto en tiempo de arar la tierra, barbechar o sembrar, y coger mayz, o papas, o quinua, o yucas, y camotes, o otras legumbres y fructos de la tierra suelen ofrecerle cebo quemado, coca, cuy, corderos, y otras cosas: y todo esto bebiendo y baylando.	To the same effect – at the time of tilling the earth, ploughing, and harvesting maize, or potato or quinua, or yucca, and sweet potato, and other native vegetables and fruit – they normally offer her burnt fat, coca leaves, guinea pigs, lambs [also alpaca lambs] and other things: and all this while they drink and dance.

Text 3: On Pachamama, Peru 1585[25]

In order to better grasp where the marked difference between colonial and contemporary understandings could lie, I will now turn to the colonial descriptions and understandings. As could be seen, it is not easy to capture the contemporary image of Pachamama, but her occurrence and conception in colonial times is even more difficult to understand. Pachamama is not as frequently mentioned by the (always male) chroniclers as are other supernatural beings. We may imagine that she "came to life again" after the destruction of the Inca empire,[26] that is, she was then noticed more clearly when the state deities had practically disappeared, i.e. been destroyed by the Spanish invaders. It is possible that due to the emphasis on Inca deities Pachamama was hardly mentioned for the pre-Spanish era, and it is also probable that the male chroniclers did not completely grasp the significance of a general, female principle of life. Moreover it is possible that the Christian view-

---

[24] Referring to the procreation *cama-* has a very complex meaning in Quechua. It was adapted by the Christian missionaries for the "creator", but in Andean terms creation is seen as a series of consecutive transformations, a succession of generations rather than a creation *ex nihilo*. (See Taylor 1974–1976 for a discussion.)

[25] Juan Polo de Ondegardo ([1585] 1985: cap. V, fol. 2r, 255).

[26] The Inca state or empire was the final, infra-structurally and logistically best organised and geographically most extended state formation before and at the time of the Spanish conquest (in 1532). It only lasted for a maximum of 120 years and was preceded by more than a millenium of gradually better organised and more complex chieftainships and states. It can justly be said that there was little (if anything) the Incas invented; rather they used and adapted existing achievements very intelligently. (For a concise description of Inca history and culture see, for example, Davies 1997.)

point of not having a female deity, but "only" female saints, may have obscured and influenced her understanding.[27]

However, in order to see whether there is any continuity backwards in time from the contemporary Pachamama (as ambiguous and reciprocal life-force) towards her earliest known manifestation, we have to look at the colonial sources, without forgetting the mentioned uncertainties and that they tend to be biased, either Inca- or Christian-influenced or both.

A reliable and relatively early chronicler is Juan Polo de Ondegardo ([1571] 1990: cap. IV, XI, XVII; [1585] 1985: fol. 2r, 255) who says that the Earth was called Pachamama and worshipped. Interestingly he ascribes to her, just like to other, male deities, her own contingent of lands,[28] chosen women to serve her, animals and other kinds of foods.

Authors who wrote around the first two decades of the 17th century mention her as well. The first known drawing shows her name, together with that of other supernatural beings, but it is difficult to interpret the south central Andean indigenous author's meaning (Pachacuti Yamqui Salcamaygua ca. 1613, fol. 13v, also ed. 1995: 36–39) unless we limit ourselves to her contextualisation in meteorological phenomena (see *Illustration 3*).

Arriaga ([1621] 1968, cap. II, 201, *cf.* cap. V, 214) describes her, in a similar way as other worshipped places (such as the sea, the springs, the rivers and the high mountains): "Mamapacha, which is the Earth, they also revere, especially the women at the time of sowing; and they speak with her saying that she should give them a good harvest. And for this they spill maize beer and ground maize, either with their own hands or through those of the witches".[29] This shows that she receives offerings which are brought to her in a ritual also involving drink and dance (see *Text 3* at the beginning of this section). It makes clear that she is associated with fertility: particularly well formed or prosperous samples of agricultural

---

[27] In this particular case it is necessary to call the readers' attention to the fact that there are entire books full of data about Inca and regional deities, but within these, the mention of Pachamama is scarce.

[28] Also Ramos Gavilán ([1621] 1879, cap. XIII, 19–20, translation SDS): "Among other interesting things found in Copacabana [lake Titicaca] there was a plot which was dedicated to the earth: *Tellus*, the goddess who also had her sacrificial altars among the idolatrous cults of the old world. As the Incas from here were kin of those from Cuzco, they brought this myth with them when they came from the capital, calling her Pachamama, which means Mother earth, to whom they offered sacrifices before working her, requesting her, as she was a good mother, she should give them everything necessary to maintain children." Original text: "Entre otras cosas notables que se hallaron en Copacabana fué un solar dedicado á la tierra: *Tellus*, diosa que tambien tuvo sus aras entre los cultos idólatras del viejo mundo. Como los Incas de acá eran parientes de los del Cuzco, al venirse de la metrópoli se trajeron ese mito, llamándola *Pachamama*, que viene á decir Madre tierra, á quien ofrecian sacrificios antes de labrarla, pidiéndole que como buena madre les diese lo necesario para sustento de hijos."

[29] Translation SDS; Spanish original: "A Mamapacha que es la Tierra, también reverencian, especialmente las mujeres, al tiempo que han de sembrar, y hablan con ella diciendo que les dé buena cosecha, y derraman para esto chicha y maíz molido, o por su mano o por medio de los hechiceros."

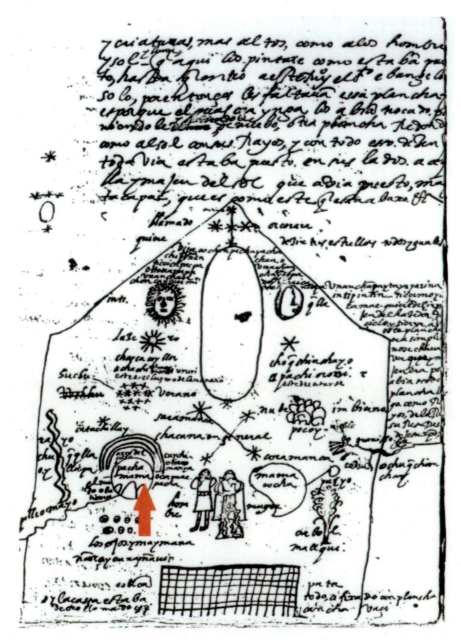

Illustration 3: Juan de Santacruz Pachacuti Yamqui Salcamaygua (ca. 1613, fol. 13v, transcription in 1995 ed., 38–39) (source see Ref. Cited).

products, such as double corn cobs or cobs which are especially colourful, are put together with the maize separated for sowing. These are called *saramama* and worshipped as mothers of corn.[30] In a 1700 annual letter a Jesuit even relates Pachamama to the warm valley areas were coca grows; he writes about the custom "actually to bury the leaves of that little plant [the coca] in the earth, in the earth with the name Pachamama, which they really call great Mother, thinking that it will be that she will, through their spreading of the little plant, gratefully answer with a sufficient harvest of the coca in the same way".[31]

Still in the late colonial era witnesses in the idolatry process (quoted by Huertas Vallejos 1981: 78) state that the mixture of soil with certain ingredients is beneficial to obtain the inclination of a beloved person. Here we can see how Spanish folk customs and old Andean earth worshipping could possibly come together.

As to season(s) in which Pachamama was particularly respected or worshipped, it is not clearly said in the sources that the deities' August festival was also dedicated to Pachamama, but it seems to have been for *all* deities. This time of the year was in Inca times used to keep oneself clean from illnesses (Molina [ca. 1575] 1989: "Agosto", 73) – not unlike the time of year and kind of activities related to the stories about the Virgin in Spain (see section "Folk concepts of the Virgin Mary in Spain").

At the beginning of the 17th century, in the Lima hinterland, a particular regional manifestation of Pachamama may have been the multi-personal female deity Chaupiñamca and her sisters, resident in particularly shaped stones, with myths and rituals related to her/them. These women are closely associated with the economic well-being of a community and in one case the cleaning of the irrigation canals. (*Huarochirí Manuscript* [ca. 1608] 1991: ch. 10).

So, in a way, Pachamama is linked in concrete terms to human economy and fertility, but only a few authors assign her the same kind of worship as to other important supernatural beings of Andean origin.

Nowhere do we find a relationship, "closeness" (as van den Berg [1990: 245] would call it) or "blending" with the Virgin Mary. On the contrary, one of the central Peruvian mid-17th century witnesses who were asked about local "idols" describes at the occasion of the birth of the Virgin that *huacas* and "ydolos" received offerings: "And in the same way he has seen that, when on many occasions the

---

[30] Arriaga (*ib.* cap. II, 204–205) explains the forms, shapes and names of particular maize cobs or items made of other materials, such as stone, which are kept with the plants for the fertility of which they are "responsible". They can be called "zaramama", "cocamama" etc. and are thereby clearly related to Pachamama.

[31] "… nempè herbulam illa, terrae immittere; terrae in/quam quam Pachamama, magnam nempè Ma-/trem vocant, mente illa, fore, vt herbula sparsa fæ-/cunda responderet messis in satis, Cocæ veluti / grata" (in Polia 1999: 557; translation from Latin into English by SDS; translation into Spanish by Polia 1999: 558).

festival of the birth of the Virgin was made, the majordomos killed llamas for their hearts and they offered their blood to the idols and Guacas and the Pucara [regional deity], and the Indians ate the meat".[32] But no mention is made of Pachamama, who in this case would have been an apt receptor of such gifts.

In way of a summary, we can quote Ludovico Bertonio, the great Aymara lexicographer (who finishes with a phrase that also reminds us of the background of most colonial authors): "Pachamama, Suyrumama: the earth which produces food, and in the times of the ancestors it was a name of reverence, seeing that the earth would give them to eat; and thus they used to say: *Pachamama huahuamaja*. Oh earth, I will be your child, or: take me, or have me as child. They spoke like the Devil taught them".[33]

4.2   The Virgin Mary

In the face of this evidence, we have to ask whether a "Virgin Pachamama" was created at all in the colonial world and if it was, by whom. We could see that the sources, whose authors were mostly clerics and which were written at the beginning of the 17th century, were mostly of anti-idolatrous character and did not relate Pachamama with the Virgin. The ones that seem to have been the first to locate the Virgin in a framework of a deity more than "just" a saint were those that aimed at providing an indigenous language translation of the Christian doctrine, to be used by the parish priests in their daily doctrinal work. The first published one was composed in 1582/83 on the occasion of the Third Lima Council (*Doctrina christiana* [1584] 1985). The editors, authors and translators had to work directly with the indo-European texts and try to find explanations which would establish a clear meaning on the basis of complex concepts.

In this context, let us imagine how the priests and the Virgin arrived in Peru. We have to think of a Christian parish priest travelling to Latin America and, in the early times, possibly taking with him his own image of the Virgin he venerates, depending on his personal and parish history, e.g. Our Lady of the Candlestick. He would then have his indigenous flock pray before this image (or later he

---

[32] Witness Martin Chaupis Ricapa (in Duviols ed. 2003: Procesos y visitas de Bernardo de Novoa, Cajamarquilla, 1656, 204; translation SDS); original text: "Y asimesmo a bisto en muchas occasiones que se a echo la fiesta de la natiuidad de la Birgen los mayordomos an muerto llamas por el corazon y la sangre la an ofrecido a los ydolos y Guacas y al Pucara y comiase la carne los yndios."

[33] Bertonio ([1612] 1984, Aymara-Spanish, 242), translation and italics SDS; original: "Pachamama, Suyrumama: La tierra de pan llenar [sic: lleuar], y acerca de los antiguos era nombre de reuerencia, por ver que la tierra les daua de comer; y asi dezian, Pachamama huahuamaha. O tierra yo seré tu hijo, o tomame, o tenme por hijo. Hablauan como el Demonio les enseñaua." It is interesting that Bertonio gives a concept which is very similar to the Quechua one, but that González Holguín's 1608 *Vocabulario*, the equivalent dictionary for Quechua, does not mention Pachamama as an entry.

Illustration 4: Bernardo Bitti: Candelaria (The Virgin of the Candle-sticks) (Church of the Jesuits, Arequipa, Peru, ca. end of 16th century) (source see Ref. Cited, with permission).

would have one made by an artist[34]) teaching them the "right" words, i.e. the *Salve* and the *Ave María*. In this way the Virgin is always a concrete manifestation with a particular (hi)story of this individual image who would be used to intercede be-

---

[34] A rather artful example is Bitti's *Candelaria* Virgin (in the Church of the Jesuits in Arequipa) (*Illustration 4*), another one Our Lady of the Expectation of San Pedro in Lima, painted around 1575–1576 by Bernardo Bitti. The comment by Strehlke (2006) on the latter describes the logistic difficulties artists were confronted with when producing this kind of painting in the early colony. We can imagine that *mestizo* and native artists carried out these works under more modest circumstances.

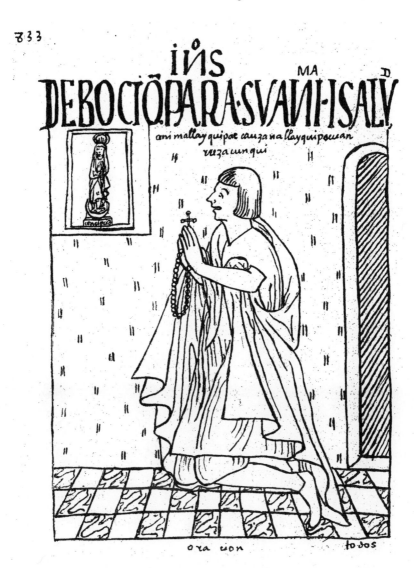

Illustration 5: Felipe Guaman Poma de Ayala: Deboción para sv ánima i salvd (Devotion for his soul and health) ([ca. 1615]: 833, 2001: [847]) (source see Ref. Cited, with permission by Copenhagen National Library).

fore God in order to help "her" parishioner, as shown by the indigenous chronicler Guaman Poma (see *Illustration 5*).

Thus, the prayers would be said in front of an image of a certain Virgin. For this purpose the mentioned Quechua translation of them would be a first contact with the Christian figures and images the native population would have had. Therefore the translator-missionaries produced texts which should have not only conveyed the message, but also done this in a way meaningful to the native new parishioner.

The Ave Maria, for example, would read as follows:

Spanish (*Doctrina Christiana* 1584)	Quechua (*Doctrina Christiana* 1584)	English from Quechua (SDS)
Dios te salue Maria,	Mvchaycuscayqui Maria	May he greet you, Mary.[35]
llena de gracia.	Diospa gracianhuan huntascan canqui.	You are full of God's grace.
El señor es contigo.	Apunchic (1) Diosmi camhuan.	Our highest mountain spirit (1) God is with you.
Bendita tu en las mujeres.	Huarmicunamanta collananmi (2) (3) canqui.	Among the women you are the most excellent one (2) – I know/have seen this (3).
Y bendito el fructo de tu vientre Iesus.	Vicçayquimanta pacarimuc (4) Iesus huahuayquiri collanantacmi,	And from your womb Jesus your son, [the one] born from there (4), is excellent – I know/have seen this.
Sancta Maria, virgen madre de Dios,	A sancta Maria virgen Diospa maman,	Oh Holy Mary, Virgin, mother of God,
ruega por nosotros peccadores agora,	ñocaycu (4) huchaçapacunapac muchapuaycu, cunan,	pray for us (4) severe sinners now
y en la hora de nuestra muerte.	huañuynijcu pachapipas.	and also at the time of our death.
Amen.	Amen Iesus.	Amen Jesus.

Text 4: *Ave Maria* in *Doctrina christiana* ([1584]: fol. 1v–2r, 1985: 22–23).

Understanding in an Andean context:

(1) *apu* (lord): refers to indigenous deities, spirits of the highest mountain peaks.
(2) *qullanan* (principal, first, noble, special, excellent): she is the highest-ranking spirit.
(3) *-mi/-m* is an evidential suffix which indicates personal experience and, in some cases, validation of affirmation or certainty.
(4) *paqarimuq* (the one [who is] born from there), derived from *paqarimu-*, "to come out of/from, to be born from" (verb); *cf. paqari-na* (noun), "the place they come/emerge from". *Paqari-mu-* is an important indigenous concept of

---

[35] This is already a formulaic usage of a Quechua form ("May God greet you", *Doctrina christiana* ([1584]: fol. 15v, 1985: 170) which would literally mean either "I will worship you" or "you were the worshipped one", depending on how one interprets the verb form *-sqa-yki-*.

the Andean peoples, referred to by several colonial authors (e.g. *Huarochirí Manuscript* [ca. 1608] 1991, ch. 24, 117, 216: where a certain group has come from; Guaman Poma [ca. 1615] 2001: 84: how the *paqarina* receive offerings; for a closer analysis see Dedenbach-Salazar Sáenz 1997: 199). Pachamama is also said to have come out of a *paqarina* (see "Pachamama today").

(5) *ñuqayku* (we <u>excl.</u>) / *muchapuwayku* (pray in <u>our</u> favour): *-yku* means that "we" belong to a different group from the one that is addressed, in this case the Virgin. The inclusive form (the speaker(s) and the addressee(s)) is *-nchik* (see *Text 6*, from the *Tercero Cathecismo*, for its usage), where in this case the speaker and his addressees, i.e. the preacher and his audience, form a group.

Another Andean term which (similar to *apu*) must have evoked associations with Andean life, in this case the Inca nobility, was used at the beginning of the *Salve*:

Spanish (*Doctrina Christiana* 1584)	Quechua (*Doctrina Christiana* 1584)	English from Quechua (SDS)
Salue te Dios reyna, y madre de misericordia Vida, dulçura, esperança nuestra[.] …	Mvchaycuscayqui çapay coya (6), huacchay cuyas [sic] mama, cauçay, ñucñu (7), suya-naycu, …	May he greet you, the Inca's only wife (6), the mother who loves the orphans, life, sweetness (7), for whom we wait. …
O clemente. O piadosa. O dulce virgen Maria.	A, llaquipayac, A, cuyapayac, A, ñucñu virgen Maria (7).	Oh, always sympathetic, Oh, always loving, Oh, sweet Virgin Mary (7).

Text 5: *Salve in Doctrina christiana* ([1584]: fol. 3r–3v, 1985: 25–26).

(6) *sapay quya* (the only Inca wife): The Inca used to have several wives, but only one "legitimate" one, called *quya*. She was his full sister. Whilst he was identified with the Sun, she was with the Moon.[36] The usage of this symbolic name and the depiction of the Immaculate Conception with the crescent moon under her feet (as, for example, shown by Guaman Poma in the context of his Christian prayers, *Illustration 5*) must have evoked memories of the Inca queen.

---

[36] In the sermon about prayers (*Tercero Cathecismo* [1585], sermon 29, fol. 189r, 1985: 725), she is even entitled as "Queen of Heaven": "hanacpachap coyan". In general, though, in the Christian texts the Andean word *quya* is avoided. In the *Tercero Cathecismo* (which was created by the same editorial committee as the *Doctrina Christiana*), wherever she is mentioned, it is normally as the "Virgen", "Sancta Maria", in both Spanish and Quechua, with the benevolent characteristics and by names typical of her and her being Jesus' mother (for example *Tercero Cathecismo*, sermon 17, fol. 100v, 548; sermon 21, fol. 124r, 595). The same is the case in how the Virgin is described in Avila's sermons (1648 *passim*).

(7) Words like *ñukñu*, "sweet(ness)", *llakipayaq*, "always, again and again, sympathetic", *kuyapayaq*, "always, again and again, loving" heighten the Virgin above human beings (including Eve) and at the same time give her chracteristics not unlike Pachamama's.

When translating these words not only into the Quechua language, but also into an Andean framework of belief, an image of the Virgin emerges which is partly different from the European mother of Christ and fits in a certain way the Andean categories and their internal relations: she is the physical mother of the most important supernatural being, who at the same time is above the human beings. She is closely related to the mountain spirits as well as to the Inca.

The only grammatical element of the text which might indicate that Mary is an intercessor, rather than an autonomous supernatural being, is the verb "muchapuaycu" because we have to interpret *-pu* as an action carried out in someone's favour (or disadvantage) by another being, i.e. "pray/worship for us". This means that the speaker of the prayer requests the Virgin to pray to someone else. Although this would have been completely clear for a Christian(ised) colonial Quechua speaker, in a recently converted Andean person it might have caused some confusion: despite having all the characteristics of a deity, Pachamama is now praying to yet another deity.

Whilst this implication of Mary as intercessor is quite straightforward, although maybe confusing for the indigenous parishioners, the translators of the prayer find it necessary to observe that "you are full of God's grace", adding the Spanish word for "God" in the Quechua text to the Spanish original version. Possibly the translators wanted to make it more explicit that the grace of Our Lady was given to her by God. However, we may doubt how much clearer it would have been as the Andean people would probably not have known the meaning of the Spanish loanword "gracia", "grace".

The only other feature which is not completely in agreement with how the reciprocal and ambiguous Andean Pachamama is conceived of, is the *Salve*'s completely positive evocation of the Virgin: she is always sweet, sympathetic and loving. However, close to the Andean idea, she is also life itself. Also the fact that the Christian God, Jesus Christ, comes out of her womb, reminds us of Pachamama's important role as producer of fertility.

These prayers seem to be the only more or less convincing evidence that there could have been a correlation, even convergence of Pachamama and the Virgin, in the colonial era.[37] This also becomes clear in the explanatory sermon about the

---

[37] Damian (1995: esp. 71–75) highlights the *coya* and the Virgin's visual similarities, but her visual evidence is of the 18th century (some of uncertain origin: 17th–18th century), and she correlates the parallels to written sources mostly from earlier times. Just by looking at the 18th century paintings, it seems to be clear that it is a fashion being presented here. Either Damian's or the painters' interpreta-

Virgin, in which it is, on the one hand, highlighted that she has a higher position than the other saints, apostles and angels; on the other hand, a certain reciprocity becomes evident in the last quoted sentence (bolded in the text) – both features are compatible with Pachamama and her relationship to other spiritual beings and to humankind respectively.

Spanish (*Tercero Cathecismo* 1585)	Quechua (*Tercero Cathecismo* 1585)	English from Quechua (SDS)
En el Aue Maria hablamos con Nuestra Señora la Virgen Maria madre de Dios que es Reyna del Cielo, y es Abogada nuestra,	Cay oracionta çocarispam, nuestra Señora Sancta Maria viñay Virgenta rimachinchic [sic] (4), paymi, ari Diospa çapay maman, hanacpachap coyan, ñocanchicpapas marcanchictac. Diosman villapuquenchictac,	As we are raising our prayer, we talk to our Lady Saint Mary, the eternal Virgin – all of us: I who speak and you who listen (4). She – we have seen it/know it – is effectively God's only mother, the Queen [Inca wife] of the Heavens, and also of our regions. She is the one who speaks for our benefit to God.
y es una señora que nos quiere mucho, y siempre ruega por nosotros, y por ella nos haze el Señor tantos bienes, y nos libra de todos males.	cay señoram ñocanchicta ancha munahuanchic, paymi ñocanchicpac viñaylla Diosta muchapuanchic, villapuanchic, payraycutacmi Diospas chica allichahuanchic, yma mana allimantapas quispichihuanchic.	This lady likes us very much, she always prays for our benefit to the truly eternal God, she speaks in our favour, and because of her also God does us much good and makes that we are saved from anything bad.
Esta señora es sobre todos los Apostoles, y sobre todos los Sanctos, y sobre todos los Angeles.	Cay mamanchicmi llapa Apostolcunamantapas, tucuy sanctocunamantapas, hinantin Angelcunamantapas payrac ancha sancta ancha collanan.	This our mother, she is even holier, more excellent than all the Apostles, all the saints together with the angels.
Y despues de Iesuchristo su hijo nuestro Señor no ay otro como esta señora, que tan alto sea, ni que tanto nos quiera.	Iesu Christo ñaupaqueyoc, payracmi, llapactapas sancta caspa, cuyaquenchic caspa yallicun,	Jesus Christ is the leader; after him she is the most exceeding one, being the foremost saint, loving us.

tions or both must be the "re-invention" of a tradition. It would be interesting to compare these representations with Mexican and Spanish ones of the same and earlier periods. Looking, for example, at the Virgins Guaman Poma ([ca. 1615: 827, 833, 2001: [841, 847], see *Illustration 5*), the indigenous Andean writer paints, we can see that they are unlike the 18th century ones and look much more like the virgins of Bitti (*Illustration 4*).

Por esso la hemos de llamar siempre en nuestros trabajos y necessidades, y tenella por madre y querella mucho, porque ella nos tiene por sus hijos y nos quiere mucho.	chaypac ari, yma muchuyninchicpipas, ñacaricuyninchicpipas payta huacyarissun, payta mamanchicpac chasquicussun yupacussun tucuy sonconchichuampas munassun, paypa munaña huahuancamancanchic.	Because of this, in whatever suffering or pain we are, we will call her, we will receive her as our mother, we will esteem her, we will like her with all our heart, so that she will love us all like her children.

Text 6: *Tercero Cathecismo* ([1585]: sermon 29, fol. 189r [1985]: 725).

However, the authors of the *Tercero Cathecismo* (*ib.* sermon 6, especially fol. 36v, 420) understood the "danger" of associating and even correlating Christian and Andean supernatural phenomena. Among others, stars, rivers, mountains and the earth must not be understood as living beings or even deities. That they are not of this kind is shown through the fact that they do not speak or feel – thus affirm these authors.

It is also expressed in the instruction of the First Commandment that it is forbidden to worship any kind of animal or natural phenomenon, especially the "fertile earth": "ama … *camac pacha*ctahuampas muchanquichu", "and you must not worship the *fertile earth*" (*ib.* sermon 18, fol. 104r, 555).

Nonetheless, a colonial Spanish author, the Franciscan Jerónimo de Oré, who lived in Peru and wrote towards the end of the 16th century, has a long "cántico" (canticle) about the Virgin ([1598]: fol. 80r–91r, 1992: 237–259) and shows how these distinctions can become blurred.

Thus she is, for example, in the poetic form of a litany compared to the crown of the saints and the house of God (*ib.* fol. 82r, p. 241; fol. 89r, 256; *cf. Illustration 6*), a typical European comparison, where we can see that in his Quechua text Oré uses the commonly applied words in prayers to the Virgin. However, he adds a characteristic which may also be considered to be typical of an Andean goddess. For instance, in one of the verbal images she is dressed like the Sun: "Çumac inctictas [sic] pachallicurcanqui", "you dress yourself [like] the beautiful sun" (*ib.* fol. 82v, 242; fol. 90v, 258).

The clearest association with Pachamama is found when Oré refers to the Virgin as "blessed and fertile earth, mountain of God": "Tú eres tierra bendita y fértil, monte de Dios" (*ib.* fol. 82v, 242; fol. 90v, 258). He even uses exactly the words which had been warned about by Polo ([1585] 1985: fol. 2r, 255, see *Text 3*): "la tierra fertil", here in Quechua as "camac allpa", and Oré's phrase also reminds us that the earth includes the mountains (*pacha* and *apu*): "Cam camac allpa, çumac orco canqui", "You are the fertile earth, the beautiful mountain". Therefore here we can see that Oré, probably without explicit intention, ascribes to the Virgin some important aspects of Andean deities.

4.3   Summary

The Virgin in the Andes is explicitly compared by the missionaries to the world of the (pre-Christian) Incas and situated in it. She is also identified with fertility, through the fact that she gives birth to Jesus, but also directly as the fertile earth. We have, of course, to recognise that the examples are sporadic; the fact that they are not consistent shows the experimental nature of the explanatory efforts in the late 16th century.

Moreover, at this stage we have to ask ourselves what influence the different authors and their work would or could have had on the indigenous population. Would it have been directly exposed to a text like a sermon or a "cántico"? – A question which so far it is not possible to answer.

Probably one or the other priest would have admonished them not to take anything in the realm of nature as an independent powerful being. Maybe someone would have used Ore's "cánticos" to perform a certain aspect of them, but the one on Mary, for example, mentions innumerable Biblical characters who would certainly have confused (not only) a 16th/17th century indigenous audience.

The other impression the parishioner may have been under, and possibly the most plausible and regular one, would have been the *Ave María, Salve* and the other main formulaic prayers (as shown by Guaman Poma [ca. 1615]: 835, 2001: [849]). The key words and concepts people may have most easily understood would have been those of Mary as excellent, special, mother of God, benevolent and defending the believers. This and even more so, the occasional association of her with the "fertile earth" would have certainly put her in the realm of a divine being – although a bit too benevolent for an Andean understanding – but we may doubt whether she would have easily be linked with their Pachamama who was not manifest and visible in certain individualised figures and images. This does not mean she would not have appealed to an indigenous Andean person, especially if we think of their richly adorned indigenous deities, but she may not have easily been (con-)fused with Pachamama.

5   The Spanish Traditions

When examining the Spanish context, the previous considerations of attempts to teach the image of the Virgin to the indigenous people are further complicated by the fact that there also was (and is, of course) a difference between a theological-intellectual tradition on the one hand and popular or folk traditions on the other, both of mutual influence. This is expressed by several authors (e.g. Pfandl 1959: 158–159, Christian 1998) and well formulated by Llompart (1968: 220–221):

The Church relies on a series of religious rites of official character, the liturgy – mass, preaching, sacraments – which are the means of communicating blessing and salvation to the faithful. Liturgy has an echo and provokes reactions in the depth of the popular soul; these have a certain dynamism and specific traits of their own. Thus beliefs, customs and habits of popular religiosity sprout, grow, interlace with each other and flower.[38]

It is therefore necessary to call attention to what I would like to see as the "two Virgins": the intellectually-theologically inspired one and the popular-folk inspired one. I will try to isolate common features, aiming to clarify whether and how the Mediterranean – theological and folk – image of the Virgin could have influenced or even formed the concept of Pachamama.

5.1   The Christian Intellectual Conceptualisation

It will become clear that the mentioned missionaries' discourse with respect to a heightened and purely loving Virgin Mary goes back to Spanish theological concepts.

When studying the 16th century Christian doctrine of the Third Lima Council and the Peruvian Franciscan Oré's imagery, we see that these are very closely modelled on the theological Mediterranean description of the Virgin: often we find her in litanies where she is equated to all important Christian concepts (bearer of Christ, advocate of the people etc.), ancient Old Testament characters, eternal spring, plants as well as unlimited beneficence. We also find her described as "chosen like the Sun" and "fertile life".

For example, Latin American colonial texts written for the Peruvian *criollos* (citizens of Spanish descent), such as the famous Lima litanies created by the archbishop Santo Toribio de Mogrovejo at the beginning of the 17th century (Arzobispado de Lima no year), reflect very much this benevolent image:

---

[38] Translation SDS, original text: "La Iglesia cuenta con una serie de ritos religiosos de carácter oficial, la liturgia –misa, predicación, sacramentos–, mediante los cuales comunica la gracia y la salvación a sus fieles. La liturgia tiene un eco y provoca unas reacciones en el fondo del alma popular, las cuales poseen un dinamismo y una propia especificidad. Así brotan, crecen, se entrelazan y florecen las creencias, los usos, las modalidades de la religiosidad popular."

Illustration 6: Vicente Macip: Inmaculada Concepción (Immaculate Conception) (ca. 1535) (source see Ref. Cited).

…	…
Elegida como el Sol	Chosen like the Sun
Amada de Dios …	Loved by God …
Estrella de la mañana	Morning star
Medicina de los enfermos	Medicine for the sick
Reina de los cielos	Queen of the Heavens
Rosa sin espinas	Rose without thorns
Aurora luminosa	Shining dawn

Hermosa sin igual	Beautiful without equal
Luz del medio día	Light of noon
Flor de virginidad	Flower of virginity
Lirio de la castidad	Lily of chastity
Rosa de la pureza	Rose of purity
Venero de santidad	Spring of sanctity
Cedro oloroso	Fragrant cedar
Mirra de incorrupción	Myrrh of incorruption
Bálsamo siempre manante	Always flowing balm
Terebinto de la gloria	Ever-green *terebinto* tree of glory
Palma vigorosa de la gracia	Forceful palm-tree of grace
Vara florida	Blooming wand
Piedra refulgente	Brilliant stone
Olivo plateado	Silver olive-tree
Paloma preciosa	Precious dove
Vida fructífera	Fertile life
Nave cargada de riquezas	Wealth-laden ship
Nave del mercader	Ship of the merchant
Madre del Redentor	Mother of the Saviour
Huerto cerrado	Enclosed orchard
Zarza que no se consume	Blackberry bush that does not wither
Gloria del mundo	Glory of the world
…	…

Text 7: Extract from Mogrovejo's litany to the Virgin (17th century) (Arzobispado de Lima no year: 6; translation SDS).

These metaphors are also evident in contemporary visual representations of the Virgin and her attributes, as can be seen in *Illustration 6*.

The imagery used in Mogrovejo's text is similar to the one, for example, of the *Doctrina espiritual* by the famous Iberian Dominican Luis de Granada ([1587] 1906, Tratado II: "Oración devotísima a Nuestra Señora", 105–107), whose "most devoted prayer" clearly represents the written style of a theologically trained author:

Oh Virgen gloriosa, bienaventurada, más pura que los ángeles, más resplandeciente que las estrellas … (*ib.* 105)	Oh, glorious Virgin, blessed, purer than the angels, more brilliant than the stars …
Tú eres luz de las tinieblas, tú eres espejo de los sanctos, tú eres esperanza de los pecadores. … (*ib.* 106)	You are the light in the darkness, you are the mirror of the saints, you are the hope of the sinners. …

| Reina de los ángeles, emienda mi vida y ordena todas mis obras de tal manera, que merezco yo (aunque malo) ser de ti oído con piedad. ... (*ib.* 106) | Queen of the angels, reform my life and organise all my work so that I deserve (although I am bad) to be heard by you with devotion. ... |

Text 8: Prayer to Saint Mary, by Luis de Granada, Spain 1587

In the examples we see how authors use poetry or prose to address the Virgin, in a more formulaic style or a more personal one respectively, but in each case she is the subject of numerous metaphors. This must have appealed to Andean addressees, as in their verbal art metaphorical expressions and descriptions were apparently much used.[39] However, it is especially difficult for the translator to render them in the target language and for the addressee to understand the meaning of the metaphors when one is not familiar with the physical objects they refer to and/or does not know the language.

It is interesting to notice that – as far as I have been able to find out – only Oré, the Peruvian writer, uses metaphors for the Virgin which can also clearly refer to Pachamama.

I would therefore like to argue that, despite these Mediterranean traits of the Virgin, some of which may easily find a resonance in Pachamama, it seems doubtful that so few similar items of an extremely long list of a multitude of characteristics would have evoked Pachamama's image in the Andean population when the Virgin was being described (especially as the long poetic texts were probably never cited to the indigenous people as a whole). The Christian priests, however, might have detected or even looked for Pachamama's traits in the Virgin. Therefore we have to ask who fomented the convergence (if we assume that there was one), and it is reasonable to suppose that it seems to have been the missionaries rather then the indigenous people.

5.2 Folk Concepts of the Virgin Mary in Spain

In looking for similarities of the Virgin and Pachamama, it is also necessary to study Medieval (and even recent) Mediterranean folk concepts and traditions of Mary in order to find out whether there are any features which might be considered coincidences with Pachamama. This is especially important as we know that the coverage of priests on the whole was rather thin in the Andes in colonial times, whereas the contact among "common" people, such as travellers and businessmen with farmers and shepherds must have been a much more common phenomenon.[40]

---

[39] See Dedenbach-Salazar Sáenz (2003: 335, 353, 451, and *passim*).

[40] Albó (1966: 275) mentions for the second half of the 17th century that there were not enough mis-

Illustration 7: Nuestra Señora de la Vega (Our Lady of the Fertile Plain) of Haro, at the entrance of the church (Virgen de la Vega, Haro, La Rioja, España). In the statue (14th century) the Virgin has, in addition to a pomegranate (which originally seems to have been an apple) a sheaf of wheat in her right hand, as a sign of the barley she had transformed into wheat (Mundo del Cofrade 2009) (source see Ref. Cited).

The oldest reference in writing with respect to the fact that the Virgin Mary had long since been understood as and equated with the Earth can be found in Alfonso X or Wise's no. 43 of his Articles of Faith in the 13th century (Alfonso el Sabio 1945: 72–76). Although they belong to an academic tradition rather than to a popular one, some of them clearly draw on folk conceptions. Thus Alfonso writes that "because those who adored the earth wanted to show very much how they prayed to Saint Mary, because she had seven things in her which were similar to the earth" – "one to work her[41]; the other one, to fertilise her, the third one, to irrigate her",[42] after that, she would carry good fruit in time, and the fruit she produced would be both beautiful and delicious, and she gave us the bread.[43] These characteristics reflect, according to Alfonso, that she was humble, like a servant; she was spotless; and she was fertile so that the Holy Ghost could take possession of her body. Of course, Alfonso himself sees these traits as metaphorical-symbolic ones, "translating" them directly into a Christian imagery, such as that the bread is Christ's body.

Alfonso tried to draw the addressee away from the earth as object of worship, but it can be supposed that this probably fomented a blending of her and the Virgin. Still today we find virgins in Spain who are associated with agricultural well-being, such as the "Virgen de la Espiga" (the "Virgin of the Corn Ear") or "Nuestra Señora de la Vega" ("Our Lady of the Fertile Plain") of Haro who, according to the (hi-)story, changed barley into the wheat which was needed to pay the plot tenancy (see *Illustration 7*; Abad y Cobreros 1990: 119–122).[44] The practice of important

---

sionaries to cover the whole territory of a province. As to meeting with common Spaniards, see Guaman Poma in the second half of his book where he writes about encounters with all kinds of Spaniards.

[41] The earth and the Virgin are also grammatically closely related as the author can use the feminine form for both because "tierra" is of feminine gender in Spanish. Therefore physical traits and their transference as a metaphor to St. Mary become closely intertwined.

[42] Translation SDS, Spanish original text: "Ca los que aorauan a la tierra queríen tanto mostrar commo que orassen a Ssanta María; ca ella ouo en sí siete cosas a ssemeiança de la tierra"; "la vna, labrarla; la otra, estercolarla; la terçera, rregarla." (Alfonso el Sabio, 13th century, Setenario, Ley XLIII, 1945: 74).

[43] Under his rule Mary gained an important role in the theological framework (Hall 2004: 33–40).

[44] Although here it seems to be clear that Mary is related to older goddesses, all other evidence, connecting her historically and prehistorically to older Mediterranean earth goddesses, is, of course, mostly speculative. However, it will be helpful to look at some of this information. According to Carroll the way that the Virgin Mary was ultimately venerated was derived from the cult to the Mediterranean goddess Cybele. This explains that the Mary cult probably did not arise suddenly or from nowhere and that it already brought its "fused" origins with it. (Carroll 1986, chs. 4 and 5, based on other scholars' research and his own hypotheses.) Gómez-Tabanera, on the other hand, calls the readers' attention to the ideas that the Mediterranean deity Demeter might have been the precursor to the Virgin, presenting her as "alive, multi-shaped, changing, mistress of life and death, of peace and war, benevolent and malevolent, omnipresent to the farmer as mother earth" (1968: 203, translation SDS, Spanish original text: "se nos presenta viva, multiforme, cambiante, señora de la vida y la muerte, de la paz y de la guerra, benéfica y maléfica, omnipresente como madre tierra al campesino …"). A multitude of sources

festivals for the Virgin Mary gives evidence of the fact that the Christian Saint-Deity was indeed associated very closely with agricultural rituals. Gómez-Tabanera (1968: 201–204) describes the Spanish tradition of the Assumption of the Virgin in August as one of many festivals dedicated to her, in the resting time between harvest and sowing, and it is documented as far back in time as the 13th century.[45]

It is therefore not surprising that in the Middle Ages and later, especially in the time of the Counter-Reformation, the Virgin appeared to many individuals. Chapels for a number of Saints and also for Mary were erected in order to give people support, e.g. against natural disasters, such as locusts and other insects, as well as hailstorm damage and epidemics, lameness and blindness (Christian 1981b: 71–72). Mary was seen as benevolent, never as angry; she would warn people of a punishment, but she would not punish (*ib.* 98).

Many apparitions of the Virgin in different manifestations are recorded in Spain in the 16th century, partly going back to the Middle Ages (Christian 1981b: ch. 3; Kamen 1993: 147 ff.). Where such an apparition or image occurred, a shrine tended to be built. The places were often found at rarely visited sites, such as mountains, caves or wells,[46] where persistent domesticated animals had made their herders follow them, or where poor farmers and women had happened to experience them; as Kamen (1993: 148) puts it: "virtually inaccessible places in the countryside, underground or in caves or undergrowth, with only a handful located in ruins."[47] Thus there are, for example, the "Virgen de la Cuevita" (the Virgin of the Little Cave), whose sanctuary, by the way, was made by Franciscan friars whose principal aim was the Christianisation of the Canary islands people (Yeyo 2006; Caballero Mujica y Riquelme 1999: 24, 37). In Cáceres, "Nuestra Señora de la Fuente Santa" ("Our Lady of the Holy Well") appeared in order to show some pilgrims a mysterious flow of fresh water (Fernández Sánchez 1994: 258–260). There was also, well known in Peru and repeatedly mentioned by Guaman Poma, the "Virgen de la Peña de Francia' ("Our Lady of Peñafrancia"; Adorno in Guaman Poma 2001: [403]) who had appeared in Asturias on a rock.

---

shows that both goddesses Cybele and Demeter had a rich oral (and later written) tradition since before Christian times (*Internet Women's History Sourcebook* 1998–2007, s. v. Rome, Goddesses). Another author, Berger (1985), shows very well how the so-called "grain protectress" developed from a pan-European deity to a saint and finally to the Virgin Mary. The fundamental difference to the Andean Pachamama seems to have been the much more concrete personification of these deities, which then, of course, continued in the Virgin Mary's many manifestations.

[45] In Spain many festivals combined ancient harvest offerings with certain calendar dates and in this way christianised older customs (Sánchez Herrero 1978: 259–263).

[46] Interestingly enough, among Pachamama's ritual sites are also wells and springs (Mariscotti de Görlitz 1978: 76).

[47] See also Christian (1981a: 207–209; 1981b: 75–78, 82–83; 1989: 63, 69, 73); Defourneaux (1970: 113).

The brief summary of popular religious practices in Spain has shown that a number of Spanish coincidences might have confirmed similar Andean phenomena so that an approximation on the folk-level(s) may have been existent in the practical sphere without having to recur to theological correlations which missionaries tried to create. In this sense, the Andean population could very much carry on with its customs which were possibly even reinforced by similar imported ones.[48]

6   Conclusion: Coincidences and Convergences

Spain, 13th century	Peru, 20th century
Alfonso the Wise writes the following about the Earth and how her characteristics became that of Saint Mary, here about the seventh trait she had which was similar to the Earth:[49]	A Quechua consultant from central southern Peru talks about Pachamama's characteristics:
The seventh because she [the Earth] gave us great benefit because the holy bread which we receive (which) is her body, which we eat every day as sacrifice, and the wine which we drink is her blood which benefits us in its quality ...[50]	She [Pachamama] really has bones and blood. Pachamama also has hair. Her hair is the pasture. Her blood is in the earth. Her blood is definitely always there; we plough her. Her blood is definitely there. And Pachamama also has milk. And the Earth, she breastfeeds us. This is how we live our life.[51]

Text 9: The Earth: the Virgin – Pachamama

---

[48] It would be interesting to study the efforts of the colonial Church to educate their Spanish overseas subjects to be "real" Christians and the reaction of the common Spaniard and *criollo* to behave like "proper" Christians!

[49] Which he then relates back to the Bible: "the prophet David said: take bread from the earth – which is understood as the body of our Lord Jesus Christ, who took it from Saint Mary ..." (Alfonso el Sabio: Articles of Faith, no. 43; 1945: 76; translation SDS). Original text: "dixo el propheta Dauid: Ssaque pan de la tierra – que sse entiende por el cuerpo de Nuestro Ssennor Ihesu Cristo, que ssacó de Ssanta María ...". Not only 16th century missionaries made enormous efforts to explain Christianity – Alfonso's rationale almost seems to distort it.

[50] Alfonso el Sabio (Articles of Faith, no. 43; 1945: 76; translation SDS). Original text: "La vii^a, que nos dió grant pro; ca el pan ssanto que nos rreçebimos que es el ssu cuerpo, comiendo cadal día por ssacriffiçio, et el vino que beuemos es la ssu ssangre, que nos aprouecha de guisa ...".

[51] Gow y Condori (1976: "Pachamama", 11, translation SDS). Quechua original: "Chiqtapunin tullun yawarnin kan. Pachamamaq pilunpis kan. Pilun pastu. Yawarnin kan allpapi. Yawarninqa kasyanpuni barbichanchis. Chaypis yawarninqa kasyanpuni. Lichinpas kasyanpuni Pachamamaqa. Paytaq ñuñuwanchis chay tirrapi. Chaywanmi kawsanchis kay bidapi."

Based on the Spanish tradition we can easily recognise (possibly) universal similarities, coincidences which may eventually have led to a convergence or fusion of
concepts,[52] but a series of these coincidences can be said to be so similar to each
other that no explicit recognition would necessarily have occurred and it will therefore be difficult to identify them as European or Andean.

We can see the following similarities:

– the concept of a "mother earth" and her association with fertility, probably
  going back to ancient Mediterranean deities but certainly to Alfonso X; a clear
  example is the Bolivian Virgin who is associated with the first crops, and certain
  manifestations of the Virgin in Spain related to fertile agricultural products;
– August as the month of resting from agricultural tasks used to especially worship Pachamama and the Virgin of the Assumption;
– the origin and appearance of the earth deity / the Virgin from particular places,
  such as wells, caves and rocks;
– Pachamama and the Virgin as warners, not implementers of disasters;
– the Virgin's body and blood as bread and wine on the one hand and, on the
  other, Pachamama's hair as pasture, and she has bones, blood and milk (see
  Text 9);
– the Virgin figures are always dressed up splendidly; the memory of Pachamama
  as a well adorned Inca deity may have made them alike also on this level.

Despite these apparent coincidences, there are also compelling differences:

– the European mother deities are more personified than Pachamama who is more
  generally conceived of as "the Earth", "the World". There is a certain similarity
  in this as well, however, because particular images of the Virgin appear in many
  places, and Pachamama (sometimes Pachamamas) is spread out everywhere and
  encompasses everything; sometimes she also seems to have the shape of little
  human beings.
– The Virgin is not ambiguous, she is always benevolent and kind-hearted, whereas Pachamama can become very angry if not treated as well as expected and
  necessary.

As can be seen, there are more coincidences (mostly in concept, time and place
of origin or residence, and character) than clear differences (mainly in the
personification[s] of the Virgin and the strong reciprocal ties with humankind of
Pachamama). This is not surprising when one takes into consideration, as shown

---

[52] And these again based on blendings, as becomes clear in Alfonso the Wise's description.

above, that especially the ancient popular European conceptions of the Virgin are very similar to those of Pachamama. If – despite the clear high-Church difference between an intercessory saint and an autonomous deity (an important theological difference) – we think of the contacts "common" people would have had from the colonial era onwards, it does not surprise that Pachamama and the Virgin's likeness could have led to a certain convergence of both beings.

The evidence indicates, then, that there are many features both the Virgin and Pachamama have in common, probably due to their similar functions. These can be noticed especially on the popular level where they must have had and still have much contact. Moreover, some colonial priests seem to have used traits of the Virgin (especially her fertility and the idea of her as *the* mother) as connecting points between both deities. The indigenous population may have taken these up and/or made associations itself.

Therefore coincidences (an accidental and remarkable occurrence of events or ideas at the same time, suggesting but lacking a causal relationship, see footnote 10) and an eventual convergence (the development of similarities in unrelated events or ideas of the same environment) of important traits is more probable than "wrapping up" the Andean in the European (which essentially translates as syncretism).

Thus, what happened was not the hoped-for conversion, but the result is a religious tradition and practice mostly rooted in some European theological aspects as well as a number of Spanish folk *and* Andean traditions, which all developed in a cultural space and climate in which both could live and prosper together and even blend into each other and thus converge.

The (super-)natural forces which make individual and social life easier or possible at all, apparently have their unconscious basis in similar ecologies and traditional economies, which would have been the reason why similar ideas and concepts could sprout.[53]

Nowadays popular and theological standpoints are practiced and debated by the people who worship Pachamama.

The indigenous people who carry out their rituals for Pachamama do not care about "Andean" or "Christian" origins or whether Pachamama is a saint or a deity (in the Catholic sense) – the most important function of Pachamama and the Virgin is to guarantee the future well-being of society. It seems that where the Virgin has traits of Pachamama and fertility, it goes back to a Spanish tradition. Where Pachamama is related in oral testimony to the Virgin, also in naming her e.g. Pachatierra, the Andean tradition may have subsumed the Spanish import. Therefore,

---

[53] This would consequently lead us to the "universal" debate, which will have to look into general patterns. This has, of course, been done within different theoretical frameworks, e.g. of syncretism, but it may be necessary to distance ourselves from pre-conceived ideas such as "religious evolution" (which still forms large part of the current discourse) and look into "a better understanding of practical circumstances", as Marvin Harris (1974: 4–5) demands and does.

although there are indications of Pachamama and the Virgin being closely associated and evidence as to their coincidences, more research is necessary to find out how this supposed relationship is being conceived of and carried out at present, that is, whether one can really understand the different rituals as convergences.

As far at the intellectual debate goes, for a number of years now the *teología india* (influenced by liberation theology) has come to play an ever more important role in the interpretation of this Andean way of living. Indigenous Catholic priests of the "new generation" interpret the Andean rituals and the Bible in new ways. By "theologising" Andean religious features, they try not only to combine an understanding and interlacing of both, but often also utter their view of what they think about colonization, old and new, and how the subaltern lives of the indigenous peoples can be changed by recognising a solidarity between the indigenous population and a Jesus Christ of their own understanding.[54]

In terms of my argument, these developments continue putting layer upon layer on phenomena and interpretations which have been converging for centuries, and thereby the "common people" as well as the intellectuals of indigenous origin live the dynamics of culture.[55]

References Cited

Abad León, Felipe (text), y **Jaime Cobreros** (photographs)
1990   Guía para visitar los santuarios marianos de La Rioja. Madrid: Ediciones Encuentro. (María en los Pueblos de España, vol. 4.) Internet (partially): http://books. google.es/books?id=sSI4Ix3Ky5wC&pg=PA119&dq=villabona+haro&as_brr=3& ei=UJ4FSIL_NJTAzATBy_yXDg&sig=B_RdwGOpFgltEX4sv58mUgskn-w#v= onepage&q=villabona%20haro&f=false (19/05/2013).

Alfonso el Sabio [Alfonso X]
1945   Setenario [Spain, 13th century]. Edición e introducción Kenneth H. Vanderford. Buenos Aires: Facultad de Filosofía y Letras de la Universidad de Buenos Aires, Ins-

---

[54] See, for example, Valencia Parisaca (1999), Preface by Arnold, 9 ("la nueva generación"); the author, 91 ("la teologización aymara") and e.g. 90 and 98 for his understanding of liberation and the role of the earth respectively. In my opinion this author's words do not call for a revolution, but it is a short step towards such ideas.

[55] Possibly already in the colonial era ideas about an earth mother were carried back to Spain with travellers. Nowadays Pachamama comes to Spain with South American migrants, for example in Madrid, in a popular festival organised by Andean embassies (Ecuador y Bolivia celebraron Inti Raymi en Madrid, 2011). Pachamama is also used in the socio-political associations of female immigrants in Madrid, for example the day centre for migrant women (Pachamama, un espacio en que las mujeres se integran, 2010) or the association of Ibero-American business women (AMEIB – PACHAMAMA, 2008). Therefore we must not imagine the transfer as a one-way path, and here we even see how Andean concepts are re-contextualised in socio-political life by their protagonists, not unlike the theology presented by the mentioned Valencia Parisaca.

tituto de Filología. Internet publication by Biblioteca Virtual Miguel de Cervantes, Alicante, 2009: http://www.cervantesvirtual.com/obra/setenario--0/ (19/05/2013).

Allen, Catherine J.
2002 The Hold Life Has. Coca and Cultural Identity in an Andean Community. Washington and New York: Smithsonian Institution. [2nd ed.; orig. 1988.]

AMEIB – PACHAMAMA
2008 Pachamama, Asociación de mujeres empresarias iberoamericanas [Madrid]. Internet: http://www.asociacionpachamama.org/ (19/05/2013).

Arriaga, Pablo José de
1968 Extirpación de la idolatría del Pirú [1621]. In: Francisco Esteve Barba (ed.), Crónicas peruanas de interés indígena, 193–277. Madrid: Atlas. (Biblioteca de Autores Españoles 209.)

Arzobispado de Lima
no year Santo Toribio de Mogrovejo – Modelo de Piedad Filial Mariana: Tema 4 – Hijo se Santa María. Internet: http://www.arzobispadodelima.org/santos/storibio/pdf/evangelizador04.pdf (19/05/2013).

Avila, Francisco de
1648 Tratado de los Evangelios, qve nvestra madre la iglesia propone en todo el año .... 2 vols. [Lima.] Internet: http://openlibrary.org/works/OL15385322W/Tratado_de_los_euangelios (19/05/2013).

Berg, Hans van den
1990 La tierra no da así nomás. Los ritos agrícolas en la religión de los aymara-cristianos. La Paz: UCB (Universidad Católica Boliviana), ISET (Instituto Superior de Estudios Teológicos), HISBOL.

Berger, Pamela
1985 The Goddess Obscured: Transformation of the Grain Protectress from Goddess to Saint. Boston: Beacon Press.

Berner, Ulrich
2007 Synkretismus – Begegnung der Religionen. In: Joachim G. Piepke (ed.), *Kultur und Religion in der Begegnung mit dem Fremden*, 47–74. Nettetal: Steyler Verlag. (Veröffentlichungen des Missionspriesterseminars St. Augustin, Nr. 56.)

Bertonio, Ludovico
1984 Vocabulario de la lengua aymara [1612]. (Facsimile edition based on the 1956 La Paz facsimile.) Cochabamba: CERES (Centro de Estudios de la Realidad Económica y Social), Instituto Francés de Estudios Andinos (IEFA), Museo Nacional de Etnografía y Folklore (MUSEF). (CERES Documentos Histórico no. 1; MUSEF Fuentes Primarias no. 2; Travaux de l'IFEA, tomo XXVI.)

Bitti, Bernardo
16th century Virgen de la Candelaria. Painting in the Jesuit Church in Arequipa. Internet: http://www.flickr.com/photos/jesuitasperu/6059595929/in/set-72157627432126734/ (19/05/2013). Reproduced with permission by the Jesuits of Peru. **[Illustration 4]**

Bonwetsch, [Gottlieb] Nathanael
1953 Saints [1911]. In: The New Schaff-Herzog Encyclopedia of Religious Knowledge.

Based on the third edition of the Realencyklopädie founded by J. J. Herzog, and edited by Albert Hauck. Prepared ... under the supervision of Samuel Macauley Jackson ... with the assistance of Charles Colebrook Sherman and George William Gilmore, etc. (Index ... By G. W. Gilmore) 1908–1914. Internet edition: New Schaff-Herzog Encyclopedia of Religious Knowledge, vol. X: Reusch – Son (Grand Rapids, Michigan: Baker Book House, 1953), 175–177: http://www.ccel.org/ccel/schaff/encyc10/Page_175.html until http://www.ccel.org/ccel/schaff/encyc10/Page_177.html (19/05/2013).

Caballero Mujica, Francisco, y María Jesús Riquelme Pérez
1999　Guía para visitar los santuarios marianos de Canarias. Madrid: Ediciones Encuentro. (María en los Pueblos de España, vol. 15.) Internet (partially): http://books.google.es/books?id=wSOdrSO1BkkC&printsec=frontcover&dq=Gu%C3%ADa+para+visitar+los+santuarios+marianos+de+Canarias&hl=es&sa=X&ei=yekAT9nzJoqj8gOOl5HDAQ&ved=0CDgQ6AEwAA#v=onepage&q=Gu%C3%ADa%20para%20visitar%20los%20santuarios%20marianos%20de%20Canarias&f=false (19/05/2013).

Carroll, Michael P.
1986　The Cult of the Virgin Mary: Psychological Origins. Princeton: Princeton University Press.

Christian Jr., William A.
1981a Apparitions in Late Medieval and Renaissance Spain. Princeton: Princeton University Press.
1981b Local Religion in Sixteenth-Century Spain. Princeton: Princeton University Press.
1989　Person and God in a Spanish Valley. New revised edition [1972]. Princeton: Princeton University Press.
1998　Spain in Latino Religiosity. In: Peter Casarella and Raúl Gómez (eds.), El cuerpo de Cristo: The Hispanic Presence in the U.S. Catholic Church, 325–330. New York: Crossroad Publishing Company. (A Crossroad Herder Book.)

Condori Mamani, Gregorio, y Asunta Quispe Huamán
1982　Gregorio Condori Mamani. Autobiografía [1977]. Ricardo Valderrama Fernández and Carmen Escalante Gutiérrez (eds.). Cusco: Centro de Estudios Rurales Andinos "Bartolomé de las Casas". (Biblioteca de la Tradición Oral Andina 2.)
1996　Andean Lives. Gregorio Condori Mamani and Asunta Quispe Huamán. Translated from the Quechua ... by Paul H. Gelles and Gabriela Martínez Escobar. Austin: University of Texas Press.

Council of Trent
1848　The Canons and Decrees of the Sacred and Oecumenical Council of Trent [1562–1564], ed. and trans. J. Waterworth (London: Dolman, 1848). Internet: Hanover Historical Texts Project. Scanned by Hanover College students in 1995. Internet: http://history.hanover.edu/texts/Trent/trentall.html (19/05/2013).

Damian, Carol
1995　The Virgin of the Andes. Art and Ritual in Colonial Cuzco. Miami Beach: Grassfield Press.

Davies, Nigel
1997　The Ancient Kingdoms of Peru. London: Penguin.

Dedenbach-Salazar Sáenz, Sabine
1997   La terminología cristiana en textos quechuas de instrucción religiosa en el siglo XVI. In: Mary H. Preuss (ed.), Latin American Indian Literatures: Messages and Meanings. Papers from the Twelfth Annual Symposium, Latin American Indian Literatures Association, 195–209. Lancaster, California: Labyrinthos.
2003   Die Stimmen von Huarochirí: Indianische Quechua-Überlieferungen aus der Kolonialzeit zwischen Mündlichkeit und Schriftlichkeit – eine Analyse ihres Diskurses. CD-ROM, Aachen: Shaker Verlag 2003. Also: http://hss.ulb.uni-bonn.de/2003/0253/0253.htm (19/05/2013) [this 2003 edition used for quotations]. Paperback edition Aachen: Shaker Verlag 2007. (Bonn Americanist Studies, BAS 39.)

Defourneaux, Marcelin
1970   Daily Life in Spain in the Golden Age. Translated [from the French] by Newton Branch. London: Allen and Unwin. [Originally published as "La Vie quotidienne en Espagne au Siècle d'Or". Paris: Hachette, 1966.]

Doctrina Christiana
1985   Doctrina christiana y catecismo para instrvccion de los indios ... [1584]. In: Tercer Concilio Provincial de Lima (ed.) 1985: 5–188. [Also on the Internet: http://openlibrary.org/books/OL24440872M/Doctrina_christiana_y_catecismo_para_instruccion_de_los_indios_y_de_las_de_mas_personas_que_han_de_ser_enseñadas_en_nuestra_sancta_fé (19/05/2013).]

Domínguez García, Javier
2008   De Apóstol Matamoros a Yllapa Mataindios: Dogmas e ideologías medievales en el (des)cubrimiento de América. Salamanca: Ediciones Universidad de Salamanca. (Estudios Históricos y Geográficos 144.)

Duviols, Pierre (ed.)
2003   Procesos y visitas de idolatrías. Cajatambo, siglo XVII. Lima: Pontificia Universidad Católica del Perú, Fondo Editorial, Instituto Francés de Estudios Andinos (IFEA). (Colección Clásicos Peruanos.)

Ecuador y Bolivia celebraron Inti Raymi en Madrid
2011   [Popular Andean festival celebration, organised by the Ecuadorian and Bolivian embassies in Madrid, includes offerings to Pachamama.] In: Ecuador Inmediato.com – El periódico instantáneo del Ecuador, 03/07/2011. Internet: http://ecuadorinmediato.com/index.php?module=Noticias&func=news_user_view&id=153058&umt=ecuador_y_bolivia_celebraron_inti_raymi_en_madrid (19/05/2013).

Fernández Sánchez, Teodoro
1994   Guía para visitar los santuarios marianos de Extremadura. Madrid: Ediciones Encuentro. (María en los Pueblos de España, vol. 5.) Internet (partially): http://books.google.com/books?id=3fHORKJcggAC&printsec=frontcover#v=onepage&q&f=false (19/05/2013).

Frommeyer, Miriam S.
2007   Das Verhältnis zwischen Menschen und Gottheiten in den südperuanischen Anden und dessen Ausdruck in Ritual und Gebet. Unpublished Master Thesis, Faculty of Philosophy, University of Bonn, Germany.

Gisbert de Mesa, Teresa
2006 The Virgin Mary and the Rich Mountain of Potosí. In: Rishel, Joseph J. and Suzanne Stratton-Pruitt (eds.): The Arts in Latin America, 1492–1820, 447. Philadelphia Museum of Art; Antiguo Colegio de San Ildefonso, Mexico City; Los Angeles County Museum of Art; New Haven: Yale University Press.

Gómez-Tabanera, José Manuel
1968 Fiestas populares y festejos tradicionales. In: José Manuel Gómez-Tabanera (ed.): El folklore español, 149–216. Madrid: Instituto Español de Antropología Aplicada.

González Holguín, Diego
1989 Vocabvlario de la lengva general de todo el Perv llamada lengua qquichua o del Inca. [Ciudad de los Reyes (Lima), 1608.] Prólogo Raúl Porras Barrenechea. Presentación Ramiro Matos Mendieta. Lima: Universidad Nacional Mayor de San Marcos. (Facsimile of the 1952 edition. Contains addenda.)

Gow, Rosalind, y **Bernabé Condori** (eds.)
1976 Kay Pacha. Tradición oral andina. Cuzco: Centro de Estudios Rurales Andinos "Bartolomé de Las Casas". (Biblioteca de la Tradición Oral Andina 1.)

Granada, Luis de
1906 Doctrina espiritual [1587]. In: Obras; tomo XIV, 3–160. Edición crítica y completa por Justo Cuervo. Madrid: Emprenta de la viuda é hija de Gómez Fuentenebro. Internet: http://www.archive.org/details/obrascue14luisuoft (19/05/2013).

Guaman Poma de Ayala, Felipe
1936 Nueva Corónica y Buen Gobierno (Codex péruvien illustré). Paris: Institut d'Ethnologie. [El primer nueva corónica y buen gobierno (1615/1616).] **[Illustration 5]**
2001 El primer nueva corónica y buen gobierno (1615/1616). København: Det Kongelige Bibliotek, GKS 2232 4° (ca. 1615). Electronic edition directed by Rolena Adorno and Ivan Boserup. Autograph manuscript facsimile, annotated transcription, documents, and other digital resources [and bibliography]. Internet: http://www.kb.dk/permalink/2006/poma/info/es/frontpage.htm (19/05/2013). [The page indications in brackets refer to the consistently numbered manuscript pages as introduced by Adorno.]

Hall, Linda B.
2004 Mary, Mother and Warrior: The Virgin in Spain and the Americas. Austin: University of Texas Press.

Harris, Marvin
1989 Cows, Pigs, Wars and Witches: The Riddles of Culture [1974]. New York: Vintage Books.

Hoggarth, Leslie
2004 Contributions to Cuzco Quechua Grammar. Aachen: Shaker Verlag. CD-ROM. (Bonn Americanist Studies, BAS 41.)

Huarochirí Manuscript
1991 The Huarochirí Manuscript. A Testament of Ancient and Colonial Andean Religion [ca. 1608]. Translation from the Quechua by Frank Salomon and George L. Urioste. Annotations and introductory essay by Frank Salomon. Transcription by George L. Urioste. Austin: University of Texas Press.

Huertas Vallejos, Lorenzo
1981   La religión en una sociedad rural andina del siglo XVII. Ayacucho: Universidad Nacional de San Cristóbal de Huamanga.

Internet Women's History Sourcebook
1998–2007   Paul Halsall (comp. and ed.) November 1998. Last Updated April 16, 2007. Internet: http://www.fordham.edu/halsall/women/womensbook.html (19/05/2013). [Part of the Internet Ancient History Sourcebook.]

Kamen, Henry
1993   The Phoenix and the Flame: Catalonia and the Counter Reformation. New Haven and London: Yale University Press.

Köstlin, Julius
1953   God [1909]. In: The New Schaff-Herzog Encyclopedia of Religious Knowledge. Based on the third edition of the Realencyklopädie founded by J. J. Herzog, and edited by Albert Hauck. Prepared … under the supervision of Samuel Macauley Jackson … with the assistance of Charles Colebrook Sherman and George William Gilmore, etc. (Index … By G. W. Gilmore), 1908–1914. Internet edition: New Schaff-Herzog Encyclopedia of Religious Knowledge, Vol. V: Goar – Innocent (Grand Rapids, Michigan: Baker Book House, 1953), 2–7: http://www.ccel.org/ccel/schaff/encyc05/Page_2.html until http://www.ccel.org/ccel/schaff/encyc05/Page_7.html (19/05/2013).

Llompart, Gabriel
1968   La religiosidad popular. In: José Manuel Gómez-Tabanera (ed.), El folklore español; pp. 217–246. Madrid: Instituto Español de Antropología Aplicada.

Madre Pachamama
2006   Madre que nutre, protege y sustenta las culturas. In: Diario Hoy, Cultura Hoy. La Plata, Argentina, 31/07/2006. Internet: http://pdf.diariohoy.net/2006/07/31/pdf/s03-sup.pdf (19/05/2013).

Mariscotti de Görlitz, Ana María
1978   Pachamama Santa Tierra. Contribución al estudio de la religión autóctona en los Andes centro-meridionales. Berlin: Gebr. Mann Verlag. (Indiana Supplement 8.)

Marzal, Manuel María
1971   El mundo religioso de Urcos. Un estudio de antropología religiosa y de pastoral campesina de los Andes. Cusco: Instituto de Pastoral Andina.

Macip, Vicente
ca. 1535   Inmaculada Concepción. Colección Fundación Banco Santander, Madrid. Internet: http://www.google.de/imgres?q=Inmaculada+Concepci%C3%B3n+vicente+macip&um=1&hl=de&sa=N&rlz=1W1ADRA_enGB419&biw=1600&bih=607&tbm=isch&tbnid=kyc0Xb5IJ5k_qM:&imgrefurl=http://commons.wikimedia.org/wiki/File:Juan_de_Juanes_-_Inmaculada_Concepci%25C3%25B3n.JPG&docid=M7w7Pvt5Ll3cpM&imgurl=http://upload.wikimedia.org/wikipedia/commons/5/5c/Juan_de_Juanes_-_Inmaculada_Concepci%2525C3%2525B3n.JPG&w=419&h=498&ei=dQioT7uvNufZ0QWlzOXvBQ&zoom=1&iact=hc&vpx=643&vpy=119&dur=405&hovh=245&hovw=206&tx=118&ty=170&sig=110345833342599040368&page=1&tbnh=128&tbnw=108&start=0&ndsp=32&ved=1t:429,r:5,s:0,i:79 (19/05/2013).   **[Illustration 6]**

Molina, Cristóbal de [el cuzqueño]
1989 Relacion de las fabulas i ritos de los ingas … [ca. 1575]. In: Henrique Urbano and Pierre Duviols (eds.), Cristóbal de Molina [y] Cristóbal de Albornoz: Fábulas y mitos de los incas, 49–133. Madrid: Historia 16. (Crónicas de América 48.)

Mundo del Cofrade
2009 La Virgen de la Vega – Patrona de Haro (La Rioja). Internet: http://mundodelcofrade. blogspot.com/2009/10/patronas.html (19/05/2013).

The New Schaff-Herzog Encyclopedia of Religious Knowledge [1908–1914]
1953 Based on the third edition of the Realencyklopädie founded by J. J. Herzog, and edited by Albert Hauck. Prepared … under the supervision of Samuel Macauley Jackson … with the assistance of Charles Colebrook Sherman and George William Gilmore, etc. (Index … By G. W. Gilmore.). New York and London: Funk and Wagnalls Co. Reprint of the Grand Rapids, Michigan, edition by Baker Book House, 1953.   Internet (1908–1914 edition): http://www.archive.org/details/ NewSchaffHerzogEncyclopediaOfReligious (19/05/2013)

Núñez del Prado Béjar, Juan V.
1970 El mundo sobrenatural de los quechuas del sur del Perú a través de la comunidad de Qotobamba. *Allpanchis Phuturinqa*, vol. 2: 57–119 [and photographs].

Ofrendas a la Pachamama
2009 Ofrendas a la Pachamama en el Arco Deustua de Puno. Video uploaded by Indigeno9 on 04/02/2009.   Internet: http://www.youtube.com/watch?v=nI8a3FAUCIE& feature=related (19/05/2013).

Oré, Luis Jerónimo de
1992 Symbolo catholico indiano [1598]. Edición facsimilar dirigida por Antonine Tibesar. Lima: Australis. (Colección Ars Historiae.)

Pachacuti Yamqui Salcamaygua, Juan de Santacruz
ca. 1613 Relacion de antiguedades de este Reyno del Piru. Ms. 3169, fols. 131–174. Biblioteca Nacional, Madrid. **[Illustration 3]** [Also on the Internet: by the Spanish National Library as part of *Papeles varios sobre los indios Incas, Huarochiris y otras antigüedades del Perú*: http://bdh.bne.es/bnesearch/CompleteSearch.do?text=& field1val=%22Per%C3%BA+Historia+Fuentes+%22&showYearItems=&field1Op =AND&numfields=1&exact=on&textH=&advanced=true&field1=materia& completeText=&view=2&pageNumber=2&pageSize=1&languageView=es (19/05/2013).]
1995 Relación de antigüedades deste reino del Perú [ca.1613]. Edición, índice analítico y glosario de Carlos Araníbar. México and Lima: Fondo de Cultura Económica. (Sección de Obras de Historia.)

Pachamama, un espacio en que las mujeres se integran
2010 [Report about a day centre for migrant women in Madrid.] In: El Comercio del Ecuador.es.   Internet: http://www.elcomerciodelecuador.es/revistaes/37- ecuatorianos-en-espana/344-pachamama-un-espacio-en-que-las-mujeres-se- integran-.html (02/01/2012).

Pfandl, Ludwig
1959 Cultura y costumbres del pueblo español de los siglos XVI y XVII: Introducción al

estudio del Siglo de Oro. Traducida … del alemán. Con prólogo del P. Félix García. Barcelona: [no publisher] (3rd Spanish ed.).

Phuturi Suni, Ciprián
1997   Testimonio: Tanteo puntun chaykuna valen. Las cosas valen cuando están en su punto de equilibrio …. Dario Espinoza, recopilador. Lima: CHIRAPAQ, Centro de Culturas Indias.

Pillsbury, Joanne (ed.)
2008   Guide to Documentary Sources for Andean Studies, 1530–1900. 3 vols. National Gallery of Art. Norman, Oklahoma: University of Oklahoma Press.

Polia Meconi, Mario
1999   La cosmovisión religiosa andina en los documentos inéditos del Archivo Romano de la Compañía de Jesús (1581–1752). Lima: Pontificia Universidad del Perú, Fondo Editorial.

Polo de Ondegardo, Juan
1990   El mundo de los incas [1571]. Laura González y Alicia Alonso (eds.). Madrid: Historia 16. (Crónicas de América 58.) [Original title: "Notables daños de no guardar a los indios sus fueros".]
1985   Instrvccion contra las cerimonias, y ritos que vsan los indios conforme al tiempo de su infidelidad [1585]. In: Tercer Concilio Provincial de Lima (ed.) 1985, 253–262. [Printed without author indication, ascribed to Polo de Ondegardo.] [Also in the Internet edition of the Confessionario para los curas de indios, by Catholic Church, Province of Lima: http://openlibrary.org/works/OL15480197W/Confessionario_para_los_curas_de_indios (19/05/2013).]

Ramos Gavilán, Alonso
1879   Historia de Copacabana, y de la milgarosa imagen de su virgen [1621]. Escrita por el R. P. Fr. Alonso Ramos, y compendiada por el P. Fr. Rafael Sans, cura interino del santuario …; con aprobación del ilustrísimo señor obispo Dr. D. Mariano Fernández de Córdova. Lima: J. Enrique del Campo, 1837. In: Album Patriótico dedicado a los suscritores de "El Eco del Misti", Arequipa, Julio 28 de 1879. Internet: http://hdl.handle.net/2027/mdp.39015027998908 (19/05/2013).

Rishel, Joseph J., and Suzanne Stratton-Pruitt (eds.)
2006   The Arts in Latin America, 1492–1820. Phialdelphia Museum of Art; Antiguo Colegio de San Ildefonso, Mexico City; Los Angeles County Museum of Art; New Haven: Yale University Press.

Sahumerio: Incense offer on the day of Pachamama
1997   1 August 1997, in Puno, Peru. Photograph Alfredo Salazar.   **[Illustration 2]**

Sánchez Herrero, José
1978   Las diócesis del reino de León: Siglos XIV y XV. León: Centro de Estudios e Investigación "San Isidoro", Archivo Histórico Diocesano, Caja de Ahorros y Monte de Piedad de León. (Colección Fuentes y Estudios de Historia Leonesa, no. 20).

Sehringer, Lisi (guión), **Cristina Palaoro** (dirección), **Fernando Palaoro** (realización)
2008   Caminos de los Andes. DVD [on Pachamama, Argentina; in Spanish]. Part of: Barros-Sehringer, Lisi and Lucía Borrero: Caminos de los Andes. Menschen und Landschaften der Anden. Stuttgart: Ernst Klett Sprachen.

Strehlke, Carl Brandon
2006   Bernardo Bitti: … Our Lady of the Expectation. In: Rishel, Joseph J. and Suzanne Stratton-Pruitt (eds.), The Arts in Latin America, 1492–1820, 416. Philadelphia Museum of Art; Antiguo Colegio de San Ildefonso, Mexico City; Los Angeles County Museum of Art; New Haven: Yale University Press.

Taylor, Gerald
1974–1976   Camay, camac et camasca dans le manuscrit quechua de Huarochirí. *Journal de la Société des Americanistes* 63: 231–244. Paris.   Internet: http://www.persee.fr/web/revues/home/prescript/article/jsa_0037-9174_1974_num_63_1_2128 (19/05/2013).

Tercero cathecismo
1985   Tercero cathecismo y exposicion de la Doctrina christiana, por sermones [1585]. In: Tercer Concilio Provincial de Lima (ed.) 1985: 333–778. [Also on the Internet: http://openlibrary.org/works/OL15435929W/Tercero_cathecismo_y_exposicion_de_la_doctrina_christiana_por_sermones (19/05/2013).]

Tercer Concilio Provincial de Lima (ed.)
1985   Doctrina Christiana y catecismo para instrvccion de indios …. [and] Tercero Cathecismo … [and further texts]. [Ciudad de los Reyes (Lima): Antonio de Ricardo, 1584/85]. (Facsímil del texto trilingüe [of the copy of the Biblioteca Diocesana de Cuenca].) Madrid: Consejo Superior de Investigaciones Científicas. (Corpus Hispanorum de Pace, vol. 26-2.)

Valencia Parisaca, Narciso
1999   La Pachamama: Revelación del dios creador. Ilave, Puno, Peru: Instituto de Estudios Aymaras (IDEA), Quito, Ecuador: Ediciones ABYA-YALA. (Colección Iglesias, Pueblos y Culturas, no. 52–53.)

Virgen de la Vega (Haro, La Rioja, España)
no year   Internet: http://es.wikipedia.org/wiki/Virgen_de_la_Vega_(Haro), photograph 2008 (19/05/2013).   **[Illustration 7]**

Virgen del Cerro Rico de Potosí
18th century   Anonymus: Die Hl. Jungfrau (Virgen) vom Cerro Rico, Potosí (reproduction from 1942). In: Margarete Payer und Alois Payer: Bibliothekarinnen Boliviens vereinigt euch! = Bibliotecarias de Bolivia ¡Uníos!: Berichte aus dem Fortbildungssemester 2001/02. – Teil 2: Chronik Boliviens.   Internet: http://www.payer.de/bolivien2/bolivien02.htm (19/05/2013).   **[Illustration 1]**

Webster
1989   Webster's New World Dictionary. Third College edition of American English. Victoria Neufeldt (Editor in Chief), David B. Guralnik (Editor in Chief Emeritus). New York: Prentice Hall. (Prentice Hall General Reference.) (1986; 4th printing, with corrections 1989.)

Yeyo
2006   Imágenes del Santurario [sic] de la Virgen de la Cuevita-Artenara. Internet: http://yeyo.lacoctelera.net/post/2006/01/26/imagenes-del-santurario-la-virgen-la-cuevita-artenara-1 (19/05/2013).